GREECE AND THE

NEW BALKANS

Signal Balkan Studies

Miranda Vickers, *Albanian Nationalism after the Cold War*

GREECE AND THE

NEW BALKANS

THEMES AND HISTORIES

JAMES PETTIFER

SIGNAL BOOKS
OXFORD

First published in 2021 by
Signal Books Limited
36 Minster Road
Oxford OX4 1LY
www.signalbooks.co.uk

A catalogue record for this book is available from the British Library

ISBN 978-1-8384630-1-4 Paper

Cover Design: Tora Kelly
Typesetting: Tora Kelly
Cover Image: Annatsach/Wikimedia Commons
Printed in India by Imprint Press

CONTENTS

In memory of my parents, John and Jeanne Pettifer,
who loved Ionian Island Greece

INTRODUCTION

OVER THE LAST FORTY OR more years, my writing, research and travel in Greece, Turkey, Macedonia and the Balkan near neighbourhood north of the Greek border have taken place in many different political contexts. Yet many of the themes that first emerged in those years long before the Cold War had ended have been consistently present ever since. They are focused on the nature of Greece's relationship to the wider Europe, the meaning of Hellenism in the contemporary world, the often confrontational relationship with Turkey and the uncertainties in the relationship with the Soviet Union, and now Russia. Before the end of the Cold War, there was, however, one great difference, in that Greece's relationships with Albania, Yugoslavia, Bulgaria and Romania might have had their good or bad periods, but were nonetheless stable and not of great security, economic or political concern in Greece. This has never applied to the relationship with Turkey.

My own connection with Greece started a long time ago as an Oxford undergraduate in 1969 under the Colonels' dictatorship. Arriving then in Thessaloniki by road from Yugoslavia after a time as a volunteer in Skopje on earthquake damage repair seemed to be like entering a Third World police state. Greece was on its knees at that time. Yet after the dictatorship there was a democratic transformation. The experiences of and reflections on that transformation from those years were the basis of my book *The Greeks: Land and People since the War*,[1] which was mainly based on study and research in the late 1980s and early 1990s concentrated on the dilemmas of the PanHellenic Socialist Movement (PASOK) government led by Andreas Papandreou. That period was referred to as 'the populist decade' by some commentators. The Papandreou government was in power against a difficult international background. Socialist government, of any kind, was anathema to the ascendant United States, when Ronald Reagan was president, and Margaret Thatcher was British prime minister in London. The processes of Greek democratization after the dictatorship fell in 1974 were still very much a work-in-progress. Although the most prominent members of the military junta were put on trial, many lesser functionaries remained in the localities. A new international orientation to secure Greek democracy seemed to be needed, given the highly problematic relationship between Greece and Turkey in NATO.

PASOK flourished in the widespread climate of anti-Americanism that had developed after the role of the US in the Turkish invasion of northern Cyprus in 1974 and the emergence of information on some US state agencies in the genesis of the Colonels' dictatorship. The central ambition of both the Karamanlis government after 1974 and PASOK after it was to obtain European Community membership, which was eventually achieved in 1981, thanks largely to the very active advocacy of France and Britain. I wrote much about the dilemmas of modernization, and inevitably raised the issues of the Greek relationship with the then much smaller and less integrated European Community.[2] At that time, in a Community with a single figure number of members, Greek influence was much greater than it is now in the much enlarged EU.

But the optimism of these years was fleeting. In south-east Europe, the end of the Cold War brought instability and violence, mass population displacement and ten years of intermittent conflicts between 1991 and 2001. The Kosovo intervention in 1999 marked NATO's first war on European soil. As the ex-Yugoslav wars developed, the question of possible Greek involvement was a major concern in the international diplomatic world, as was the conflict that was developing between the Greek government and the government of the newly independent FYROM/RM, Former Yugoslav Macedonia/Republic of Macedonia. The term I coined - drawing on the past - to designate the crisis as 'The New Macedonian Question' has become widely current in both academic and diplomatic debates ever since.[3] At the heart of the matter were problems with Greek external relations that had existed for many years, some since the days of the Versailles settlement after World War I, but which at that time were largely lost to view given the pseudo-stability in the southern Balkans since the end of the Greek Civil War in 1949 and the rigidities of the Cold War international boundaries in the region.

The gradual democratization of the country after 1974, with the legalization of the Greek Communist Party (KKE), the return of significant numbers of political exiles from abroad, and the energization of the trades union movement and civil society organizations, was to bring profound changes to the nation. A different type of politics became possible, exemplified by the PASOK phenomenon and later the SYRIZA government in the period of the financial crisis. Although the centre-right New Democracy party contained and still contains many patriotic and sensible democrats, the right was never able to re-establish the ideological and political hegemony it had enjoyed throughout the

Cold War. This weakening of the right was also linked to the growth of foreign contacts through increased tourism. Greece was becoming a much more 'open society', and the break with the world of the Colonels was not only a political rupture but also involved the renewal of many different social and economic impulses that had been dormant for many years.

Yet always periods of apparent progress were interrupted or halted by crises elsewhere in the Greek 'near abroad', just as Cyprus crises had often determined events in Athens a generation before. The onset of the border crisis with Albania from mid-1991 onwards was a central factor in increasing Greek involvement with the northern neighbours. After social order had begun to break down in the Albanian cities and countryside tens of thousands of migrants flooded into Greece, introducing a 'Balkan' factor in Greek society that has remained divisive up to the present day. It was followed by the border blockade and crisis over Macedonia.

Prior to the end of the Cold War in 1990-1991 there was little sense among the Greek political class, with a few honourable exceptions, of the scale and magnitude of the emerging crisis to the north. The end of Yugoslavia was strongly resisted in Greece, and different Athens governments engaged in more or less active collaboration with the Milosevic regime in Belgrade, in the hope that some kind of reformed and modernized Yugoslavia might emerge from the chaos. There were particularly close relations between Serbia and the Mitsotakis government for part of the Milosevic period. All Greek political parties, including the communist KKE, were firmly set against compromise with the new state entity in Skopje over Macedonian issues.

My writing from the early 1990s in *The Times*, *The Wall Street Journal* and *The Scotsman* and in the Royal Institute of International Affairs journals *International Affairs* and *The World Today* was increasingly dominated by the unfolding and often very dramatic events to the north of the Greek border. Events were making the liberal orthodoxy of progress and convergence in Eastern Europe that had prevailed after 1989 increasingly unreal, and as well as reporting on events, all serious writers were drawn into to trying to understand the causes of what at first seemed to be an almost unbelievable level of violence and social conflict. This regional unrest has resulted in my books, particularly *Kosova Express*,[4] and those written by similarly involved contemporaries like Tim Judah, Misha Glenny, Miranda Vickers, Martin Bell, Noel Malcolm and other later analysts and historians who had all started originally in journalism as eyewitnesses to events. It also seemed necessary to think through and develop new political and analytical concepts to understand what was happening, and the mid-1990s saw the emergence of the term 'kleptocracy', from the Greek meaning 'government by thieves', as a new post-communist norm for many Balkan governments, as my Chatham House journal paper reproduced here indicates.

Recent twentieth-century history involving outside Powers also began to impinge, as while the ex-Yugoslav wars dragged on, external nations began to reproduce regional bilateral roles that had been thought to have been much reduced or disappeared after the end of World War II. This obviously applied to the British-Greek relationship, but there were many other active dimensions, as between Russia and Serbia, and the US and Albania, and Germany and Austria with Croatia. New small nations in the Southern Balkans emerged as political actors, principally Montenegro after independence in 2004, and Kosovo after independence in 2008. Yet they emerged with a very lengthy history and it seemed necessary to investigate what the consequences of that history might be in terms of the new nation and state identity. Thus my paper on the nineteenth-century German historian von Ranke and the history of Montenegro was written, while closer to home, my reflections on the history involve in some cases people I knew personally like Nigel Clive and C.M. Woodhouse who spent lifetimes involved in Anglo-Greek relations. The von Ranke study emerged indirectly from a paper I had published with Averil Cameron on the general nature of current identities in Montenegro and the *longue durée* of their historical and clerical roots.[5]

The history of the so-called 'Chatham House version' of Middle East history is frequently referred to in academic discourse, and it is likely that the same institution will be seen as having played a similar seminal role after 1991 in developing the understanding of the 'New Balkans', with the Royal Institute of International Affairs Balkan programme organised by the British-Croatian intellectual Christopher Cviic.[6] Although some of the work undertaken was seen as very controversial in official London and elsewhere, as it was judged to be hostile to traditional British-Serb and British-Yugoslav relationships, it did open up new understandings of the Balkans based on detailed knowledge of the contemporary realities. This was at a time when particularly under the Conservative government between 1993 and 1997, British foreign policy appeared to most of us inextricably linked to the survival of Yugoslavia, almost irrespective of the ethics involved, and the human and physical costs of that policy.[7] If there was a Chatham House version for the Balkans, it was a story of the acceptance of fragmentation and recognition of the inevitable creation of new small countries, and the emergence of hitherto suppressed minorities and minority ethnic groups and nationalities. For that reason, the theme of the Chameria Albanians in Greece became current in my work, given the central role British political actors such as Woodhouse had played in World War II and its immediate aftermath in the region.

I have written extensively elsewhere on the situation as it developed when the war began to spread from Albania into Kosova after 1997, and I have not reproduced here papers from that period, or the issues are covered in earlier books: *Albania: From Anarchy to a Balkan Identity* (with Miranda Vickers, London and New York, 1997) and *The Albanian Question: Reshaping the Balkans* (with Miranda Vickers, London and New York, 2007). The current development of the Macedonian issue is explored in a new book *Lakes and Empires in Macedonian History: Contesting the Waters.*[8]

This collection, however, is focused on Greece and the immediate northern border neighbours and the final section in a direct sense 'returns' there, mimicking the Greek popular concept of a human life as completing a circle. The vulnerabilities of Greece within the European Union had always been known to observers, and internal uncertainties existed, going back thirty or more years to allegations that the Greek economic data had been faked up to permit entry into the Eurozone.

Thus the final section of the book concerning the Greek crisis after 2009, its effect of the Republic of Macedonia/Former Yugoslav Macedonia and its impact on other neighbours is in a sense a continuing story, still with real implications today. The security implications of a collapse of Greek society after 2010 brought concern in the UK and US governments about what the future might be, and my text on that period was published digitally (only) by Penguin in London. 'The Making of the Greek Crisis' was in origin based on written analysis I produced for the Conflict Studies Research Unit in the UK Defence Academy.

Greece and Albania continue to have a frequently tense relationship, currently over the delineation of rights for oil and gas exploration on the Adriatic Sea coast and in offshore waters. The post-2010 trauma was not, and is not, merely an economic crisis but also a crisis which reflects deep currents and themes in Greek history, and the wider crises in the Eastern Mediterranean. It is ironic - although all Greek history, particularly in the post-Ottoman period, is never short of ironies - that the nation escaped unscathed in the Yugoslav wartime period, except as a destination for a very limited number of refuges, only to find itself close to social and economic collapse in peacetime after 2010 with the onset of the debt crisis. The refinancing of the Greek debt after the

2015 crisis and the succession of 'bailouts' has meant a major loss of sovereignty over the economy, and the spreading perception that the EU was determined to 'punish' Greece for what in Brussels and critically, Berlin, was seen as irresponsible political and financial behaviour. The shabby treatment of Greece by the EU has opened the possibility of a renewal of the Greek relationship with Russia, although it remains to be seen what will develop in that direction in the next years.

At the time of writing a degree of financial stability has been achieved by 2020, but at an appalling human cost in terms of poverty, unemployment and above all emigration. An estimated half a million or more people have left the country since 2010. In the Balkan neighbourhood the illegal NATO- and US-enforced Prespa Agreement on the Macedonian name dispute has increased regional instability and was a major factor in the fall of the SYRIZA government in Athens in 2019. The situation has been worsened by the economic effects of the Covid-19 pandemic which in 2020 drastically reduced revenue from tourism, so that, at the time of writing, the national debt is approaching 200% of GDP. The Greek nation feels threatened, justifiably or not, by an ebullient and resurgent Turkey and depends for security on a diminishing number of nations, principally France and, controversially, the US and Israel. Prediction is always something for analysts and historians to avoid, but it is hard to believe that NATO membership will continue to have the same level of support in future generations in the region as it has had in the past.

I would like to thank James Ferguson of Signal Books for suggesting this project, Miranda Vickers for editorial advice, Averil Cameron for comments on a part of the draft, Tora Kelly for her design skills, and the publications and publishers indicated in the footnotes to individual articles where earlier drafts of some articles first appeared.

James Pettifer
St Cross College, Oxford, 2021

1   J. Pettifer, *The Greeks: Land and People since the War*, London: Penguin, 1993.

2   See J. Pettifer, 'Greek Polity and the European Community, 1974–1993', in P. Carabott (ed.), *Greece and Europe in the Modern Period: Aspects of a Troubled Relationship*, London: Centre for Hellenic Studies, King's College London, 1995, and J. Pettifer, 'Greek Political Culture and Foreign Policy', in K. Featherstone and K. Ifantis (eds.), *Greece in a Changing Europe: Between European Integration and Balkan Disintegration?* Manchester: Manchester University Press, 1995.

3   Independence from Yugoslavia was formally achieved by a referendum in autumn 1991.

4   London: C. Hurst and Co, 2005.

5   A. Cameron and J. Pettifer, 'The Enigma of Montenegrin History: The Example of Svac', *South Slav Journal*, London, vol. 28, no. 1-2, 2008.

6   See E. Kedourie, *The Chatham House Version and other Middle Eastern Studies*, London: Weidenfeld & Nicolson, 1970. Christopher Cviic's most influential book was *Remaking the Balkans* (London: Pinter/RIIA, 1991), which its numerous critics in the Foreign and Commonwealth Office and elsewhere in mainstream thinking saw as a closet programme for an independent Croatian state and the end of the second Yugoslavia. As one of the group of RIIA members who contributed materials towards the final draft, I would say that it was at least in part a product of the collective and recent experience of RIIA members with detailed up-to-date knowledge of the scale of the looming crisis, rather than a personal manifesto by Cviic.

7   There is a very large and growing secondary literature on this subject, in many books and articles from the authors mentioned above, and also those of Alan Little and Laura Silber. The most reliable historical guidance is to be found in the writings of Sabrina P. Ramet, and Nada Boskovska in Zurich on the inter-war period pre-1939. On Milosevic and British diplomacy, see I. Roberts, *Conversations with Milošević*, Athens GA: University of Georgia Press, 2016.

8   Forthcoming, London and New York: Bloomsbury, 2021.

AFTER THE COLD WAR

THE NEW MACEDONIAN QUESTION[1]

1 First draft published in *International Affairs* (London), vol. 68, no. 3 (July 1992), pp. 475-87.

ALL BALKAN TERRITORIAL DISPUTES HAVE their mythologies; that of the Macedonian Question is among the most bloody, complex and intractable of all in a small peninsula already well burdened. But it was also the conflict that, perhaps more than any other, socialist Yugoslavia seemed to have superseded. So what gave rise to some of the most acute political turmoil of the inter-war period, particularly the recurrent Macedonian assassinations and bombings, seemed to have been 'solved' by Tito's creation. It is in its way appropriate then, that it is only with the final demise of Yugoslavia, symbolized by international recognition of the independent Croatian state, that the new Macedonian problem is emerging.

The purpose of this chapter is not to try to put forward any blueprint for a 'solution' of the issue; that would be wholly inappropriate, as the outlines of the new 'Macedonian' state are only becoming apparent, and it is very far from clear what shape many aspects of its political and military orientation will take. All that is possible is to try to indicate what the basis of the old Question was, and to suggest some comparisons with the past and present; and in that light to try to see what the problems for the international community may be. There is every indication that the process of remaking the Balkans is spreading southwards; and the centre of gravity of events may soon focus on Macedonia, as it has done in the past. It will be disturbing if international attention is distracted from this process simply because armed conflict between Serbia and Croatia has been brought to an end, at least at the time of writing.

Macedonia: The Eastern Question, and the Shortage of Macedonians

In one sense, Macedonia throughout the nineteenth century was no different from its four immediate neighbours, Serbia, Greece, Albania and Bulgaria, in that all these peoples were struggling to throw off rule from Constantinople and the declining power of the Sublime Porte. In the different phases of the Eastern Question the standing of the different candidate nation-states waxed and waned, generally linked to the power of their larger non-Balkan backers and different diplomatic imperatives, arising in many cases from events far outside the Balkans themselves. Throughout the peninsula border issues were paramount, for as the distribution of population under the old Ottoman system of government was determined on the *millet* system, where religion rather than race or language was taken as the basis of administrative organization, existing Ottoman governmental divisions often bore little relation to the aspirations of the majority of the inhabitants living within them.

But unlike Serbia or Greece, in Macedonia there was no basically homogeneous population that could form the basis of a new nation-state. There was, however, and still is, a plainly dominant majority in the cultural sense in that there are more people of Slavonic origin living there than of any other group - but only within a patchwork of extreme complexity, with Turks, Greeks, Albanians, Vlachs, Pomaks and Gypsies living alongside the Slavonic majority; and, moreover, that majority is itself subdivided into Serbian, Bulgarian and Macedonian elements.

Under the Ottoman regime no detailed statistics were kept of the Macedonian population, and substantial changes in numbers were caused by the Balkan wars of 1912 and 1913. But according to UK Foreign Office papers from 1918, there were in the ethnic territory of Macedonia, before 1912 about 1,150,000 Slavs, 400,000 Turks, 120,000 Albanians, 300,000 Greeks, 200,000 Vlachs, 100,000 Jews and 10,000 Gypsies. Although these figures would probably be disputed then and now by partisans of the different nationalities, there seems to be no reason why they should not be taken as at least a rough approximation of the position at that time.

Although there have been substantial changes since, they have not produced a more homogeneous population, but merely changed the mixture. Given the problems with recent Yugoslav censuses, in which boycotts for political reasons have been common, figures now are no more exact than they were in 1912, but the main developments have included: Nazi persecution; a greatly reduced Vlach presence due to the heavy losses this community of pastoralists suffered in the second Balkan war, and subsequent assimilation; a substantial increase in numbers of Gypsies; a very great increase in numbers of Albanians; a reduction in those of Greeks; a stable Turkish presence; a small immigration of northern ex-Yugoslav groups such as Croats and Montenegrins; and the open split of the Slavonic group into Serbian and Macedonian identities. There were also, until very recently, some people who preferred to regard themselves as Yugoslavs.

According to the 1981 Yugoslav census, probably the last where figures have any substance before the whole process was vitiated by political manipulation, the population of the Socialist Republic of Macedonia was 1,912,257 of whom 1,281,195 were Macedonians, 377,726 Albanians, 44,613 Serbs, 39,555 Pomaks, 47,223 Gypsies, 86,691 Turks, 7,190 Vlachs and 1,984 Bulgarians, plus a small number of people from six other ethnic groups. The main change since then has been the inexorable rise in Albanian numbers, which may now amount to as much as a quarter of the whole population, with a disproportionate age bias towards youth so that over the next 20 years or so the Albanian element is certain to increase further. The overall shortage of Macedonians is compounded by the fact that some ethnic groups, particularly the Vlachs, have tended to call themselves Macedonians if they have become urbanized, while retaining a de facto Vlach identity in cultural and domestic life, particularly if, until recently, they were country-dwellers.

What is most important about these figures is that they indicate a consistent and unresolved problem for any Macedonian state based on Skopje, whether before the First World War or now, in that a predominantly urban political elite of Macedonians is ruling over a country where they have almost no presence at all in very large rural areas (for example, the Albanian regions of western Macedonia), and that in nearly all these cases, like that of the Pirin Bulgarophile Slav population, the non-Macedonian minority is, or has been, wooed by the neighbouring nation-state. This is the origin of the famous Macedonian fear of the 'Four Wolves' which surround the country: Greece, Albania, Bulgaria and Serbia. Although now all four neighbouring states have said that they have no claim on Macedonian territory, there are substantial political parties in all of them, with the partial exception of Greece, which do have claims over Macedonian territory or who want a revision of the position of their compatriot minorities that would have a profoundly destabilizing effect on the new Macedonia.

The Original Macedonian Question: The Heritage of IMRO

The seminal date for the original issue was 1878, after the Treaty of Berlin had overthrown the short-lived 'Greater Bulgaria' established by the Treaty of San Stefano. Under the earlier treaty much of what is now Macedonia had been given to Bulgaria, but the Great Powers, fearful of the possibility that a Greater Bulgaria could dominate the whole peninsula, had subsequently changed their minds. The first phase of the question is dominated by the efforts of a revisionist Bulgaria to recover what was lost in 1878. At the same time Serbia was actively expansionist in the south, calling Macedonia 'South Serbia' and establishing Serbian schools and churches there. Greek policy followed a similar pattern dominated by the breach in Orthodox ranks many years before, caused by the establishment of the Bulgarian Exarchate in 1870. About 1,400 Greek schools existed by 1895 while Vlachs, speaking a language related to Romanian, had persuaded the Bucharest government to pay for over 30 Vlach language schools.

Underlying the vigorous cultural struggle for the allegiance of the population was a much deeper and longer history, on the Greek side at least. Although it is difficult for non-Greeks to understand, as the generally negative international reaction to Greek objections to European Community (EC) recognition of Macedonian independence has shown, the existence of Macedonia as a part of Greece has a fundamental place in the Greek political psyche. Alexander the Great was a Macedonian and the period of his empire has a much greater hold on the Greek popular imagination than outsiders can easily appreciate. There is, of course, some dispute about the Greekness of the world of Alexander, and numerous volumes have been produced by partisans of the different nationalities to prove or disprove particular arguments. The best known statement of the Greek position is made by Dascalakis in his book *The Hellenism of the Ancient Macedonians*,[2] in which he sets out very fully the literary and archaeological evidence as he sees it. Slav scholars usually concentrate their arguments on the passage in Plutarch where the ancient historian describes the struggles that took place between Alexander's successors, referring to the troops as 'shouting in Macedonian'. The Slav lobbyists usually conclude that this shows the existence of an autochthonous Macedonian people who were colonized by a Greek-speaking ruling class. And so on. Like many other academic disputes, the shortage of evidence means that both sides can continue their polemics more or less indefinitely. But in terms of practical political rhetoric, the disputes are very important and very much alive, particularly those aspects of them which threaten to disturb normal Greek assumptions about the nature of Greek identity throughout recorded history being based on the use of the Greek language. Another point which should be borne in mind when considering what may at first sight seem to be the exaggerated Greek response to the new state is the traditional Greek fear of instability and invasion coming from the north. Generally speaking, nearly all invasions of Greece from the time of the Slavs in the Dark Ages to the German and Italian motorized divisions of the Second World War have followed the same routes down through the northern mountain passes towards Athens, with similar results. For Greeks, the Macedonian problem awakens ancestral fears that had been conveniently forgotten for many years after the improvement of relations with Tito's Yugoslavia and the end of the Greek civil war. They are not, of course, fears of invasion at the moment, merely of chronic instability and involvement in Balkan feuds; but the fears are nonetheless real. The border of northern Greece

---

2 C. Dascalakis, *The Hellenism of the Ancient Macedonians*, Thessaloniki, Institute of Balkan Studies, 1981.

with Albania, Macedonia and Bulgaria is very long, and the Greek army and police will be very stretched to defend it in the event of a breakdown of good relations with the states to the north.

So in terms of the neighbours of the new Macedonia, the heritage of the Internal Macedonian Revolutionary Organization (IMRO) is represented by the creation of a new political vacuum as much as anything else. The type of Greater Macedonia that was envisaged by the nineteenth-century nationalists was a much larger state than the present one, with an opening to an Aegean port. The problem now is best summed up in one sentence uttered to me by an inhabitant of Skopje not long after the independence referendum last autumn: 'What are we going to build a new state with? Tobacco plants?'

Whatever political complexion the new state may have, the underlying realities are likely to be dominated by the extreme economic weakness of the country, and it is apparent that many Serbs in Belgrade still feel that this critical weakness may mean that Macedonia eventually, or perhaps quickly, will have to come back towards some sort of new Yugoslav federation, led by Serbia, as the only means of Macedonian economic survival. There are few competitive modern industries, and it is unfortunate that agriculture is dominated by the production of a single crop, tobacco, which is already in oversupply within the EC. The actual condition of the soil is frequently poor, with over-cultivation and soil erosion common problems, and although extensive investment could generate substantial improvements in production, the means to accomplish this are not in sight.

Foreign exchange reserves to back the new Denar are almost non-existent, and there seems to be a strong possibility that in the absence of a stable and internationally recognized Macedonian currency to replace the almost worthless ex-Yugoslav Dinar, the currencies of the adjoining states will circulate in neighbouring Macedonian regions and become the *de facto* currency there. There is some evidence of this happening already in the Pirin area adjoining Bulgaria. No great leap of the imagination is required to see the likely political consequences that flow from this, where the regions concerned start to look towards Sofia or Thessaloniki, rather than Skopje, for economic and political leadership. But whatever form this process takes, it is likely that one of the central respects in which the new Macedonian Question will differ from the old will have to do with the primacy of economic survival. The Macedonia that IMRO envisaged in the nineteenth century would have consisted almost entirely of semi-subsistence peasants and pastoralists: and Macedonian tobacco was worth, proportionately, a good deal more then than it is now. That entity would not have had the pretensions of a modern industrialized state within Western Europe, which is perhaps the Achilles heel of the new nation. This is despite the fact that throughout the Yugoslav era, Macedonia was at the bottom of the federal heap in terms of wage or output levels, literacy, social and educational provision, or any other measure. The non-party government of experts at present in power in Skopje has in effect placed its salvation at Brussels' door. If no investment and economic help from the EC of the scale needed to transform the situation is forthcoming, then the policies of Macedonia's neighbours will be crucial in determining the future. The government sees this process as having two main stages, the first concerned with getting widespread international recognition of statehood by the EC in particular, which the second, international investment, will follow. But in the absence of recognition, the power of Macedonia's neighbours will be decisive.

Albania, Greece, Serbia and Bulgaria: Wolves or Lambs?

It is not possible to set out in full detail the positions of all the different significant currents of opinion in all four of these countries towards the new Macedonian state; all that is attempted below is a general survey of the main factors that are likely to affect the situation in the immediate future.

Albania

In Albania, the formation of the new state has been welcomed, primarily because it is seen as a counterweight to Serbia and an irritant to Greece. Cultural relations were reasonably close for some time under Tito and the latter years of Yugoslavia, and although recently the Albanian government has taken up the human rights issues raised by the Albanian minority in Macedonia, as their position compares favourably with the very bad conditions endured by the Albanians in Serbian-ruled Kosovo, the issue has not been pursued very energetically. But Albanian nationalism is growing, particularly in the northern parts of western Macedonia adjoining Kosovo where Albanians dominate in population terms. A referendum held in January this year produced an overwhelming majority for Albanian autonomy. The de facto border imposed between Kosovo and Skopje by the Yugoslav federal army has been strongly resented. There are also growing trade links with Albania proper, for despite the appalling problems of the Albanian economy, there is a reasonable amount of hard currency in circulation there, which can be used to pay for Macedonian goods that with the collapse of inter-Yugoslav trade arrangements had become almost unsaleable. Quite sizeable quantities of wine, for instance, are being imported into Albania. But it should be noted that this trade, as elsewhere, depends on the availability of hard - or at least, respected - currency, in the neighbouring state. It is also axiomatic that little if any of the revenue generated will find its way back to the government in Skopje, in any shape or form.

It appears that for the time being, in terms of the regional dimension of the Macedonian issue, the Albanian government will try to achieve supportive and good relations with the new state. If hostilities develop between Albania and Serbia over Kosovo, which is a very real possibility and accounts for much of the current concern in Tirana over army re-equipment, Macedonia will become strategically important to both parties, and Tirana is currently unlikely to back the claims of the Tetovo-based Albanian parties in Macedonia too far. That said, relations in Macedonia between the Albanian minority and Skopje are poor, and worsening. The boycott of the original independence referendum by the Albanians in September 1991 was felt to be very much a stab in the back, and there have been calls in some quarters for the two Albanian parties to be banned. Although there are one or two Albanians at high levels in the new government, in general they are excluded from most important decision-making processes in Skopje. A particularly critical issue will be the composition of the new 35,000-strong Macedonian army which the government is in the process of creating. It appears that few, if any, Albanians will be allowed in senior positions. Since the parties representing ethnic Albanians are dissatisfied with the number of Albanian officers in the new army, they have called on youth to boycott conscription. But by and large, Macedonia is not now a central issue in Albanian politics, and this is likely to remain the case for the immediate future.

Greece

In Greece, the demise of Yugoslavia was accepted later and with more reluctance than in almost any other state in the world. Important Greek trade routes pass through Yugoslavia, and Yugoslav stability was important for many economic reasons. But the economic problem, critical for only a short phase of the Yugoslav crisis which resulted in the loss of most of a year's peach exports, pales into insignificance beside the emergence of the new proto-Macedonian state - a development which all Greek politicians would have regarded as unthinkable as recently as nine months before. The problems regarding the ancient cultural heritage have been referred to above. A more potent heritage in terms of recent history is the legacy of bitterness from the civil war, in which many of the Slav-speaking minority of northern Greece became active communists and were deeply involved in the guerrilla army. It has been estimated that there were as many as 40,000 Slav-speakers in the communist forces in the last phase of the civil war that ended in 1949. Many went into exile in Skopje, and have risen to influential positions. There is an element of revenge here in the view of some in Athens. Across the mainstream political spectrum it has been suggested that the left-wing side in the civil war was some sort of minority Slav conspiracy rather than a mass movement that had widespread support throughout Greece only two or three years before. In addition to reopening a difficult international and regional issue, the new Macedonian Question also risks reopening some of the wounds and unresolved internal controversies in Greece arising from the civil war and how it was won by the Right with foreign support. There are also difficult questions for the Greeks concerning human rights in relation to the treatment of the remaining Macedonians left in Greece after the civil war. In the far north, the writ of Athens has seldom ever run easily, and turmoil and border problems of the kind now appearing may stretch the fabric of Greek democracy itself. There have already been accusations of quite serious human rights abuses against Greek security forces on the Albanian border. But equally, there is a growth of banditry in these regions, with armed gangs making raids into Greece, and a deterioration in the economy of already poor northern cities such as Florina. A strong mood of militant Greek nationalism is developing across the political spectrum, tinged with popular concern at the apparent failure of Athens politicians to deal with the Macedonian problem firmly enough in its early stages.

The official responses of the Greek government to the emergence of Macedonia are well known and have been well publicized in the last few months. The Greek approach has been to use whatever leverage it can within the EC to prevent recognition of a state called 'Macedonia' and to attempt to base diplomatic initiatives on the assumption that some sort of new Yugoslav federation may well emerge that will include Macedonia as a component part. In essence, this differs little from the previous policy of backing Serbia to the hilt, and there is a general correspondence between Athens and the main currents of thinking in Belgrade. The private visit made to Athens by the Serbian president in March this year to discuss the synchronization of policy is very significant. But it must be very doubtful how much longer this policy can remain viable. The first major victim has been the Greek foreign minister, Mr Samaras, who was sacked in April this year by Prime Minister Mitsotakis for taking a hard line over Macedonian recognition, in line with the wishes of EC leaders eager for a settlement. But Mitsotakis miscalculated the degree of feeling against recognition among the Greek public and was forced into a vote of confidence in parliament which was only survived with some difficulty. With a majority of only two in parliament, and a substantial body of opinion in the New Democratic Party (ND) supporting the positions of Mr Samaras (particularly members from northern Greek constituencies), the Macedonian issue is clearly capable of bringing down the government. It should also be noted that Greece's President Karamanlis is of Macedonian origin.

At some point in the short term, the Greeks will be forced into an open choice between the EC and Serbia, but it should not be assumed that the Greek public will easily back the European line: preparations for the Single Market, with the austerity programme monitored by EC officials in Athens leading to some quite dramatic rises in the cost of living, and a resurgence of support for the PASOK opposition, which would probably be returned to power if an election were held now, have increased the unpopularity of the EC in Greece.

But however the issue is dealt with in the short term in Athens, it is presumably clear in Brussels that without major external assistance the new Macedonia is likely to collapse economically, and there is no prospect whatsoever of international investment in a state that does not have diplomatic recognition, as the shadowy existence of the 'Turkish Republic of Northern Cyprus' has shown. The prospects for democracy would also be as poor. In the light of the developing crisis in Bosnia, there is no reason to suppose that the re-integration of Macedonia into a new Yugoslav federation is practicable. The federal army has been systematically withdrawing from Macedonia, and border posts, even with Albania, are now controlled by Macedonian officials. In so far as the federal army is the decisive force on the ground, it shows every sign at the moment of being willing to abandon Macedonia to its fate.

Unfortunately some early actions of the Skopje government have been insensitive to Greek concerns, especially the draft banknote design showing a prominent historic building in Thessaloniki as 'Macedonian', at least by implication.

Although there are well-founded rumours of splits in the Greek foreign policy establishment over Macedonia, it is hard to see what new policy could be formed without abandoning vital Greek positions, as Mr Mitsotakis discovered in April. The disputes with the EC have fundamentally affected public opinion, and he has little room to manoeuvre. In the immediate future, the most important developments affecting Macedonia are likely to be in Greece, as the government there attempts to find some compromise between European pressures and domestic viewpoints. As in other problem areas of the Balkans recently, the EC has on this issue often seemed deeply insensitive to the legitimate concerns of people about their cultural identity, to the detriment of the EC's political influence.

Serbia

In Serbia, the government does not at the moment appear strong enough to risk a confrontation with Skopje, in particular given the care with which the Macedonians have attempted to proceed in such a way as to avoid war. Although there is a single substantial Serbian enclave in Macedonia, at Kumanovo, the inhabitants do not at present seem to feel threatened and have not resorted to the proclamations of armed 'independent' Serbian 'republics' that have so bedevilled peace efforts in the north, although pro-autonomy referenda have been held in some places. Serbs have traditionally controlled some of the most prominent economic enterprises in Skopje, and in some cases seem to be turning themselves into honorary Macedonians, in order to benefit from the privatization process. How long this uneasy equilibrium will last is doubtful.

The main dimension of Serbian policy is to allow Macedonia to become a dependent statelet; but if any of the surrounding powers, especially Bulgaria, increased their influence in Skopje dramatically, or took matters as far as territorial revision, then Belgrade would consider itself forced to act. At the moment Serbian interests are served by a policy of inactivity, with the hope that Macedonia will fail to become a viable state and will turn to Serbia as its least offensive neighbour for protection. But Serbian leader Slobodan Milosevic has in the recent past allied himself with the advocates of a Greater Serbia including Macedonia, who claim that it is really 'South Serbia', exactly as it was described in the 1890s. The leader of the Serbian far right, Vojislav Seselj, has spoken in favour of a partition of Macedonia between Bulgaria and Serbia, with a few small areas given to Albania. The Serbian Orthodox Church considers its Macedonian co-religionists as renegades, and that the bishopric of Skopje should be Serbian. The Macedonian Orthodox Church was to all intents and purposes set up by Tito.[3] Although at the moment Serbia is unable to pursue a forward policy towards Macedonia, that state of affairs could rapidly change.

---

3 It remains in schism with all other Orthodox churches, and is itself very divided in the Macedonian diaspora, particularly in Australia.

Bulgaria

Bulgaria has traditionally been the power with the most direct designs on Macedonian territory. In the late nineteenth century quite sizeable sections of the Macedonian population fled to Sofia, and to this day some western Bulgarian cities are made up of people of almost wholly Macedonian origin. Many scholars consider the Macedonian language to be basically a dialect of Bulgarian. In the 1956 census, 187,000 people declared themselves to be Macedonians, despite political pressure from the regime not to do so.

The territory of the contemporary Macedonian state is, however, far from that of nineteenth-century irredentist ambition. The key element in Bulgarian irredentism then was the *Drang nach Saloniki*, the opening to the Aegean and the great port on the Vardar estuary. This would have transformed the economic and political potential of Bulgaria to the detriment of Greece. It is a disturbing sign of the potential for this issue to re-emerge that the largest party in the current Macedonian parliament, the VMRO-DPMNE, the lineal descendant of IMRO, has as its policy the recovery of these territories, and although its influence in Skopje has declined in recent months, it still exists as a major force.

There are also mainstream political parties in Bulgaria which share this ambition. But the economics of it all are doubtful. Macedonia now has little to offer Sofia except people, land and many problems, and no revision of the Greek border could be achieved without a major war. Greece has made it clear that it would call upon its Western military allies to assist its defence of the status quo, although given the nature of the Balkan crisis in 1991-2 it is perhaps doubtful how readily many of them would do so, given that the whole exercise would be strongly reminiscent of many forms of Great Power involvement in Balkan disputes in earlier periods. Apart from the diplomatic dimension, there is in Greece a legacy of popular bitterness from memories of the Bulgarian occupation of parts of Greece during the Second World War, and there is no doubt that any Greek government, of whatever complexion, would have overwhelming popular support for more or less any imaginable policy directed towards the defence of Greek territorial integrity. It should also be noted that wider Macedonian attitudes to Bulgaria were affected in a similar way by the Bulgarian occupation there in the Second World War. But Bulgaria was the first country to recognize the independence of Macedonia, and doubtless plans to involve itself deeply in its affairs. It remains to be seen how far the natural struggle for a regional sphere of influence will be seen by other neighbouring states as an attempt at economic and later, political and military, integration. It is also possible that the long-quiescent notion of a Balkan Federation will re-emerge as an expression of Bulgarian policy.

A European Question

Perhaps the central short-term question for Europe is how far it is going to allow a Serbian-Greek stranglehold on Macedonia to develop. When the EC did not recognize the new state on 15 January 1992, it allowed time for this pressure to develop. The 1991 policy of Macedonian President Gligorov has failed, to the extent that there is no sign of the emergence of a new Yugoslav confederation between the remaining republics. It is independence or nothing. The possibility exists that a viable, if poor, small state could develop with Skopje as a capital if sufficient EC assistance is forthcoming, and a willingness in Brussels and the other EC capitals to stand up to Greek pressure. There is certainly a government in Macedonia now which is deeply – and some may feel, a little naively - committed to a Europe without borders. But the window of opportunity may not last long: external political and internal economic pressures may encourage disintegration and violence if the Macedonians are left to their fate within the ruins of the old Yugoslavia. So perhaps it is possible to conclude with the thought that while the classic features of the Macedonian Question are beginning to reappear in terms of population and territory, the area of decision already extends to a wider Europe, which was not always so in the past, and that the single great power of the European Community has replaced the competing northern European powers of the late nineteenth century. Whether this will mean the issue can be resolved more easily, though, is extremely doubtful, as EC initiatives so far in the region seem to founder on the contradiction that a transnational organization is a poor arbiter of the competing claims of new nationalisms.

THE GREEK MINORITY IN THE ALBANIAN UPRISING

THIS YEAR HAS SEEN THE collapse of the 'pyramid' investment schemes in Albania, followed by an armed uprising in the south of the country against the government of Dr Sali Berisha. The high-interest banks collapsed in January and February, and the widespread street unrest that had been endemic in southern Albanian cities in those months grew into a full-scale armed uprising in early March. It was originally focused in the Adriatic coastal town of Vlora, where two of the largest pyramid schemes, Gjafferi and Populli, had been based. In the first week in March, the Berisha government declared a state of emergency and attempted to regain control of Vlora and other rebellious areas by the use of the security police (SHIK) - all heavily-armed northerners loyal to Berisha - and the army. Opposition leaders in Tirana were harassed and often arrested. Draconian restrictions on the Press were introduced, which were condemned by Western leaders such as the then British Foreign Secretary, Malcolm Rifkind, and hurriedly withdrawn. The people nevertheless believed that the Berisha regime was proposing to introduce a dictatorship.

The clumsy and inefficient military operations precipitated precisely the situation the government was trying to avoid. The army did not prove capable - or willing - to take effective public order measures at street level, but their intervention allowed local community leaders within the rebellious areas to argue that armed resistance to a prospective dictatorship was necessary, and in March there were widespread seizures of weapons from local magazines and military stores. Berisha-appointed officials generally fled and local 'national salvation committees' rapidly became the only effective 'government' in many places.

The Greek Minority in the south played a full part in these events, although their position is often complex and contradictory. The Minority has undergone many changes since the end of communism, and is no longer the generally socially and economically homogenous group of oppressed Orthodox villagers that it was in 1990. Emigration of young people to work in Greece has been very high, which has resulted in severe depopulation in many villages, particularly on the coast between Himara and Saranda. Some political exiles have returned from abroad and repossessed property expropriated under communism. Other ethnic Greeks have become prominent in the new commercial culture post-1991. Ethnic Greeks have generally done well out of the land privatization process. But elderly people left behind in rural areas have a very uncertain existence, dependent on remittances from abroad.

I was in Argyrokastro (Gjirokastra) on 8-9 March when the town changed sides and went over to the rebellion, and many of the difficulties of the position of the Minority can be seen in the events of that day. Roughly speaking, ethnic Greeks in and around the town fell into four groups with very disparate political attitudes. The first group was the Greek shopkeepers, nearly all ex-emigres, who had done well out of the privatization process and who were generally Berisha supporters. Without exception these people had fled, or were preparing to do so. Their shops had already been smashed and looted. The second group, much the largest in the town itself, were mostly unemployed young men, who were enthusiastic supporters of the rebellion. The third group, small in numbers but politically very significant, were ex-army and ex-police officers who had been dismissed by the Berisha government on political grounds. They provided a core of older leaders. The last group were the villagers in the Droppul valley, who were usually elderly and were trying to keep their heads down and avoid involvement in the anarchy.

The town fell to the rebellion when the government sent Special Forces troops in helicopters to try to secure the local magazine, the largest in southern Albania. At about 12 o'clock the river valley below the city was suddenly full of armed men. But they were prevented from reaching the town by fire from local SHIK and troops who had mutinied and seized weapons from the town police HQ. I subsequently discovered that in the mayhem the SHIK men had driven their boss away, and the local police chief had actually led an attack on his own police station to secure weapons.

The pro-Berisha troops retreated to their helicopters and returned to their base north of Tepelena. This town had been in rebel hands for two days. Within a few minutes, the main army magazine had been opened, and soon literally thousands of weapons of every description were being distributed to the population. Tanks were seized and moved to guard the river bridges. Ethnic Greeks were prominent in all this alongside Albanians, and I understand from my fellow *Times* correspondent, Anthony Loyd, who had spent time in Saranda the previous day, that this was the case there also.

Elections in June brought a substantial Socialist victory and the ultimate fall of Berisha, but there was no immediate handing in of weapons or restoration of order. The new government is a Socialist-dominated coalition but with important ministries, such as the Interior Ministry, held by a centrist, the National Director of Archaeology Dr Neritan Çeka.

It is obviously impossible to foresee the future of the Minority after these tragic but not unexpected events, but although everyone is by definition endangered in the anarchy, the ethnic Greeks are not, per se, particularly singled out for popular anger, apart from the 'outsiders' who returned from exile abroad to repossess property. It is difficult to see this group having any role in the reconstruction process, but the basis of Minority life and culture should survive elsewhere, if in very testing circumstances.*

* This article originally appeared in *Anglo-Hellenic Review*, London, no. 16, Autumn 1997, pp. 8-16.

THE GREEK MINORITY IN ALBANIA IN THE AFTERMATH OF COMMUNISM

Introduction

BILATERAL RELATIONS BETWEEN GREECE AND Albania have often been severely strained since the demise of communism in Albania, with breaks in diplomatic relations, violent border incidents involving military fatalities, and the expulsion of tens of thousands of Albanian migrant workers from Greece. At the heart of these growing tensions is the fate of the sizeable ethnic Greek community in southern Albania. This paper examines the historical basis of this national minority, its status and political behaviour during the communist period, and the current factors contributing to ethnic tension in post-communist Albania. The dynamic interplay between Greek-Albanian bilateral relations, the sub-national divide among ethnic Albanians themselves, and domestic inter-ethnic politics, it will be argued, hold the key to determining the ethnic Greek minority's ability to pursue and achieve its interests, and thus to the development of a stable Albanian polity.

The emergence of ethnic tension, it should be noted, stands in sharp contrast to traditional western understandings of Albania. During the communist period, Albania was generally viewed from abroad as an ethnically homogeneous state (although its Balkan neighbours were well aware of the existence of the ethnic Greek minority within the country).[1] Even insofar as it was involved in international bodies under the isolationist communist regime established after 1944, this view was nonetheless maintained by an international community generally ignorant of most aspects of Albania's history and political development. As a small, relatively obscure country with neither a strong tradition of statehood nor a well-known and independent culture, the perception encouraged by Enver Hoxha's regime thus effectively structured foreign understandings. These assumed, in essence, a united country freed from the Turks by its hardy mountain people, who then emerged into nationhood as a homogeneous society with a strong national culture underpinned by shared traditions. Albanian political integration was further seen to be reflected in, and reinforced by, the struggle to free the country from Axis occupation during the Second World War and the partisan struggle which brought Hoxha and the communists to power.[2]

---

1 See Enver Hoxha, *Two Friendly Peoples* (Tirana: 8 Nentori, 1985) for a general view of how the Albanian communists viewed the Greek minority issue after 1944 and under communism. It is clear that Hoxha had little information on the early stages of the Greek Civil War and its effects on the Greek minority in Albania.

2 See Institute of Marxist-Leninist Studies, *History of the Party of Labour of Albania*, 2nd ed (Tirana: 8 Nentori, 1982) for the official communist view of Albanian history. See also Stefanaq Pollo and Arben Puto, *The History of Albania*, trans. Carole Wiseman & Ginnie Hole (London: Routledge & Kegan Paul, 1981).

And, while the outside world regarded the country as a grim, poverty-stricken *gulag* ruled by the world's most hard-line communist regime, a European equivalent of North Korea under Kim Il-Sung, the prevailing view nonetheless presupposed that rigid political uniformity implied the absence of cultural and ethnic diversity.

Both images were misleading. First, while Albania did experience a growth of national consciousness in the late nineteenth century, it was quite slow in throwing off the Ottoman yoke, becoming in November 1912 the last Balkan state to declare its independence, which was formally recognized at the London Conference of Ambassadors in 1913. Achievement of national statehood had been impeded by the Ottoman authorities' strategy of dividing the Albanians among four imperial provinces and blocking the establishment of an Albanian-language educational system, with no common written alphabet being developed until 1908. The result was a lingering heritage of cultural differences and political divisions, particularly between the two regionally-based sub-groups of the Albanian people, the Ghegs and the Tosks, whose relations were marked by only limited cooperation during the national renaissance and in opposing Ottoman rule.[3] In fact, until the 1930s, large areas of northern and central Albania had no relationship with the capital (Tirana) as a legitimate state centre in the modern sense, and still lived according to the feudal code of *Kanun i Lek Dukagjinit*, the medieval body of lore and convention regulating the operation of the blood feud.[4] This code remains influential in the north up to the present day.

The absence of cultural-territorial unity was again reflected politically within the anti-Axis resistance movement in 1943 and 1944, with bitter conflicts between communist and non-communist groups corresponding for the most part to the geographical divide between the distinct Albanian communities in the north and south of the country. In the south, the Tosks generally supported the left-wing National Liberation Movement organized and dominated by the communists following the party's establishment, under the leadership of Enver Hoxha, in 1941. The northern Ghegs divided their support between the Balli Kombetar, composed of right-wing pro-republican nationalists, and the royalist Legality Organization. The latter, supported by the northern Mati tribe, sought the restoration of fellow Mati Ahmet Zogu,

---

3 See Stavro Skendi, *The Albanian National Awakening*, 1878-1912 (Princeton NJ: Princeton University Press, 1967). See also Miranda Vickers, *The Albanians: A Modern History* (London: IB Tauris, 1995), pp. 32-53.

4 Vickers, *op cit.*, chapter 5.

who had established a monarchy in 1928 and ruled as King Zog I until he fled the country when Italy invaded in April 1939.[5] Significantly, beneath the external uniformity imposed by the communist regime that Hoxha established in 1944 and led until his death in 1985, such regionally-centred patron-client relationships persisted, the main difference being that the social base of the new regime shifted to the south. Kinship, tribal links, and the rigid friend-foe distinction central to the Kanun were retained as key elements of the system, accounting for many serious political and economic conflicts in the post-war years, including within the communist establishment itself.[6]

Second, in addition to the division among ethnic Albanians, there was, and remains, a Greek minority, as well as a number of smaller groups of Vlachs, Roma (Gypsies), Jews, Armenians, 'Macedonians', Serbs and Montenegrins. In political terms, the Greek minority is by far the most consequential group. But, while culturally and politically more integrated within Albanian society, the other groups have some importance, if only to the extent that their persistence calls into question the universalist assumptions propagated by the communist regime and, to a significant extent, by post-communist Albanian governments.

5   The history of Albania during the Second World War has been highly controversial, with most of the protagonists in the argument British ex-Special Operations Executive officers involved in the anti-Axis campaign. The best general account is to be found in Reginald Hibbert, *Albania's National Liberation: The Bitter Victory* (London: Pinter, 1991). For a contrary view, see Julian Amery, *Sons of the Eagle* (London: Macmillan, 1948). A good account of an important part of the military campaign is to be found in Brigadier T Davies, *Illyrian Venture* (London: The Bodley Head, 1952).

6   For an analysis of how elements of clan-based social organization and its core principles of unbending loyalty and honour have influenced Albania's post-communist political culture, see Fabian Schmidt, 'An Old System Blends into the Present', *Transition*, vol. 2, no. 18 (6 September 1996), pp. 50-53.

The Ottoman Adriatic Coast

The Demographics of Albania's Ethnic Minorities

Most members of the Greek minority live in the south of the country and in Tirana and are estimated to comprise 3 per cent of a total population of about 3.4 million, although this is a highly contentious question.[7] Two thousand Serbs and Montenegrins live predominantly in the villages north of Shkodra around Vraka, adjacent to Montenegro. The 15,000 Macedonians, who speak a mixed dialect with Bulgarian and Serbian elements, live either in the Peshkopi area in north-east Albania, or around Lakes Prespa and Ochrid in the south-east. The number of Albanian Roma is unknown, but may be as high as 75,000. Their settlement is scattered throughout the country, with all main towns having a Roma quarter, most of which are long-established and appear to date from early Ottoman times (if not before). The 80,000 Vlachs generally live in the southern mountains, with particularly large concentrations in the south around Korca, Selenitsa and near Vlora, although the latter group has been seriously affected by industrialization and has become almost entirely assimilated into Albanian urban society. The Jewish community of about 800 people lived mainly in Tirana but migrated to Israel en masse in 1991, although some families have since returned. The Armenian community, of similar size, exists in Tirana and Vlora, and is made up of qualified professionals, some of whom seem to have emigrated from Albania in the last two years, casting doubt on the general future of this group. There are also a number of individuals of direct Turkish descent. None of the communities of Soviet and Chinese citizens that existed temporarily in Albania under communism have remained, and there has been no evidence to date to suggest that they have had a lasting influence on patterns of ethnic minority settlement.[8]

The Politics of History: The Greeks of Southern Albania

Census figures from the communist period do not provide accurate information about ethnic minorities in Albania, and in any case controversy over the size of the Greek minority long predates communism. While historical memory and collective myths are always and everywhere of considerable importance in framing cultural identity and its political expression, in the case of Albania and its ethnic Greeks, ancient history is especially important in this respect.

---

7   The figure of 3 per cent is taken from estimates by the US Central Intelligence Agency, *CIA World Factbook*, 1994.

8   Miranda Vickers & James Pettifer, *Albania: From Anarchy to a Balkan Identity* (London: C Hurst, 1997), chapter 10.

The ancient Illyrian tribes from which the modem Albanians claim descent occupied most of the territory of the present state of Albania, as well as adjoining parts of the Balkans, until the Roman conquest. Before, however, there had been ancient Greek colonization of the coast, beginning in the fifth century BC with the establishment of important ancient Greek settlements at Dyrrachium (modem Durres), Apollonia (near modem Fier) and Butrint (near Saranda). In addition to this colonization, in southern Albania south of the River Shkumbin there were large numbers of people known to the ancient geographer Strabo (writing in the first century AD) as Epirot. These people spoke and wrote mostly in Greek, although he recorded that some tribes, such as the Bylliones, were bilingual.

While most ethnic Greeks claim direct lineal descent from the ancient Epirot tribes, Albanian historians argue that all of these tribes were Illyrian in origin, even if they had begun to speak Greek as a result of coastal colonization. In contrast, Greek nationalists claim that most of Albania in the Tosk-dominated area south of the Shkumbin is Vorio Epirus (northern Epirus) and essentially Greek from ancient times, and that it should therefore ultimately be regarded as a part of Greece itself. Albanians claim that the minority as it currently exists is the result of population movements under the Ottoman Empire, and that the great majority of the Greeks arrived in Albania as indentured labourers in the time of the Ottoman *beys*.[9]

In the modern period, as the struggle for Albanian independence developed under the disintegrating Ottoman Empire, many parts of southern Albania were subject to violent inter-communal conflict, as Greek irredentists attempted to integrate parts of what is now southern Albania into a 'Greater Greece'. Given its large Greek-speaking population, the city of Gjirokastra (in Greek, Argyrokastro), in the Vjosa (Aoos) River valley, only twenty miles from the Greek border, was a particularly active centre of irredentist ambition. Outbreaks of ethnic violence in the area were particularly serious immediately after Albanian independence was declared and during the Second Balkan War, as some Albanian-speaking villages in Epirus fought on the side of the Turks against the Greek-speaking villages. In February 1914, a Pan-Epirote Association was founded in Gjirokastra, and the town and its vicinity were proclaimed a part of Greece. In May 1914, the Great Powers signed the Protocol of Corfu, which recognized the area as

---

9   For a clear and accessible account of ancient history in the area that is now Albania, see the essay by Frank Walbank, 'Albania in Antiquity', in James Pettifer (ed,), *Blue Guide: Albania* (New York: Norton, 1996).

Greek, after which it was occupied by the Greek army from October 1914 until October 1915. Greece's administration under the Protocol was short-lived, however, and collapsed after the Italian invasion of 1915.[10]

Northern Epirus reverted to Albania under Italian protection, a state of affairs that was formally ratified in 1925 by the delineation of Albania's southern border under the December 1913 Protocol of Florence, which Greece still has not officially recognized. Under King Zog, the Greek villages suffered considerable repression, including the forcible closure of Greek-language schools in 1933-1934 and the ordering of Greek Orthodox monasteries to accept mentally sick individuals as inmates. During the Second World War, the Greek minority supported the anti-Axis resistance, and when the Partisan campaign was started under communist leadership, a separate battalion of ethnic Greek partisans (the Thanas Ziko battalion) was established.[11] During the national liberation struggle in the later stages of the war, the Albanian communists were able to prevent contact between the Greek minority and the right-wing *andartes* of Napoleon Zervas (EDES) in southern Epirus, who sought to unite northern Epirus with Greece. In 1946, with Hoxha's regime already in place, Greece attempted to reincorporate northern Epirus into its territory at the Paris Peace Conference, but failed.[12]

Thus, southern Albania and its Greek-speaking population have represented a chronic point of contention - continuing to the present - in Albania's post-independence history, manifested mainly as a territorial dispute between Albania and Greece, but also as a struggle to define a distinct Albanian ethnicity and national heritage. And, as has been common throughout the Balkans in the twentieth century, central to these struggles are the ongoing historiographical debates that suffuse history, whether ancient or modern, with nationalist meaning. Indeed, as Albanian communism would clearly demonstrate, where nation- and state-building have been the order of the day for successive generations of political elites, the definition of minority status, crucial in reflecting and altering the balance of political power within multi-ethnic states, transcends the regime types according to which that power is exercised.

---

10 For the best account of the destruction caused in Epirus and southern Albania by inter-communal violence during this period, as well as the main diplomatic intrigues which affected this region, see Rene Puaux, *The Sorrows of Epirus* (Chicago: Argonaut reprint, 1963).

11 Hoxha, *op cit.*, p. 15ff.

12 There has been very little study of the Northern Epirus issue in this period. For an interesting but highly pro-Greek view, see Pyrrus Ruches, *Albania's Captives* (Chicago: Argo Press, 1964).

The Ethnic Greek Minority under Communism

An inquiry established in 1922 by the League of Nations to study the question of the Greek population in Albania concluded that there were about 25,000 Greek-speaking people in Albania. However, the area studied was confined to the southern border fringes, and there is good reason to believe that this estimate was very low.[13] At present, organizations in Greece pursuing issues concerning northern Epirus claim that the number is as high as 400,000 in Albania as a whole. The figure used by Greek governments in public statements and documents is generally lower.

In contrast, Albanian governments use a much lower figure of 58,000 which rests on the unrevised definition of 'minority' adopted during the communist period. Under this definition, minority status was limited to those who lived in 99 villages in the southern border areas, thereby excluding important concentrations of Greek settlement in Vlora (perhaps 8,000 people in 1994) and in adjoining areas along the coast, ancestral Greek towns such as Himara, and ethnic Greeks living elsewhere throughout the country. Mixed villages outside this designated zone, even those with a clear majority of ethnic Greeks, were not considered minority areas and therefore were denied any Greek-language cultural or educational provisions. In addition, many Greeks were forcibly removed from the minority zones to other parts of the country as a product of communist population policy, an important and constant element of which was to pre-empt ethnic sources of political dissent. Greek place-names were changed to Albanian names, while use of the Greek language, prohibited everywhere outside the minority zones, was prohibited for many official purposes within them as well.

Although some Greek-language education existed under communism, pupils were taught only Albanian history and culture, even in Greek-language classes at the primary level. In general, some secondary-level provision for Greek-language education existed, but, again, only for towns and villages within the designated minority areas and with the additional proviso that there was a majority of Greek-speakers in each class in the school. Because school curricula in the Greek language in the designated minority areas were *de facto* identical with the standard Albanian-language curriculum, efforts to study many of the greatest works of ancient Greek literature were rendered impossible. Nor, with the exception of archaeology (which flourished during the communist period), was it possible to study other aspects

---

13 See *Albania* (London: Naval Intelligence Handbook, 1945), p. 178ff.

of classical Hellenistic culture once opportunities for travel abroad to Moscow State University ended following Albania's 1961 break with the Soviet Union.

At the same time, even the formal obligation to provide Greek-language education was often evaded by the regime's continuous efforts to transfer ethnic Greeks to other parts of the country from villages containing a bare majority of Greek speakers. Much of the knowledge that we have of this process necessarily relies on anecdotal evidence, as no official records of population displacement exist from the communist period and the number of people involved was quite small. Nevertheless, the process appears to have left considerable political and cultural traces in the remaining Greek-speaking areas, while the continuous threat of arbitrary administrative action by Tirana has sown a heritage of distrust that underlies some of the contemporary problems affecting relations between postcommunist governments and the Greek minority.

The repression of minority culture and education (with the exception of some independent cultural activity, such as folk dancing) was continuous with the policy pursued by the royalist regime of King Zog, under which Greek-language education had been attacked and eventually virtually eliminated in the 1930s. However, this process was further intensified in the post-war years under communism, particularly with the onset in 1967 of the campaign by Albania's communist party, the Albanian Party of Labour (PLA), to eradicate organized religion, a prime target of which was the Orthodox Church.[14] Many churches were damaged or destroyed during this period, and many Greek-language books were banned because of their religious themes or orientation. Yet, as with other communist states, particularly in the Balkans, where measures putatively geared towards the consolidation of political control intersected with the pursuit of national integration, it is often impossible to distinguish sharply between ideological and ethno-cultural bases of repression. This is all the more true in the case of Albania's anti-religion campaign because it was merely one element in the broader 'Ideological and Cultural Revolution' begun by Hoxha in 1966 but whose main features he outlined at the PLA's Fourth Congress in 1961.[15]

---

14 For a collection of documents, see Basil Kondis & Eleftheria Manda (eds), *The Greek Minority in Albania - A documentary record* (1921-1993), (Thessaloniki: Institute of Balkan Studies, 1994). For background, see also Basil Kondis, *Greece and Albania, 1908-1914* (Thessaloniki: Institute of Balkan Studies, 1976).

15 The best account of this period can be found in Peter R Prifti, *Socialist Albania Since 1944* (Cambridge MA: MIT Press, 1978).

While the inability to draw such a clear line makes it difficult to assess the full contemporary political implications of previous policies, their unambiguous impact on ethnic survival explains why the definition of 'minority' remains highly controversial. If a minority member is defined as someone who speaks Greek at home and at work, actively practises Greek Orthodoxy and lives in a Greekspeaking town or village, then the figure put forward by both communist and postcommunist Albanian governments may have some coherence. But there are undoubtedly much larger numbers of people who are in general Hellenist in their descent, cultural identity and beliefs. This number has increased in recent years owing to acculturation of numerous Albanian migrant workers in Greece. Generally, members of the Greek minority in Tirana and other cities appear to have been much more closely linked to the communist regime than were the rural majority of ethnic Greeks, who remained in the minority's heartland around Dervician and Gjirokastra. The latter have generally remained culturally conservative, anti-communist and Orthodox. For some, a private adherence to the old ideal of unity with Greece must have remained alive, and, although there are no records of oppositional political activity during the communist period that would demonstrate this definitively, individual minority members were occasionally arrested and tried for 'anti-state' offences.[16]

Assessing the consequences of the old regime's repressive measures is further complicated by the difficulty of arriving at an exact view of the role and status of ethnic Greeks within the PLA and the Democratic Front, the two main popular organizations officially sanctioned under communism. As with the rest of the population, most ethnic Greeks belonged to the Democratic Front, the umbrella organization, but the PLA's membership records did not register ethnicity. It is likely that the number of ethnic Greeks in the party, along with the size of the Greek minority as a whole, was augmented by the wave of refugees fleeing Greece following the end of the Greek civil war in 1949. In the main, these were leftists, and some were active communists who rose to important positions in the Albanian regime.[17] Their orientation was secular and anti-clerical, and they appear to have played little part in activities opposing the regime. At the same time, however, apart from a few prominent figures, it appears that many ethnic Greeks did not feel secure with their cultural identity as Greeks within the party, often

---

16 See *Albania: Political Imprisonment and the Law* (London: Amnesty International, 1984).
17 Some important Albanian communist leaders were wholly or partly Greek, like long-serving Politburo member Spiro Koleka, who came from the predominantly ethnic Greek Minority town of Himara on the Albanian Adriatic coast.

adopting Albanian names and severing any remaining links with the Orthodox Church during the period in which it remained legal. Indeed, with no provision for higher education in Greek at Tirana University or travel abroad for such purposes after 1961, entrance to elite cadres for the nearly two-thirds of Albania's population born after the Second World War was restricted to those who affirmed, at least outwardly, an entirely Albanian cultural identity.

It is in the light of this legacy of state treatment of Greek-speakers in pre-communist and communist Albania that contemporary Greek demands must be understood. Moreover, this legacy serves to influence aspects of present-day Albanian government officials' understanding of how problems concerning the Greek minority should be managed. To be sure, the assertion of ethnic minority demands is partly a consequence of the opportunities for political entrepreneurship afforded by the fluid domestic context of post-communist politics. Most importantly, however, in the case of both the pre-communist and communist regimes, policies designed to impede the maintenance or growth of a distinct Greek ethnic identity within Albania were implemented within, and were powerfully shaped by, an environment of official irredentist claims by Greece. Following a brief *rapprochement* in the post-communist period, contemporary ethnic relations and official treatment of the Greek minority within Albania have been somewhat conditioned by the sub-national division among the ethnic Albanian majority as well.

After Communism: Developments in Inter-Ethnic Relations

With the communist regime's collapse in the winter of 1990-1991 and its replacement by a democratically elected National Unity government the following spring, independent ethnic minority organizations were quickly established. For example, the Vlachs formed the National Vlach Association, with offices in Tirana under the chairmanship of Themistocles Cule, the Armenians organized the Armenians of Albania, and so on. The Greek minority formed the Omonia organization in February 1990. In all cases, these were originally loosely-organized human rights associations established with the aim of winning ethnic minority rights within a functioning multicultural civil society operating along Western lines. In general, they came into being as a result of popular movements imitating those seen across Eastern Europe on Italian and Greek television broadcasts. Thus, there were no established leadership structures; instead, prominent individuals who had some knowledge of politics gained a more or less spontaneous following of friends, neighbours, and acquaintances within the community. Conceived within a political context in which the one-party state was at least formally still in existence, even if its coercive powers had collapsed, their chief priority was the establishment of genuine cultural and political independence for their members.

In fact, many of the new leaders of the Greek minority in the south had at one time been part of the old political establishment, with the important consequence that the duration of Omonia's initial organizational disarray was relatively short. As has been noted, some ethnic Greeks achieved considerable prominence in the post-war years under communism, particularly ex-partisans from towns in the south such as Saranda, Himara and Vlora who had fought alongside Hoxha against the Germans. And, as has been true throughout Albania, long-time communists, whether at the local, regional, or national level, were able to metamorphose successfully and retain their positions within the political elite after the regime's collapse - often through a nationalist 'switch in time' that has benefited elites in much of Eastern Europe. At the same time, defence of Greek rights appears to have led in many cases to expulsion from the Party for promoting 'nationalism' or 'separatism', particularly in the late 1980s, while subsequent links with the opposition rendered the political past of these ethnic Greek leaders entirely unimportant. On the contrary, during the popular turmoil and street politics from 1989-1991, it appeared as though burgeoning political pluralism would usher in a new dawn both for minority identity and those political elites who sought to capitalize on it.[18]

Given the centrality of Orthodoxy to Slavic and Greek ethnic identity, the restoration of religious rights played a large part in the activities of several groups. The ferocity with which the communist regime repressed religion, particularly in the years until Hoxha's death in 1985, meant that much of the country's religious infrastructure was decimated by the time the ban on religious observance, codified as Article 37 of the 1976 constitution, was rescinded in early spring 1989. For Omonia, the restitution of Church property lost during the forced appropriations of the late communist period became a clear priority. Thus, almost immediately after Omonia's formation in 1990, a delegation of ethnic Greeks met the Albanian government to discuss religious issues.

Because the early leadership of Omonia was in some part composed of former communists, they were often well connected in Tirana and able to bring effective pressure to bear on the government. On the whole, their demands, as well as similar objectives on the

18 Vickers & Pettifer, *op cit.*, chapter 10.

part of other groups, were accomplished without much difficulty or official obstruction. Title to Church property was clearly delineated in the localities, with few of the competing ownership claims that have complicated the restitution process throughout Eastern Europe. Under the chaotic conditions prevailing in Albania at the time, most local communities simply seized back their old church or mosque buildings from the state without official sanction.[19] In most cases, the buildings had been used for agricultural storage purposes, and villagers simply removed their contents and began to restore them for religious use with makeshift altars and furnishings. For a time, there was a significant degree of inter-religious cooperation in these developments, as in 1989 and 1990 in the northern city of Shkodra, where Muslims, Catholics and the region's few Orthodox Albanians combined forces to bring pressure on the local and national government to reopen religious buildings for worship.

In fact, most religious groups found that they were pressing at an open door with respect to the 1989-1991 Tirana governments. Despite the constitutional ban, relaxation of official repression of religion as such, not merely Orthodoxy, had begun in 1988-1989, exemplified by improved relations with the Catholic Church, which culminated in Mother Theresa's visit to Albania in February 1989. Reformist communist leaders such as Fatos Nano and Ramiz Alia, who led the PLA's successor, the Socialist Party, after its decisive victory in the 1991 elections, were well aware of the gross human rights violations that had occurred during Hoxha's effort to make Albania an atheist state in the 1970s. They viewed generosity towards the various religious groups and Churches as both a morally and politically desirable policy, one also likely to win approval from the international community. Indeed, foreign investment was being courted not only from the West, but also increasingly from Islamic countries, making a clear policy of religious tolerance essential.

This liberalizing trend with respect to religion was accompanied by an initial extension of formal national minority rights in political institutions. Faced with a multitude of pressing economic, social and political problems, the last communist government in 1989 and the first National Unity governments in 1990 and 1991 had little difficulty in agreeing to such demands. In the south, Greek minority representation

---

19 See my report in *The Independent* (London), 6 February 1991. The best account in English of the outlook of the northern Greek bishops on the persecution of the Orthodox Church under communism is to be found in Metropolitan Sevastianos of Dryinoupolis, *Northern Epirus Crucified* (Athens, 1986).

already existed, in a tenuous form, through many local decisionmaking bodies. Ethnic Greeks who were communists or who, if not, were prepared to work with the one-party system, were often involved in local administration in the southern minority areas and were thus able to assist with the projection of wider minority demands in Tirana. Indeed, Omonia's early success was greatly facilitated by the fact that already at this early stage, as in most later political debate, it acted as a united body with a clear and well-supported local and national leadership (who, given the geographical concentration of the minority, were often the same people). As a result, a generally agreed-upon agenda of human rights demands, in addition to those concerning religious exercise, quickly emerged. One of the most important demands, the right to travel, was immediately secured, thereby allowing ethnic Greeks, often after a fifty-year hiatus, to visit relatives in Greece.

Rising Tensions in Albania's Ethnic Relations

Despite Omonia's early achievements in the immediate aftermath of communism's collapse in 1990 and 1991 - a period culminating in the March 1992 election of the first completely non-communist government under Dr Sali Berisha - problems for the Greek minority soon began to surface. While such basic human rights as freedom of religious worship, publication and travel had quickly been secured, hopes on the Greek side for sustained progress in institutionalizing harmonious relations with the ethnic Albanian majority were not realized.

This reflected a change in atmosphere that was partly linked to the Albanian economy's growing dependence on income from migrant workers in Greece. Following the removal of border controls in December 1990, large numbers of poor Albanians fled to Greece as illegal migrant workers, contributing to increased tension between the two countries.[20] Within Albania, the economic status of many Greek communities quickly began to rise above that of ethnic Albanian communities, as minority members found work and residence rights in Greece easier to obtain. This disparity in treatment by Greece led to conflict, first over ethnic Greeks' demands for greater Greek-language educational provision. While ethnic Greeks resented a continuing absence of teachers and resources, as well as little interest at the national level in altering the communist-era definition of minority areas entitled to Greek-language schools, ethnic Albanians regarded Greeks as having access to financial aid from Greece and the Greek diaspora that was unavailable to them, as well as medical treatment and other benefits in the northern Greek town

20 Vickers & Pettifer, *op cit.*, chapter 10.

of Ioannina. In 1991, Greek shops were attacked in the coastal town of
Saranda, home to a large minority population, and inter-ethnic relations
throughout Albania worsened.

There was also a widespread view among ethnic Albanians that the
Tirana government disproportionately favoured the Greek minority in
the process of land privatization. This perception was in turn nurtured
by the underlying division within the ethnic Albanian majority. Berisha's
newly elected anti-communist government, dominated by northern
Ghegs, was viewed as attempting to buy off ethnic Greek radicalism while
providing few benefits to ethnic Albanians in the Tosk-dominated (and
historically far more pro-communist) south. In fact, the Greek minority
was regarded by the Berisha government as being highly susceptible to
extremist Orthodox revivalist propaganda broadcast from expanding
irredentist organizations based in northern Greece. However, while
religious differences among Albanians, who adhere to Catholicism,
Eastern Orthodoxy and Sunni and Bektashi Islam, have historically
played little role in shaping domestic political conflict, Tirana's suspicion
embraced Orthodox Albanians as well, as they too have often been
influenced by anti-government propaganda from northern Greek
bishops. With very few Orthodox Albanians in the north, the Berisha
government, composed almost entirely of Sunni Muslims, demonstrated
its lack of sympathy for either Orthodoxy in general or the Greek
minority - all of whose members are Orthodox - by proposing in 1994 a
requirement that all heads of religious groups be Albanian-born. While
the constitutional draft containing this provision was voted down in a
referendum in November 1994, an important reason for its rejection was
that the Albanian Orthodox Church had invited Archbishop (Eparch)
Anastasios Giannulatos, a Greek citizen, to lead it temporarily in its
effort to rebuild.[21]

Thus, what many southern Tosks saw as an alliance between the
Greek minority and the Gheg north could be (and for many Orthodox
Tosks evidently was) interpreted as Gheg power exercised with a view
to asserting northern interests over those of the south as a whole. With
respect to the Greek minority's demands for recognition of cultural
difference, this meant that ethnic Albanians' deep-seated suspicion of
Greek irredentism, which could be expected under any government, was
exacerbated by the sectionally-based Gheg hegemony - justified partly
in terms of hostility toward residual communist influence - extended
throughout its region of settlement.

---

21 See Fabian Schmidt, 'Between Political Strife and a Developing Economy', *Transition*
(1994 in Review: Part 1), p. 8.

The most visible focus of the Berisha government's fear of Greek irredentism was the Northern Epirus Liberation Front (MAVI), which claimed responsibility for the car bombing of Albania's ambassador to Greece in 1991 and was accused in 1994 and 1995 of orchestrating attacks on Albanian border posts and military personnel.[22] However, the MAVI threat could be magnified only after relations between ethnic Albanians and Greeks had already deteriorated following the attempt by the Socialist-led government to prevent Omonia's participation in the 1992 elections on the grounds that it represented exclusively ethnic interests and was therefore illegal. Following strong protests by the Conference on Security and Cooperation in Europe, the Council of Europe, the United States, and other powerful international actors, this decision was reversed. However, while Omonia ultimately did participate, under the name of the Party of Human Rights, and won seven seats in the 140-seat Assembly, the episode was extremely damaging to interethnic relations. The government attempted to improve matters with the mixed electoral system introduced by Vilson Ahmeti's interim government prior to the 1992 elections: 100 seats are allocated on a majority basis in single-member districts, with the remaining forty seats divided proportionally among parties receiving at least 4 per cent of the popular vote.[23] The concentration of ethnic Greeks in and around centres of Hellenism such as Saranda and Gjirokastra could guarantee their election there, but nowhere else in the country is success for an Omonia-based candidate possible. While it has been possible for the overwhelmingly ethnic Greek villages along the Aoos River valley stretching toward the Greek-Albanian border to secure majorities on municipal councils, the same electoral calculus generally applies at the local level. Faced with their inability to secure significant representation in national bodies, disagreement began to arise within Omonia, and among the Greek population generally, as to the surest means toward amassing the political power necessary to secure their demands, particularly expansion of Greek-language education to areas outside the old communist-designated minority zones. This debate over means rapidly developed into a debate over ends.

---

22 It is not clear to what extent MAVI was a significant political and paramilitary formation rather than merely a fanatical splinter group. At the time, the Albanian government claimed that Greek army and secret police personnel were involved in the attacks. The name is adopted from the wartime Northern Epirot organization which fought as a separate resistance group against the Axis in 1943. It was destroyed in vicious fighting with the German occupiers and the Albanian nationalist forces of the Balli Kombetar, and it played no part in the final liberation of the country.

23 See Fabian Schmidt, 'The Opposition's Changing Face', *Transition*, vol. 1, no. 11 (30 June 1995), p. 50.

As the internal debate that accompanied Omonia's evolution from a human rights association into a political party became marked by the formal emergence of moderate and radical wings, the absence of either Albanian or Greek government support for their agenda quickly put party moderates at a serious disadvantage. The moderate wing has campaigned for ethnic Greek interests within a modified framework of the current Albanian state, while Omonia's radical wing calls for border revisions and *enosis* (union with Greece). An important turning point came in April 1992, when Omonia's chairman, the moderate Sotir Qiriazati, wrote an open letter to Greek Prime Minister Constantine Mitsotakis, calling for an autonomous region to be established in southern Albania and requesting substantial Greek government support for the region's social and economic development. These proposals were rejected not only by the Albanian side, which unanimously views ethnic territorial autonomy as tantamount to eventual secession, but also by Athens. This failure resulted in a transfer of the political initiative within Omonia to the radicals, who, entirely unbeholden to Albanian government support, argued that only a strategy guided by *enosis* would secure the necessary commitment from Athens.

The moderates' view of the Greek minority's position within the Albanian polity has been weakened further by the highly constitutive role of religion in ethnic Greek identity. Indeed, disputes between Omonia's moderate and radical wings have been subsumed in the complex history of the autocephalous Albanian Orthodox Church, with religious leaders playing a central part in defining alternative conceptions of the ethnic group's political status.[24] The radicals were supported by the influential Orthodox Bishop of Konitsa in Greece, the late Metropolitan Sevastianos, whose diocese includes parts of southern Albania, while Archbishop Giannulatos is a leading moderate who has attempted to mitigate irredentist claims. However, while the lack of trained clerics led Albanian Orthodox authorities in 1990 to invite the Patriarchate of Constantinople (Istanbul), with Albanian government approval, to appoint ethnic Greeks to senior positions in the Church, many Albanians view this as part of a Greek effort to gain lasting control over Albanian Orthodoxy. Thus, given that the Albanian Church's establishment in 1929 and independence (recognized in 1937) represented a key element of state-building in interwar Albania, and that Orthodoxy alone underpins the Greek conception of southern

24 For a comprehensive overview of church history from a Greek perspective, see, in Greek, 'The Albanian Autocephalous Orthodox Church' by Apostolis Glavina, Thessaloniki, 1992. See also Sevastianos, *op cit.*

Albania as northern Epirus, Archbishop Giannulatos' mere presence in his religious role has served to emphasize the ambiguity of his political position.

Against this background, it is not surprising that the first substantial open conflict in the Gjirokastra region, in the spring of 1993, occurred after the expulsion of an ethnic Greek Orthodox priest, Archimandrite Chrysostomos Maidonis, for allegedly taking part in subversive, anti-Albanian activities. He was accused by Tirana of abusing his ministry by preaching separatism and *enosis* among the Greek minority. In widespread unrest in the Greek villages, local leaders were arrested and there were well-attested accounts of human rights violations in the area, including the sentencing of the Mayor of Dervician, a minority village, to six months in prison for raising the Greek flag on Greece's national day.[25] This was followed by a noticeable expansion of surveillance of the minority by the reformed secret police in the minority areas, as well as a revival of the population movement controls that originated under the communist regime. The Greek government's response was swift: it stepped up deportation of Albanians working illegally in Greece and cancelled three official visits to Tirana after pro-Maidonis demonstrations outside the Albanian embassy in Athens led the Berisha government to recall its ambassador.[26] Thus, the increase in the level of Albanian repression, and the Greek government's reaction to it, demonstrated how porous boundaries between politically salient organizations and actors at the sub-governmental level in the 'home state' and the 'kin state' can shape official behaviour in ways dangerous for inter-ethnic, and inter-state, peace.[27]

Bilateral Politics, Emigration and Domestic Ethnic Relations

Since the end of communism, there has been a considerable increase in Albanian-Greek trade, with the very large illegal migrant workforce in Greece representing a major factor in bilateral ties.[28] Greece is the second largest source of foreign investment in Albania, after Italy. Road links

---

25 Vickers & Pettifer, *op cit*, chapter 10.

26 Marianne Sullivan, 'Mending Relations with Greece', *Transition*, vol. 1, no. 15, (25 August 1995), pp. 11-16.

27 Focusing on the role of such organizations as the Orthodox Church thus represents an important qualification and extension of Rogers Brubaker's very useful 'triadic' framework for analyzing ethno-politics in Eastern Europe, where twentieth-century border movements have left national minorities in 'home states' adjacent to their ethnic 'kin states'. See Rogers Brubaker, 'Home States, Kin States, and Ethnic Minorities in the New Europe', *Daedelus* (1995).

28 See Economist Intelligence Unit, Albania Country Reports (London: EIU, 1992-1997).

with Greece have expanded rapidly, particularly with the improvement in the Ioannina/Kakavia border route and the rebuilt road connection to the south-eastern frontier post at Kapstica. These link the Korca region with the northern Greek region around Kastoria and offer good road connections to the economic centre of Thessaloniki.[29] A new border post has been opened in the Timfi mountains, north of Konitsa, in 1999.

This represents a major change over the past decade. There was virtually no trade at all between the two countries until 1976, when an economic agreement between Tirana and the Karamanlis government was signed. Even then, a formal state of war, dating back to the Italian invasion of Greece from occupied Albania in 1940, remained in effect until 1981. In the years between 1976 and 1989, electricity imports from Albania were integrated into the Greek national power grid and a number of smaller-scale bilateral relationships developed. Recently, plans have been proposed for a new major hydroelectric scheme on the Aoos River, although the proposals have been strongly opposed by environmentalists and it remains to be seen whether they will come to fruition.

These economic ties have been augmented by a new and central relationship: the very large sums of money remitted to Albania by the migrant workers. While accurate official data is not available, independent analyses have estimated that as much as one-third of Albania's total hard currency earnings emanate from this source, with as many as 300,000 workers active in the Greek economy at any one time. This amounts to $400 million per year and contributed significantly to the stability of the Albanian Lek for much of the post-communist period. (Smaller sums are remitted from Italy, the USA, Germany, and Switzerland, as well as from other countries with a sizeable Albanian diaspora.)

The Greek remittances have given Greece a great deal of leverage over the Albanian economy, as was demonstrated following the expulsion of Maidonis in 1993 and again in the autumn of 1994 with another mass expulsion of Albanian migrant workers by Greece after five Omonia activists were charged with espionage and arms possession in connection with a MAVI raid on an Albanian army barracks in which two Albanian soldiers died.[30] At the same time, the pattern of migration in search of

---

29 See generally *Blue Guide: Albania, op. cit.*
30 *Balkan News* (Athens), November 1994. A great deal of other material related to the 'Omonia Five' appeared in the Greek press at the time. The Greek police later began their own investigation of MAVI, arresting three Greek citizens and four Greek Albanians following another thwarted border raid in the spring of 1995. Confirming Albania's earlier accusations, the police said MAVI was likely headed by Anastasios Giorgos, a former Greek army officer, while the Greek press suggested that the Greek secret service may

employment has extended this leverage over Albanian governmental policy to the Greek minority to a much greater extent than its relative size would indicate, significantly affecting Albanian domestic politics. The centrality of emigration and employment policy at the meeting between Greek Foreign Minister Karolos Papoulias and his Albanian counterpart in March 1995, for example, is a clear indication of how Greek diplomacy has focused on balancing both visas and economic aid against issues affecting the Greek minority.

At the same time, however, emigration patterns into Greece have proven to be a source of disruption and increased ethnic tension for many of Albania's Greek communities. With the demise of authoritarian rule and the advent of freedom of movement, a substantial number of ethnic minority Greeks, too, immediately began to work in Greece as part of the estimated 100,000 Albanian nationals in the current Greek labour force. Greek Prime Minister Constantine Mitsotakis appealed to the northern Epirus villagers in 1991 to remain in Albania in order to preserve the area's 'Hellenism' but this had little effect. As a result, some villages have suffered from severe depopulation, with quite serious consequences for the social structure of many localities, particularly those on the coastal fringe between Saranda and Himara, where an absence of able-bodied young men has caused additional burdens to fall on women and the elderly.[31]

These developments became politically salient to the extent that they structured controversy surrounding the land privatization process around the ethnic divide. While accurate statistics are unavailable, visual inspection confirms that large areas of fertile privatized land in and around ethnic Greek villages lie derelict and uncultivated due to ethnic Greek migration, whereas neighbouring ethnic Albanian villages, whose inhabitants find it difficult to obtain visas to work in Greece, are clearly land-hungry. Indeed, in addition to the belief that ethnic Greeks benefited from a political alliance with the Gheg-dominated government, the slightly higher birth-rate within the Albanian villages, has exacerbated the communal relative deprivation that fuels perceptions among ethnic Albanians in the south. Moslem towns near Greece like Konispol remain impoverished, while Greek minority towns nearby like Saranda are enjoying good economic development. Thus, inter-ethnic relations have been affected not merely by political developments at the national level,

indeed have been either involved with the organization or had overlooked its activities. At the same time, a former Greek government minister, Theodoros Pangalos, admitted that the Omonia Five had 'very probably been linked' to MAVI. See Sullivan, *op cit.*, p. 16.

31 Vickers & Pettifer, *op cit.*, chapter 10.

but also by the local-level politics of resource scarcity. While decisions made in Tirana regarding the treatment of Albania's Greek minority have clearly shaped these relations, the politicization of ethnicity must also be viewed in terms of the operation of economic forces and social change driven by the opening of an often unruly border.

The Uncertain Political Future of the Greek Minority

Since the demise of one-party rule, the Greek minority has thus far been the only ethnic minority in Albania to pursue independent political participation. In all other cases, minorities are either very small and have confined their activities to cultural and human rights campaigns, or have failed to overcome internal obstacles to collective action (particularly the Roma and, to a lesser extent, the Vlachs). Others, such as the Jews, have left the country altogether, while, given their economic acumen, external links and cultural cohesiveness, the ethnic Greeks' position corresponds in many ways to that of the Jews in Hapsburg (or Armenians in Ottoman) society, attracting similar political distrust. Unlike these groups, however, the acute climate of anti-Greek feeling in Albanian politics and society produced by the Greek minority's assertiveness is linked to deep-rooted problems in bilateral relations.

Although there are no significant explicitly racist or chauvinist political parties in Albania, there are many individual politicians who adhere to very strong anti-Greek views, which in turn affects the orientation of virtually all ethnic Albanian political parties.[32] In fact, problems concerning the minority have been manipulated by the widespread use of xenophobic stereotypes on both sides of the border. Even quality newspapers in Greece often discuss Albania as though it were a protectorate, while many well-educated Albanians appear tacitly to believe that their country will become one if Greek minority demands are met. Yet again, it is important to bear in mind that such anti-minority prejudices are manipulable in the post-communist period and serve to politicize religious, cultural and economic cleavages along ethnic lines precisely because they are entrenched in the irredentism of the post-independence and inter-war periods and the national division among Albanians reinforced during the wartime resistance.

These factors have combined not only to make Omonia's inclusion in any governing coalition in Tirana in the near future unlikely, but also call into question whether Omonia will continue to participate in

---

32 Rightist forces such as the group led by Tomas Dosti within Berisha's Democratic Party, for example, played a prominent role in shaping the government's repressive anti-Greek measures from 1994 to 1996.

the electoral process at all. Greek policy may well be influenced by the probably irresistible demand of ethnic Albanian-dominated Kosovo for independence and possible eventual union with Albania. In such a scenario, the demands of Kosovar Albanians for independence may well reinforce those of the Greek minority in Albania. While neither Greek leaders within Albania nor their protagonists in Greece have ever called for reconsidering the Greek minority's position as part of a wider Balkan settlement involving Kosovo, the Berisha government's 1992-1997 period of intermittent repression should be understood in part as a reaction to Greek minority demands for an autonomy arrangement similar to that enjoyed by Kosovar Albanians prior to Serbian President Slobodan Milosevic's own crackdown on the province.[33]

In these circumstances, it is likely that government pressure to restrict Greek aspirations will continue, even if some of the more extreme methods of surveillance and control adopted by the Berisha government were defeated by internal opposition in 1997 or modified by international pressure. This is true despite developments since late 1996, when serious strains linked to the growth of high interest 'pyramid' investment schemes began to appear in the Albanian financial system. By December, a financial collapse, beginning in Vlora and Tirana, but soon affecting the entire country, had become imminent. After a period of chaotic street protest, anarchy overtook many southern cities. The Berisha governmen's attempts to restore order failed, and an armed population took control of most towns.[34] The Greek minority played a significant role in these events, with some of the strongest oppositional activity focused in the most densely Greek-populated areas.[35] Although allegations of Greek involvement in the leadership of the uprising were made by the Berisha government, there was no evidence of ethnic conflict between Greeks and Albanians in the popular struggle leading to early elections and the return of the Socialist government in June 1997. On the contrary, while many of Berisha's right-wing supporters (particularly ex-émigrés) had their property ransacked, ethnic Greeks were left alone.[36]

33 These themes have frequently been aired in Albanian public debate, particularly in such newspapers as *Rilindja*, in which Kosovar influence is apparent.

34 See Fabian Schmidt, 'Pyramid Schemes Leave Albania on Shaky Ground', *Transition*, vol. 3, no. 3 (7 March 1997), pp. 8-10.

35 See reports by Anthony Loyd and James Pettifer in *The Times* (London), 7-21 March 1997. The Greek minority in Saranda scored the first military success for the opposition by capturing a government tank on 6 March.

36 For a more detailed examination of the role of the Greek minority in the uprising, see James Pettifer, 'The Greek Minority in the Albanian Rising', *Anglo-Hellenic Review*, no. 16 (Autumn 1997), included in this collection.

Nevertheless, there may be some truth in the view held by many Berisha supporters, including Kosovar Albanians, that the victory of the Socialist Party - with its predominantly southern support base - was a victory for Greece and Greek regional influence. During the transition period between the Berisha government's resignation and the election of the Socialist government, the emigration question reemerged to dominate the bilateral agenda, with the Greek government promising to make available to Albanians an extensive work permit scheme that would legalize tens of thousands of guest workers. However, although relations between the two Socialist governments appear amicable, there has been significant parliamentary and public opposition to the proposals in Greece, and it is doubtful that real progress will be made on other traditionally divisive issues.[37] Revealingly, an agreement on improving Eparch Athanasios Giannulatos status and position, concluded during Greek Foreign Minister Papoulias visit to Tirana in 1995, has done virtually nothing to diminish controversies concerning the appointment and influence of Orthodox Church personnel.[38]

At the same time, it seems unlikely that the Greek minority in Albania will be able to insulate itself from the wider fate of the country, which is bound to be uncertain and fraught with social and economic tensions for the foreseeable future. Even prior to the outbreak of widespread civil unrest following the collapse of the investment schemes in early 1997, the attack on the United States Embassy in Tirana by over one thousand youths in March 1995 provided a strong indication of the very high social tension within Albania caused by mass employment and inflation. Such factors may very well aggravate national security concerns whose resolution awaits a wider Balkan settlement. For, while the removal of Sali Berisha's highly confrontational and polarizing government has benefited bilateral relations and contributed to regional stability, particularly in terms of economic cooperation, the more fundamental and historically ingrained cultural, religious and social divisions that have shaped Albania's polity and political regimes will remain.[39]

37 Indeed, a new problem has emerged, as it is widely believed in Tirana that a large sum of aid money was stolen by the government, and/or people close to it, and placed in Greek banks. However, given restrictive Greek banking legislation, recovery will likely prove difficult for Fatos Nano's Socialist government even if criminal activity can be demonstrated.

38 For example, conflict over Greek control of the Orthodox Church arose in 1996 in Elbasan.

39 At the time of writing there is also increasing interest in the Chameria/Cameria issue. For an Albanian view of the subject, see 'British Imperialism and Ethnic Cleansing' by NG Zhagu, Tirana, 1995; also ed K Naska, *Dokumente per Camerine 1912-1939*, Tirana: Dituria, 1999, and Albert Kotoni, *Cameria* Denoncon, Tirana, 1999. The late

CM Woodhouse refers in passing to the Cham controversy in some of his historical and polemical works; see for instance, *Apple of Discord*, London: Hutchinson, 1948, p. 93ff, for his views of the Cham role as alleged pro-Axis collaborators. Modern Greek scholars tend to differentiate between different groups of Chams, so that the Epirus coast stretching from the Albanian border north of the old Ottoman port of Sagiada down to Preveza is acknowledged as Cham, whereas the inland areas are claimed to be Greek-inhabited. This distinction would have an important effect on the current Albanian property claims. Albanians generally see the town of Filiates as the centre of Cham settlement in the region in modern times.

In the event of the Cham controversy developing internationally, this distinction is likely to encourage discussion of the British role in the events of the Second World War, as it is generally believed that the EDES royalist militia leader Zervas was acting on Woodhouse's orders in moving against the Chams in 1943-44. Woodhouse has defended his decisions over the Chams by claiming that the interethnic conflict in Epirus, and also fighting between different wings of the Greek anti-Axis movement, meant that two divisions of the communist controlled ELAS popular army were tied up in Epirus and this helped save the British force under General Scobie in Athens from defeat in the Battle of Athens in 1944.

THE RISE OF THE KLEPTOCRACY

THE DAYTON AGREEMENT ON BOSNIA was expected to benefit southern Balkan states too. They avoided following the old Yugoslavia into violent disintegration and anticipated that the end of UN sanctions and the Greek economic blockade of former Yugoslav Macedonia (FYROM) would increase economic activity and political stability. As with other aspects of the post-Dayton period, reality has proved more complex and less encouraging.

In the southern Balkans, the abstract threat of the spread of an orthodox war has been replaced by the actual spread of localized terrorist and *Mafiya* violence, with politics and economic elements inextricably intermingled. The Croatian and Bosnian wars have caused fundamental changes in the social and economic structure hundreds of miles away. The relations emerging in the post-Dayton period show all the classic features of anarcho-capitalism. UN sanctions during these wars were central in providing an ideal climate for *Mafiya* growth.

The ending of United Nations sanctions removed very large quantities of hard currency generated by petrol smuggling from many localities in the southern Balkan region, particularly in Bulgaria, FYROM and northern Albania bordering Montenegro. As a direct result, their currencies have experienced serious pressure in the past year, with a drop of about 20 per cent in value in Albania, and almost total collapse in Bulgaria.[1] The Mafia organizations that had grown during the sanctions period turned their attention to other activities, with an upsurge in drug and arms trading.

A Balkan Development

Political violence has also grown, in different forms, in the different countries. In Albania, Mafia groups undoubtedly played a part in the violence associated with the Albanian general election in May 1996. In Bulgaria, the assassination of the former Prime Minister, Andrei Lukanov, was only the most prominent in a growing number of political killings; and in FYROM, the political climate is still heavily influenced by the assassination attempt on President Kiro Gligorov in October 1995.

This growth of violence could, at one level, be seen merely as a reassertion of local traditions - a 'Balkan' development that was only to be expected. In some sense this is, of course, true. The Lukanov assassination in Sofia last October could, in every detail, have been an Internal Macedonian Revolutionary Organization 'execution' from the 1920s, as could the Gligorov car bomb. But there is evidence

---

1   See article by James Pettifer in the *Wall Street Journal*, 30 September 1996, for more detail.

to suggest that the wider growth in violence is part of a change in the political climate and very fundamental structural changes in the economies.

An important factor is the end, for the immediate future anyway, of the practical possibility of real integration into Western institutions, the European Union in particular. Thus, the elites have no pressing motive to modify their behaviour to conform to European norms, which are themselves becoming increasingly subject to criticism.

As such, anarcho-capitalism has wider significance than merely increasing the risk for Western companies operating locally. The 'Mafiaization' of the former communist states in the southern Balkans also has wider implications for Mediterranean and regional security.

Fortress Greece

The shape of many, perhaps most, post-Dayton societies in the southern Balkans is becoming visible, and it is not an encouraging picture. This is particularly so for Greece, as the only EU and NATO member on the Balkan peninsula, with a long land border with all three states.

Although most of the new arsenal being purchased by Greece is concerned with defence against what is seen as an expansionist Turkey, there is also a substantial element of a new 'Fortress Greece' requirement to defend the long northern borders and control illegal immigration – with helicopters and light military vehicles in particular. The problem of population movement in the north is being faced by the Simitis government.

The changing social and economic structure is the key to growing anarcho-capitalism. Geography is important. Albania, FYROM and Bulgaria, despite many differences in ethnicity and history, have many common features. They have relatively small populations - all three countries together support fewer people than London and the Birmingham region. The proportionately large land mass includes many mountainous and remote areas, declining or derelict industry and a large number of peasants living at semi-subsistence level.

Free to Move

The power of central government, particularly law enforcement agencies, is weak outside the main cities, and often corrupted within them. The young and educated are taking advantage of post-communist freedom to go abroad, if possible, or to the cities, if it is not.

The rural areas stagnate and suffer depopulation and the end of any effective public order enforced from the centre,[2] while the cities grow and have a rapidly increasing underclass of ambitious but frustrated and unemployed young people with Western aspirations but no job and little money.[3]

All three countries have conscript armies and most young men have some knowledge of weapons. They are a ready recruiting ground for organized crime and businesses which, while not necessarily criminal in the literal sense, nevertheless use coercion and violence as part of their normal modus operandi.

Worthwhile former state-owned assets from the old industries have become closely concentrated in the hands of the old nomenclatura, embodied in holding companies which are often based outside the country and are not subject to government regulations. In Bulgaria, Multigroup is the classic example - a profitable combine dealing in metals, tourism and other activities generating large quantities of hard currency, integrated vertically and managed from Switzerland. In Albania, VEFA Holdings is managed by ex-army figures and a key element in its portfolio is the old state arms trading company MEICO. VEFA is also involved in high interest-rate 'pyramid' investment schemes, food production, shops, and tourism and is the most prominent organization emerging in a 'parallel' economic world.[4]

Eternal Flows of Cash

These and many similar smaller organizations act as intermediaries between the rural hinterland and the cities, and recycle substantial amounts of foreign aid into local hands. This would be a positive feature if there were a legal framework so that they could also contribute tax to central government, but in all three countries this is often not the case.

Local elites appear to assume that foreign aid flows will flow eternally. This creates some local interest in the maintenance of a degree of political instability, as foreign aid would probably be considerably reduced if settled conditions returned to the Balkans. This can also be seen in Bosnia, where Dayton has produced a society where the Mafiaization of areas like Mostar depends on foreign aid flows for 'government

2 This subject is extensively analysed by the International Organization for Migration, IOM, Geneva, Switzerland 1995, in an important report, *Profiles and Motives of Potential Migrants from Albania*. This shows that the desire to migrate has not diminished at all under the Berisha government.

3 Male unemployment in every Balkan capital is over 20 per cent, and in some, such as Sofia and Tirana, it is much higher.

4 For much valuable material on Multigroup, VEFA and similar organizations, see *East European Newsletter*, London, between 1993 and 1996.

reconstruction' in the hands of EU officials with no functioning local state to govern.

Bankruptcy Beckons

In these conditions, the decisive feature of anarcho-capitalism in these countries is becoming clear: the collapse of central government finance. Most worthwhile currency is in private hands and state bankruptcy beckons. In Bulgaria, the whole economy is collapsing and default on the nation's enormous debts seems inevitable.[5] Albania's debt was recycled in 1995 to avoid this situation, while the FYROM economy is so small that the value of the currency is held by what amounts to direct transfers from World Bank and IMF funds.

'Government', in so far as there is any, consists of the finance of a central bureaucracy and, importantly, growing police forces that are ineffective against organized crime but target political unrest or dissent from the policies of the ruling group.

All Balkan leaders in the post-communist period appear to have learnt a good deal from the way President Milosevic runs Serbia - President Berisha of Albania, in particular. Western policies have unintentionally assisted these tendencies by their emphasis on strong presidential governments in the Balkans as a factor for 'stability'. The relationship between these satrap-type presidents and actual state power and democracy does not seem to have been much considered, either at the level of safeguarding human rights or a democratic and efficient law enforcement system.

Throwing Money at It

There has as yet been little attempt by Western governments to link Balkan economic aid to decent human rights criteria or the key issue of legality, except in the 'Republica Serbska' and with the principled position the US government has taken, tying the lifting of the 'outer wall' of UN sanctions to the improvement of human rights in Kosovo by the Milosevic regime. The practice, so far, could be characterized by the famous phrase of the Deputy British Prime Minister Michael Heseltine, of 'throwing money at problems and hoping they would go away'. But only a small minority benefits from the money.

Under Balkan anarcho-capitalism, welfare, health and education provision declines or collapses. Economic activity is based on direct cash

---

5   See *Bulgarian Economic News*, Sofia, September 1996. Although political factors were important in the run on the banks then, it seems clear that the basic problem is the absence of real assets to support the currency value.

transfers of hard currency, and most local banks are technically bankrupt or act as money-laundering organizations, without real balance sheet assets. Bulgaria is again the most prominent example. Only the military is exempt from the state financial crisis. In Albania and FYROM, the armed forces are trained and financed externally from the United States, while Bulgaria still has close links with Russia. This is very much a return to historic patterns of Great Power dependency.

The rise of the *Kleptocracy*, to use the Greek term for 'government by bandits', poses new problems for foreign governments. In FYROM, European Union emergency humanitarian aid programmes have tried to help the bottom 20 per cent of the population facing a daily struggle for existence. In Skopje, the only functioning and properly financed ministry is the key Ministry of the Interior, totally unreformed since communist days. The government does not appear capable of, or interested in, taking responsibility for most social issues - and has little money to do so anyway.

Perhaps half the urban population in Bulgaria will face serious food and heating shortages this winter, and the newly elected President, Peter Stoyanov, has called for an emergency humanitarian aid programme.[6] In Albania, the buzz of economic activity around Tirana cannot disguise the continuing desperate poverty of most rural areas where there is evidence of the recurrence of malnutrition and epidemic diseases on a scale not seen since the 'Winter of Anarchy' of 1990-91.

The proponents of market economics argue that this is a temporary phenomenon, that the 'trickle-down' effect will soon begin to reach the rural and poorer areas. On the contrary, it seems that the structural changes outlined above, with elites able to appropriate assets and much EU aid for their own benefit and channel it abroad, will impoverish the vast majority.

Terror: the Weapon of Choice

Terrorism may become a characteristic political weapon for many groups in the southern Balkans, as it was pre-war. Tradition, the vast imbalances between country and city, and the absence of parliamentary government offering the possibility of strong opposition within a peaceful framework, will drive it now as then. Western support for familiar, entrenched presidents assists these regressive processes. The FYROM parliament was produced by a heavily manipulated election in November 1994, and in Albania it is scarcely functioning after the

6   See articles in *The Times*, by James Pettifer on 3 October 1996, and by Roger Boyes on 26 November 1996. A large programme started in December 1996.

corrupt election of May 1996. Opposition under anarcho-capitalism is likely to be anarchic itself, with the symbolic act of violence becoming ever more common, as President Gligorov, ex-Prime Minister Lukanov, the head of the Albanian prison service and many other less prominent people have found to their cost in the past year.

To reverse these trends would require rural investment and social development, and the modification of existing aid policies. Alternatives could include aid targeted at preserving traditional labour-intensive, family-based agriculture, so discouraging the flight to the cities; an end to banking secrecy; efforts to control small arms transfers and demilitarize the Balkans; clear supervision of EU aid so that it is not stolen; and making dispersal dependent on the evolution of parliamentary government.

The PHARE programme, the main channel for EU aid, could be disentangled from its present subservience to local power elites, dedicated to the elusive dream of the resurrection of old industrial bases from the communist period. The anthropomorphic worship of strong presidencies as a sign of democratic development should be ended since the results increasingly resemble old-style Third World dictatorships. Social stability in the post-communist and post-Dayton Balkans has to be built on a traditional, rural economic foundation, involving the mass of the people. It is most unlikely to result from financing a kleptocratic elite.*

---

* An erarlier draft of this article was published in *The World Today*, London, vol. 53, no. 1, January 1997, pp. 13-17.

THE ALBANIAN UPHEAVAL

KLEPTOCRACY AND THE POST-COMMUNIST STATE

The Hubris of the Berisha Regime

THE WIDESPREAD CHAOS AND DISORDER in Albania in the spring of 1997 following the collapse of the pyramid banking schemes has brought international concern that this small Balkan country could prove to be a model for other transitional societies and their governments in Eastern Europe which are failing to satisfy popular expectations of Western capitalist society. This fear has been expressed in particular relation to Russia, which has many of the same features of transitional society such as mass impoverishment, some nostalgia for communism, a dissatisfied and possibly rebellious military, a popular culture where the use of weapons is common, and a very small, very rich elite whose business practices have been heavily influenced by mafia operations. This society has been described by Solzhenitsyn and others as a 'kleptocracy', the Greek term meaning 'government by bandits'.

High hopes for Albania have been followed by disappointment, both for Albanians and international sympathizers of the Berisha regime. Albania had been seen by many right-wing and mainstream commentators in the West as a model for post-communist economic development, with a strong pro-market government, high growth rates, accelerating foreign investment and a satisfactory orientation towards NATO and European Union policy on Balkan political issues. It was in particular seen as the diametric opposite of its neighbour, Serbia, which was none of those things.[1]

The International Monetary Fund, the European Bank for Reconstruction and Development and the World Bank had been very supportive to the Berisha government, the latter in particular. This project has now collapsed in disaster, with the state incapable of exercising the most basic functions, most of southern Albanian under the control of local 'salvation committees' after the armed rising of March 1997, and the north and Tirana under the control of pro-Berisha armed groups. Albania has become the second Balkan country, after Bosnia, to fall under international military control, with the advent of the Italian-led humanitarian intervention force in April 1997. It is unclear what real power the Socialist government elected in May will have to change this.

The mass seizure of weapons from army stores, usually the Albanian-model copy of the Kalashnikov AK-47 assault rifle (although there are many heavier weapons in circulation), coupled with the easy availability of large quantities of ammunition from Albania's own plants, has led to

---

1   See most literature produced by the World Bank and International Monetary Fund on
    Albania between 1992 and 1996 for examples of the special pleading applied.

the creation of an armed population on a scale that has not been seen
in the Balkans or elsewhere in Europe since the World War II period,
even in the wars of ex-Yugoslavia.[2] The nearest comparable situation
may well be in the late Ottoman Empire, and the mass armed popular
risings of the Balkan peoples against the Porte, such as the Ilinden Rising
in Macedonia in 1903.[3]

The background to the current crisis is well known. After a long
period of anarchy and political turmoil as communism collapsed
between 1989 and 1992, the government of Dr Sali Berisha was elected
in the spring of that year and produced apparent stability. His strong
anti-communist rhetoric led to large financial, moral and political
support from the West (the US, Germany and Britain, in particular)
although there was little real investment.[4] The United States, as well as
the neo-Habsburg, predominantly Catholic bloc of Germany, Austria,
Slovenia, Croatia and Hungary, supported Albania against British- and
French supported Serbia. Dr Berisha, in turn, tried to underwrite his
dominant political position with a new constitution in 1994, but was
rejected overwhelmingly by the people in November of that year. It
seems clear that Albanians feared it would provide the framework for
a very authoritarian 'presidential' state, with little real role for political
opposition or judicial independence. Politics remained in crisis until
an attempted resolution in the election of May 1996, won by Berisha's
governing Democratic Party. The election was judged to be very corrupt
by the vast majority of international observers present, including the
OSCE delegation. The election was marked by violent attacks on
opposition activists, particularly on members of the Socialist Party, a
monopoly of television by the governing party, coercion of independent
journalists and media institutions, and government party custody of
ballot boxes after the elections.[5]

At the same time, pyramid banking schemes had been growing
rapidly, offering very high rates of interest, which soaked up the greater
part of émigré remittances and people's savings in general. Remittances,
mostly from Italy and Greece, may make up as much as a third of

2 See *The Complete Kalishnikov Family of Assault Rifles* by Duncan Long (Boulder CO,
   1988) for a technical analysis of the Albanian version of this weapon.
3 For information on this subject, see *Macedonia: Its races and Their Future* by H.M.
   Brailsford (London, 1906).
4 For background on US support and policies, and a general analysis of the nature of the
   Berisha regime, see *Albania: From Anarchy to a Balkan Identity* by James Pettifer and
   Miranda Vickers (London, 1997).
5 See article by James Pettifer in *The World Today*, Chatham House RIIA, London, June
   1996.

Albanian GDP. There are strong grounds for believing that many of the operators of these pyramid schemes had close links with Dr Berisha's party.[6] There was general concern that the collapse of the schemes might be imminent in autumn 1996, and the IMF issued warnings to the government in October 1996. It seems, however, they were not made with sufficient vigour, and the sycophantic and uncritical relationship officials of the international financial organizations had developed with the Berisha apparatus did not assist them. Market capitalist society in Albania was seen to have 'no limits'. This, of course, was not the case. As Marx once remarked, some businessmen only discover the law of gravity when the ceiling falls in.

The collapse of the first pyramid schemes began in December 1996, and rapidly accelerated after Christmas, bringing widespread social tension and street disorder. A major revolt against the government began in the southern cities of Vlora and Saranda, followed by armed rebellion in mid-March 1997 throughout southern Albania. A key date was 10 March, when the southern regional centre of Gjirokastra went over to the rebellion, after which it spread rapidly northwards in the next few days. All political authority of the Berisha government was destroyed in the south in this process and, after international intervention designed to prevent a nascent north-south civil war, a 'government of national unity' under Socialist Bashkim Fino was installed, with the task of organizing democratic elections under international supervision. After a complex and difficult negotiation process designed to produce multi-party agreement on a new electoral law, elections are due to be held in June 1997. At the time of writing, much of the country is still under the control of various armed groups, and a modicum of public order is maintained in the cities only by a heavy paramilitary presence. The conditions that could lead to full scale civil war still prevail. It is not clear whether the elections will result in effective or stable government.

The March Rising and the Kleptocracy

In the quality press there have been many speculative assertions about the nature of the uprising and the degree to which it developed as a result of conscious political planning and organization, and the degree to which it was a spontaneous and inchoate movement of protest against the loss of assets in the pyramid banks, and against the increasingly undemocratic character of the Berisha regime. This is an important issue, in trying to establish whether the social and political breakdown in Albania might be a model for what could happen elsewhere.

6   See *The Wall Street Journal Europe*, 28 January 1997.

The following observations are fairly exclusively based on my own experiences in the south in March 1997, and in Gjirokastra and Tepelena, which were at the heart of the rebellion at the time, and later in Korca in May 1997.[7] Major factors in the situation were:

1) There was widespread and long-standing dissatisfaction with many aspects of the Berisha government, both on a range of practical issues and because it was dominated by northern Gheg Albanians. (Those living south of the Shkumbini river are called Tosks, and speak a different dialect of the language.) Under communism, southern Tosks had always been well represented in the government and had often dominated it. The years 1992-96 had seen a steady advance in the control of the local state, the security apparatus in particular, by Berisha placemen, usually from north-east Albania.

2) The economy of the south had become increasingly dependent on remittances from émigré workers in Greece, and links with Greece were in any case strong due to the presence of at least 40,000 ethnic Greeks in southern Albania.[8] Many southern Albanians had become accustomed to the higher standard of living and a functioning modem industrial society in Greece, and had become increasingly impatient with what they saw as the lack of economic and social progress under the Berisha government.

3) Although this factor was probably exaggerated considerably by the Berisha government in their portrayal of the uprising, some residual elements from the old communist security apparatus and its functionaries remained in the south. Under communism, these coercive state organs had been filled almost exclusively by southerners. Informal networks certainly remained in some places.[9] Some of these people had gone into exile in Greece and Italy after 1992 and may have interacted with the Mafia and organized crime in general prior to the rising. But there has been no concrete evidence produced to support allegations made in pro-Berisha circles that a planned pro-communist conspiracy lay behind the rising.

---

7   See *The Times*, London,10 March 1997.

8   There is a detailed analysis of the situation of the Greek Minority in the Minority Rights Group report, *The Southern Balkans* (London, 1995).

9   See article in *The Times* by James Pettifer, 3 March 1997

4) Under communism, senior echelons in the army had been dominated by southerners. Many of these men had been made redundant in the US supervised military reforms between 1992 and 1995 and were often unemployed and highly dissatisfied with the end of their careers. Promotion prospects for younger talented southern officers were poor under the Berisha regime, even if they could keep their jobs, as northerner Ghegs were strongly favoured in the military. This produced a pool of potential leaders of the rising at local level, with military training and experience and knowledge of the current disposition of stored weapons in the localities. This was augmented by the fact that Albania's arms factories are in the south, near Berat, and were a target for the rebellious soldiers.

At the heart of the movement was a split among the military, particularly on the key day of the revolt, 9-10 March, when Gjirokastra changed sides and went over to the anti-Berisha opposition. This city had been attempting to maintain a precarious neutrality in the second week in March but, when Berisha Special Forces in helicopters arrived in the town to secure the arms store, local leaders in the army and in the police and security apparatus mutinied. The revolt began with the leader of the local police organizing an attack on his own police station against pro-Berisha elements from the security police (SHIK).

When the weapons held in the police station were seized and distributed to the population, resistance to the pro-Berisha forces arriving in helicopters was possible, and the town fell to the rebellion very easily. The main arms store was then stormed and opened and very large quantities of weapons were distributed to the population. The government forces retreated northwards to their bases.

This sequence of events corresponds very closely to the partisan model of popular resistance established in the Second World War. The partisan tradition is very strong in the south, and the way the rebellion spread north up the mountain valleys after the fall of Gjirokastra followed very closely events in 1943-44.

As elsewhere in the Balkans, organized crime had been growing as a major force in the country after the end of communism. In the south, particularly on the Adriatic coast, a particularly favourable environment existed for its development, with Albania lying on a direct route for heroin imports from Turkey to Europe, the proximity of the coast of southern Italy with many Mafia-dominated towns, and the ease with which large-scale cannabis plantations can be concealed in southern

Albania. The city of Vlora had been affected by lawlessness for a long time. In this environment, many supporters of the Berisha regime became involved with organized crime and became highly unpopular locally, where people saw a steady criminalization of society developing. This criminalization very seriously affected the working class, the old, the poor and minorities, therefore augmenting mass support for the unrest.

The exact nature of Albanian organized crime will need careful analysis in the future if policies are to be devised that will assist the de-Mafiaization of society. It appears that one of the major defects of Western policy towards the Berisha regime was in the near-total incapacity of most governments to see how destabilizing to society crime had become, even though there are notorious examples of 'gangster states' - as President Clinton has called Colombia - in existence elsewhere in the world. The link between free-market fundamentalism and the establishment of ideal conditions for kleptocratic rule, with the abdication of the state from many areas of Albanian life, is very strong, and in this sense the rising is merely an extension of trends that had already existed strongly in Albanian society. It also illustrates a major crisis in one aspect of free-market ideology as it has developed towards Eastern Europe. In Russia, for instance, the 'Mafia' seems to have been accepted by the West as a permanent feature of society, and has not inhibited continued large-scale economic support for the Yeltsin government.

This criminalization led to some of the classic features of a kleptocratic society, with the end of any taxation of normal business activity and the collapse of what remained of most education, health and other public provision.[10]

The development of the Mafia had been greatly assisted by the United Nations sanctions against Serbia during the ex-Yugoslav war. The social structure of normal economic activity has been seriously damaged a long way away from the areas on the Balkan peninsula where actual fighting has been taking place, but very little of the international aid and reconstruction funds has been allocated outside Bosnia (where Western liberal concern has been focused by the media).

As a result, an enormous and little understood sense of historic grievance against the West, the United States in particular - as the main architect of Dayton - has spread across the southern Balkans. This is linked to the massive growth of popular protest against social and economic conditions and against existing regimes that spread across the region in the winter of 1996-7. The West is widely seen to have cheated

10 See article by James Pettifer in *The World Today*, Chatham House RIIA, London, January 1997, reproduced as a later draft in this collection.

these countries. All feel they have made considerable efforts to enforce sanctions (even if some, like Romania, did not) but have received little or no real compensation for the economic losses involved.

The Lessons of the Albanian Rising and the Future

Although it is very unclear what will happen in Albania, a number of preliminary observations can perhaps be made about the situation:

1) The rising has illustrated that there are limits to what the poorer and dissatisfied sections of society will take in Eastern Europe, in terms of a reversion to authoritarian rule linked to ultra-free market economics. It seems that it is possible for very traditional mass protests to occur that can challenge accepted notions of an 'inevitable' market process of development.

2) The links between organized crime and the Albanian population mean that the process of revolt is itself anarchic, destructive and violent, far beyond what is required to defeat local political opposition. There is a strong 'Luddite' element - witness the total destruction of all computer shops in Tirana as an example in the early stages of the March rising there. In that sense, the Albanian events have more in common with peasant revolts under the Ottoman Empire than any traditional Marxist industrially based movements linked to 'class'. This is likely to be the case if similar revolts occur elsewhere in Eastern Europe, as the combination of de-industrialization, post-communism, emigration and the technological revolution destroys much of the old industrial working class. Faith in 'technocratic development' based on the progress of industry has disappeared in whole sections of society. Many Muscovites, for instance, although living as urban workers, actually survive in their families only by cultivating small plots of land. Peasant values and attitudes are thus reasserting themselves throughout society. In the Balkans, whole societies have reverted to small-scale agriculture, with the collapse of whole segments of a viable industrial society, as in much of Bosnia, former Yugoslav Macedonia (FYROM), parts of Bulgaria, Serbia and throughout Albania.

3) In this world, debates of interest to Western left-wing ideologists on issues such as post-modernism have little place or relevance. The whole liberal/left Europeanist agenda has little meaning in the Balkans, and probably in many places elsewhere

in Eastern Europe. An example is perhaps the difficulties the Bosnian war caused this constituency of Western opinion.

4) The most fundamental lesson from the Albanian events is the need for a return to political economy, whatever model of transition in Eastern Europe is adhered to. It is clear that in pre-1997 Albania there was a complete divorce between politics and economics in the way this society was seen in the West, coupled with a large dose of the politics of public relations around President Berisha himself.

5) It should also be clear that building up over-powerful presidencies is no short cut to development or 'stability'. There is no alternative to the struggle to build up democratic institutions based on popular consent in the region, but socialists in the West should recognize that many of their assumptions about social and economic development may appear totally irrelevant in Eastern Europe. This is the case both with the modernist, personalist agenda ('political correctness') and the old left programme based on class.

Changes in the economy and mode of production, coupled with the strong revival of religion everywhere in Eastern Europe, are bringing back highly conservative modes of small-scale collective social and family life, and a revival of ideologies that were thought to have been superseded long ago. With them comes a return of primitive, direct-action, populist methods of struggle.[11]

---

11 This article first appeared in *Labour Focus on Eastern Europe*, Oxford, no. 57, 1997, pp. 4-13.

HISTORIES

Montenegrin Historical Writing

Writing

Ranke and His Legacy

'THE EXISTENCE OF THE MONTENEGRINS, so long precarious, was beginning to acquire stability: the prolonged conflict between the Balkan mountain and the Porte was attracting the attention of Civilised Europe ... blessings were showered on the heroic mountaineers by their Christian neighbours'

Leopold von Ranke, *A History of Servia* (1829)

In addressing this question it is necessary to think clearly about how the history of the Montenegrin region and people was written in the past, and how it has been seen and understood both inside and outside Montenegro. It is a truism to say that until the twentieth century most Balkan history was oral, in societies where mass literacy was not achieved in most places until after the Second World War. In countries like Bulgaria and Serbia where in the nineteenth century there had been greater progress in establishing a modern national primary education system, oral tradition still played (and plays) a very major part.

It is clear that the major external cultural relationship between the emerging history of Serbia and Montenegro in the first period of nation building in the late eighteenth and early nineteenth centuries was with German-speaking central Europe, and above all the heritage of German Romanticism, particularly that of Johann Gottfried von Herder. As Robert Wilton has pointed out, Herder did articulate ideas that were of particular relevance to the development of identity in the Balkans, and 'he serves as an appropriate representative of the body of Western philosophy and influence.'[1] Few people read Herder nowadays. His ideas of the purity of national popular cultures where a culture is a unique and unchangeable essence of a community sit uneasily in a world of globalization and multiculturalism, as does the concept of a 'Volksgeist' in a century that saw German and Italian fascism occupy the Balkans. Herder nevertheless provided a theoretical model for Serbian folksong and poetry collector and lexicographer Vuk Karadzic's work. It was the collaboration between Karadzic and Ranke that led to the writing of Ranke's *History of the Serbian Revolution*. Herder saw the role of the poet in

---

1   See Robert Wilton's important article, 'Writing the Nation, Writing the State: Compromise and Conflict in 19th Century Balkan Cultural Identity', in *South Slav Journal*, London, vol. 25, Spring-Summer 2004, p. 3.ff. His claim that ideas of national awakening based around cultural identification had been articulated in time for the first Serb uprising in 1804 is perhaps questionable. This is what the Serbs have always wished the world to think, but evidence is mostly lacking and the whole idea is essentially one of transference from the modern Greek experience, which Diaspora intellectuals had achieved for Greek nationalism by 1821 with great success. Serbia did not have a similar intellectual Diaspora until much later, as the lonely prominence of Vuk Karadzic in the heroic Byronic period indicates.

nation formation in a dramatic way, exemplified by his phrase: 'A poet is the creator of the nation around him; he gives them a world to see and has their souls in his hand to lead them to that world.'[2]

The main recent mediator of Herder's ideas with the English-speaking and reading world in the twentieth century was the Oxford philosopher and cultural historian Isaiah Berlin , who is also probably studied less now than in his working heyday.[3] Berlin's Herder is predictably idiosyncratic. The Prussian philosopher and aesthetician is seen as a pluralist and precursor of cultural relativism in historical understanding, as opposed to the moral and practical certainties of the ironclad rationalism of the Enlightenment theorists. This is also the case with the Marxist philosopher G.A. Cohen, who wrote:

> Montesquieu and Herder found it necessary to insist on what for us is obvious. Their assertion of the existence of different coherent ways of being human opposed that tend within the Enlightenment which conceived men as fundamentally alike across space and time, and which looked to a science of man whose generalizations would be as free of reference to particular ages and places as were the laws of the modern science of nature.[4]

Herder and those who thought like him in the central tradition and articulation of German Romanticism were major influences on Leopold von Ranke, the Prussian historian and author of *Die Serbische Revoluzion* (translated as *A History of Servia and the Servian Revolution*), which was first published in Berlin in 1829.[5] Ranke's *History* fulfills all the main Herderian criteria for a national epic story of a self-sustaining *ethnos*, with the sub-section on Montenegrin history a complement to the main narrative. The genesis of this book is very interesting, if unclear in some details. It embodies transference from oral tradition as mediated through Vuk Karadzic in personal dialogue with Ranke, who then wrote a history that mediated Serbian oral tradition further into the mainstream

---

2   From Johann Gottfried von Herder, *Auszug aus einem Briefwechsel über Ossian und die Lieder alter Völker*, Weimar, 1773. For background, see G. Iggers, *The German Conception of Historical Thought: from Herder to the Present*, Chicago: Wesleyan University Press, 1983.

3   See Isaiah Berlin, 'Vico and Herder', in *Three Critics of the Enlightenment*, London: 2000, and Wilton, *op. cit.*

4   See G.A. Cohen, *Karl Marx's Theory of History: A Defence*, Oxford: 1978. In the chapter on 'Images of History in Hegel and Marx', he emphasizes the novelty of many of Herder's ideas.

5   For a cogent modern discussion of Ranke and his importance, see Felix Gilbert, *History: Politics or Culture? Reflections on Ranke and Burckhardt*, Princeton NJ: 1990.

of European academic historiography. This process took place very soon after Ranke had effectively abandoned classical studies and teaching for writing 'modern' history. He finally gave up classics in the Gymnasium at Frankfurt an der Oder in 1825, during the period of his interchanges with Karadzic. The *Serbische Revoluzion* book was widely read and translated into several languages and remained in print throughout the nineteenth century and played an important part in helping to establish Serbia as the central state in the Balkans in outside perceptions. It was the foundation for Ranke's later study, *Serbien und die Turkei im Neunzehnten Jahrhundert* (1879). Vuk Karadzic had got to know the young Ranke in Germany, at a time when Ranke was in most senses still primarily a classical scholar, and Karadzic gave Ranke most of the material for this book. They spent some time in the Imperial capital of Vienna together, but Ranke is not thought to have ever visited the Balkans then, or later, and was a Brandenburg classical scholar seeing Serbia and Montenegro through the eyes of a local folklorist while still saturated in the works of Roman authors like Tacitus and Livy.

Prussian education and culture then was a heady mixture of inherited neo-classicism derived from the Enlightenment period under Fredrick the Great and his predecessors, with a wash of Romanticism from the turn of Goethe and his contemporaries away from neo-classicism. Karadzic had met Goethe in 1823-24 on more than one occasion and had made a good impression on the ageing Olympian of Weimar. Goethe admired the lyrical Serbian songs Karadzic had collected but did not rate the warrior epics as highly. This was not a general perception. The development of the Greek revolution against the Ottomans after 1821 had produced a new impetus of interest in 'national literatures' celebrating military virtues in revolt against external oppressors from which Karadzic's work benefited. The collaboration with Ranke on a publication of a history of Serbia and Montenegro could not have been more timely. In Ranke's Berlin circle, the warrior virtues of the Serbs were important. Like the Prussians and the Greeks, they were committed opponents of the Hapsburg Empire as well as of the Ottomans. Although in the debates in Berlin University in which he participated after he gained a post there in 1825 Ranke took the anti-Hegelian side and rejected the great philosopher's view of history as an unfolding universal story, he in many ways found such a story in the Serbian epics, and used it to construct his own master narrative. The self-determination of the *ethnos* from the transnational Ottoman Empire was then (as now) a liberal agenda but it could also appeal to a moderate conservative such as Ranke with his view of the task of the historian in tracing the unfolding of the work of

God in human history. Ranke's God was a very Prussian Protestant God and the Serbian and Montenegrin Orthodox churches (as *Volkskirchen*) could find a respected place in his narrative by comparison with the decadent transnational religions of the Roman Catholic Venetians and Muslim Ottomans. Ranke saw the Serbian uprisings as legitimate, not only because they were anti-Ottoman but as a step towards religious freedom for an oppressed people, the workings of God in human history. In this he made the working model for the thought of a later statesman like the English Prime Minister Gladstone and his espousal of the anti-Ottoman cause of the Christian Balkan people, particularly Bulgaria after the Batak massacres.[6]

The shadow of Tacitus' *Germania* also falls heavily over *A History of Servia*. The writing of Ranke echoes Tacitus' observations of what in essence are depicted as often virtuous and rational barbarians, but they are for all their virtues, barbarians nonetheless. This is shown at a subjective level in the famous note in Ranke's diary in 1828, saying that 'Of all the barbarians I have known, Vuk is the only one who has never taken the wrong direction intellectually.'[7] The Serbs and Montenegrins are seen by Ranke as virtuous primarily because of their successful attempts to have a parliament, a national church and to escape the Ottoman system. He also admired their fighting spirit, noting that,

> I got to know a people which has been living in subjection, with patriarchal customs and a poetic way of thinking, capable of transforming these into the hard reality of war, when the time came to liberate itself – the Serbs whose poetry you will certainly have seen.[8]

The travails of the contemporary rulers of the Obrenovic dynasty which Ranke depicts in gripping detail do not affect this general narrative structure at all, and are clearly a product of Karadzic's own serious difficulties with the crude and semi-dictatorial nature of Belgrade rule under them, and their concessions to and deals with the Sultans. Their government was a denial of all the values of the high-thinking post-Congress of Vienna optimists on new and emerging liberal states and gave rise to the image of Serbia as a country ruled by brutish and

---

6 In 1876 a massacre of about 3,000 Bulgarian Orthodox insurgents took place at Batak in the Rhodope Mountains of southern Bulgaria. It was reported in a famous story by J.A. MacGahan and his account played a major role in turning public opinion against the Sultan's attempts to repress Bulgarian nationalism.

7 See *Wilson*, op. cit., p. 228. *Wilton?*

8 Letter from Ranke to his brother Heinrich, in 1828.

unscrupulous pig keepers in the heart of south-east Europe. It was convenient for Karadzic to have Ranke named as author only, even if Ranke regarded the Serb as an equal co-author, in view of the relatively objective treatment in the *History* of Milos Obrenovic's gangsterish repression of his Karadjordjevic dynastic political rivals. Karadzic needed to find financial support for his research work from the Obrenovic rulers in Belgrade. Ranke's inherited classicism shows through clearly here, where a *volk* might be poetic and theoretically virtuous but where its rulers remained barbarian at heart.

Little is known in detail about the relationship between the Serbian folklorist and ethnologist and the Prussian classicist, except that they later remained in lifelong contact and mutual esteem. Ranke always paid Karadzic half of the royalty earnings from the book, and later noted in his papers that he had worked 'from Vuk's papers'.[9] But the book bears out Karl Marx's caustic view of Ranke that he was in his own output very frequently at odds with the theories of historical writing he put forward in his later life. There is no evidence of a principled objectivity, the 'noble dream' of the historian, or any significant (or insignificant) use of historical documents at all in the book, and it is unashamedly partisan towards the national aspirations of the Serbs and Montenegrins.

Vuk Karadzic was the only source in most respects, although Ranke later claimed that he had also checked all the facts himself, but there can be no doubt Karadzic saw what now would be called an 'advocacy role' for the book, to advance the national cause of the Serbs and secure him favour from the Obrenovic dynasty and the Russian Tsar. Was Ranke duped by the Serb, and was the publication perhaps one of the first examples of a Western intellectual love affair with a small country where the outside intellectual was not fully or well informed? This seems unlikely. Ranke was a keen and often disrespectful student of Hapsburg politics and would have been happy to offend Vienna. The same was the case with Ottoman issues. The structure of the 'Eastern Question', the ultimate future of the dying Ottoman Empire, had not yet been consciously articulated in Germany in a way it was in Britain after the Congress of Berlin but the outline of what it became was certainly present in the mind of a supremely intelligent man like Ranke at the centre of Prussia's dynamic intellectual life.

Some Ranke scholars have seen the *History* as a young man's experiment and tend to exclude it from discussion of his main corpus but there can be no doubt that it was and remains one of his most practically influential works. It legitimized a view of Serbia and Montenegro in

---

9   *Wilson*, op. cit., p. 228.

Western culture for a century, and its English translation's publication in 1852 in London and New York was a symbol of the respectability of the new Serbian state in intellectual life in Europe and the United States. Ranke effectively manufactured an academic historical tradition for Serbia where none really existed before him (outside the Church). Karadzic was fortunate in his choice of historian made nearly thirty years before, as by the English publication in 1852 Ranke was at the height of his fame and influence in the increasingly important nineteenth-century Pan-European cultural context of German universities and historical scholarship in general.

How does this relate to issues of later Montenegrin national historiography? In the *History* Ranke presents the Montenegrins as like the Serbs but further removed from 'civilisation' in their mountain fastnesses and bound by codes of immutable tradition. They are in a sense the 'true' Slavs with a fixed inner *ethnos* identity, whereas the lowland Serbs have had to adapt more to the pressures of their neighbours. In cultural terms, if Herder's and Hegel's ideas lived on in the historian's subconscious as far as the Serbs are depicted, with the Montenegrins the 'natural man/noble savage' of Rousseau is also present in the background. Or in modern historical terminology, the Serbs had a more transnational existence whereas the Montenegrins did not. Their main activity was in removing themselves from the rule of two transnational powers, that of Venice and the Ottomans. As a critic of decadent modern empires, Ranke clearly admired the Montenegrins' emancipation from Venetian rule, and particularly their warrior virtues. Ranke saw Venice in the Adriatic as an antiquated and obsolete construct, and thus the Homeric virtues of the Montenegrin warriors who ejected it from their coast as a force for modernization as well as construction of a new society.

It is perhaps significant that the long section of the *History* about Montenegro has always received much less attention than the main Serbian section. This is not simply because Serbia is a larger and more populous nation than Montenegro, but the writing on Montenegro embodies the radical side of Ranke in this work, his clear endorsement of what nowadays would be termed a guerrilla war of liberation. He sees the Serbs as having staged a successful revolution, but much more at a political and constitutional level, whereas the Montenegrins had waged a guerrilla military insurgency. It is also significant that a scholarly commentator of the last generation from the main British Yugophile and Serbophile tradition like Duncan Wilson gives little consideration to the Montenegrin aspects of Karadzic's corpus in his otherwise authoritative study of his work even though some of Karadzic's most fruitful folksong and legend collecting took place there.[10] Wilson does not discuss the Montenegrin part of the joint Ranke volume at all either, an illustration of how British Yugocentrism often elided Montenegro from historical perception. This elision was also sometimes the case with the nineteenth-century historians. After Ranke, serious consideration of Montenegrin history almost died in Europe, only to revive in England after the Congress of Berlin. An amateur historian like the late-Victorian cleric Denton draws heavily on Ranke for his even more developed view of the 'virtuous barbarians' with their Victorian moral probity in matters of sex and marriage and disinterest in money.[11]

There are in fact several 'histories' of Montenegro. There is the strong oral and poetic tradition, with its heroic ballads of resistance to outside invaders and oppressors, principally the Ottoman Turks. These are the songs of love and war. Then there is the Ottoman history itself, for although Montenegro was not conquered or integrated into the Empire in an orthodox manner, many of its main trade, cultural and external relationships for hundreds of years were with the Imperial lands. The Venetian coast was indeed just that and with the decline of Venice in the seventeenth and eighteenth centuries more and more links developed with the growing urban centres of semi-independent *pashliks* like that of the Bushatis in Skadar/Shkodra. Much of this Ottoman history is still little known or researched although the very welcome full opening of the Ottoman archives under the current Turkish government should change this over time. There is the history merged with geographical exploration in the numerous travellers' narratives that started to emerge after about 1830.

Another narrative is that of the Montenegrin Orthodox Church with its transnational origins in Byzantium and the medieval Serbian Empire. It is this latter story that was most influential in the twentieth century. The rulers of the post-Congress of Berlin Montenegrin state with its micro-capital in Cetinje were priest-kings and operated a paternalist theocracy. The poetic tradition of the Romantic generation represented by Karadzic had merged with the Christian traditions of Orthodox belief and a 'national' church was necessary to embody it. The current travails

---

10 This made possible the major volume published in Stuttgart in 1837, *Montenegro und die Montenegriner, ein Beitrag zur Kenntnis der Europäischen Turkei und des Serbischen Volkes.* Karadzic had published an important earlier paper in 1834, 'A View of Montenegro', in which he sought to counter the prevailing view in the German-speaking world that Montenegro was only a brigand society, as expressed in the Brockhaus encyclopedia and elsewhere. The resemblances with contemporary debates about the influence of 'organized crime' in the Balkans are unavoidable.

11 See W. Denton, *Montenegro Its Peoples and their History*, London: 1877.

and schisms in the Montenegrin church illustrate how much this is still a live and very difficult issue at the beginning of the twenty-first century. The formation of the new Montenegrin state after 2006 has brought the need for a unified national church that can embody the spiritual *ethnos* of the new political unit. Montenegro also continues to face the issue of transnationality, now embodied in the European Union, which the Montenegrin government wishes to join. Joining the European Union would involve a loss of sovereignty much greater than Montenegro had given up within either royalist or communist Yugoslavia.

Are Ranke and his writing still relevant to this new agenda? Some of the modern historians of Montenegro would appear to think not. The *History* is not mentioned or cited at all in Elizabeth Roberts' *Realm of the Black Mountain,* or in the Italian historian Antun Sbutega's *Storia del Montenegro: Dalle origini ai giorni nostri.*[12] When it appeared in Britain Roberts' work was praised extravagantly by ex-European Union foreign policy representative Christopher Patten in the *Times Literary Supplement* in London, who clearly did not like Montenegrin leader Milo Djukanovic, describing him as 'A Prime Minister before he was thirty, he is tall, good looking, charming and no more trustworthy than you would expect of a survivor of the breakup of Yugoslavia.' This might perhaps be read as fair comment from a negotiator who strove mightily for some years to prevent, as he puts it, 'Montenegro's escape from Serbia'. But Patten does not escape the spell of Ranke's tradition, even if he is unaware of it, when he goes on to write:

> Perhaps those from whom so much heroism has been expected find it difficult to countenance moderation. The courage has never been in doubt... In the Partisan struggles against the German and Italian occupiers in the Second World War, Montenegrins - Djilas prominent among them - played more than their proportionate part in that heroic fight against the odds. More than a third of the Partisans' generals came from Montenegro. Djilas - Tito's leading dissident critic - is the nearest person in Roberts' book to a real hero. Should we now add to his the name of Milo Djukanovic, the guileful Prime Minister and President who maneuvered Montenegro through the shoals of Serbian and European politics to the achievement of Independence?[13]

---

12 E. Roberts, *Realm of the Black Mountain A History of Montenegro,* London: 2007, and A. Sbutega, *Storia del Montenegro: Dalle origini ai giorni nostri,* Rome, 2006.

13 *Times Literary Supplement,* London, 1 June 2007. Patten does not face the issue of supercessionism implied in the European Union policy, that the EU itself represents a

The civilized man - Christopher Patten - as a moderate humanist, the 'European' - is counterpoised to the Balkan man - Milo Djukanovic - the product of the *ethnos*, who is untrustworthy and difficult to deal with, as Tacitus' disciple Ranke describes Milos Obrenovic and other Serbian leaders two centuries ago. The barbarian, heroic in war but untrustworthy in peace, is always there in some European eyes in the Balkans, whether in nineteenth-century Prussia or twentieth-century Brussels. For Milo Djukanovic read Milos Obrenovic, the flawed descendant of heroic resisters who destroyed Venetian and Ottoman power, just as Milo Djukanovic is the 'descendant' of the heroic Montenegrin Partisan generals whom Tito sent to Goli Otok forced labour camp.

The modern Montenegrin state was constituted on the basis of the Versailles treaty borders. Although Versailles was disastrous for Montenegro in many ways, it did bring one clear gain, the recognition of the modern borders which in turn formed the borders of the Montenegrin socialist republic within the first Yugoslavia and now the modern independent state. Yet in another sense it was a confidence trick - for there were no internal borders within Yugoslavia that mattered, except the northern borders of Kosova in periods of tension and crisis there. Montenegro was open for colonization from other Yugoslavs, as Croatia was, and the proportion of the population that was born outside Montenegro grew with industrialization and most of these immigrants were from Serbia.

The real question about Ranke and his inheritance ultimately goes back to Herder, and as Isaiah Berlin saw him, as a critic of the Enlightenment. Ranke was not very interested in borders and writes little about them. In his time the *ethnos* seemed always to have been there. The *ethnos* is at the heart of Montenegrin nationalism, and always has been, while the European Union is a pure child of the Enlightenment and looks forward to a borderless Europe. As has been written about the post-communist history of the important archaeological site at Svac/ Shesh near the border with Albania:

> The plethora of new states will all need new historical definition.
> No less than seven new countries, Bosnia, Croatia, Slovenia,
> Serbia, Montenegro, Macedonia and probably soon Kosova,
> will have emerged from what was the former Yugoslavia, and
> in most cases local historians see themselves as 'rescuing' a
> lost national narrative from the distortions and illegitimacy of
> communist history.[14]

transnational ideal that 'supersedes' ordinary national feelings and identities.

14 A. Cameron and J. Pettifer, 'The Enigma of Montenegrin History: The Example of Svac',
South Slav Journal, vol. 28, no. 1-2 (107-108), July 2008.

So Montenegrin historical authors will now also find themselves working against the pressures of the Europeanists on their fluid and robust *ethnos* traditions.[15]

---

15 An interesting example of this pressure are the changes in school textbooks demanded by the European Union before Montenegro can become a member.

Woodhouse, Zervas and the Chams

Exploring the Second World War Heritage

THE HISTORY OF THE EVENTS in Epirus and Chameria in the Second World War in the Greek Civil War period is only beginning to receive serious study by historians. There are three main countries obviously involved in the enquiry, Greece, Albania and Britain, but for different reasons little serious historical work was done in any of them during the Cold War period.

In Britain this was because the Greek Civil War was a painful and difficult episode, with several different dimensions. It was a long, complex conflict that passed through several phases between 1943 and 1949. British involvement was a major factor in the outcome, but there were many different political actors involved and competing strands of policy. Britain effectively had to withdraw from its previously dominant role between 1945 and 1947, largely as a result of the financial crisis of the post-war government in London.[1] This was a symbol of British imperial weakness, like the loss of India at the same time, in 1947-49. The victory of the right in Greece was only obtained through the financial and military resources of the United States, linked to the wider circumstances of the Tito-Stalin split in the international communist movement in 1948.[2]

Greece at the end of the Civil War period saw the birth of the 'Truman Doctrine', which was to become a central plank of the modus operandi of the Cold War.[3] Secondly, within Britain, the long and winding struggle of resistance to occupation and civil conflict aroused extremely strong emotions among those who had taken part as British advisers to the resistance movements led by army officers in the Special Operations Executive. The leading Special Operations Executive British Liaison Officer (BLO) concerned, C.M. (Monty) Woodhouse, was also

---

1   For an excellent account of this process, see 'The British Labour Government and the Greek Civil War - the imperialism of non-intervention' by Thanasis D. Sfikas, Keele, 1994. For a good general account of US policy development, see 'American Intervention in Greece, 1943-1949' by Lawrence S. Wittner, New York, 1982.

2   For a general survey of the pre-war background, see 'Greece and the British Connection 1935-1941' by John S. Koliopoulos, Oxford, 1977; for the Second World War Two period, 'British Policy towards Greece during the Second World War 1941-1944' by Procopis Papastratis, Cambridge, 1984. The standard American book in the Cold War period was *The Greek Civil War 1944-1949* by Edgar O'Ballance, London, 1956. On the Tito-Stalin split and its effects on Yugoslav communism in a key period for Greece, see *With Stalin against Tito - Cominformist Splits in Yugoslav Communism* by Ivo Banac, Cornell, 1988.

3   For the background in Greece to the complexities of the Anglo-American relationship, see *Anglo-American Relations with Greece - The Coming of the Cold War 1942-47* by Robert Frazier, London, 1991, and *The Truman Doctrine of Aid to Greece - A Fifty Year Retrospective* ed. E.T. Rossides, New York, 1998, and *Anglo-American Politics and the Greek Problem 1945-1949* (in Greek) by Basil Kondis, Thessaloniki, 1986.

a prominent Hellenist, secret agent and, later, a Conservative Party politician and historian of Greece in post-war Britain.[4] He essentially provided an *ex cathedra* view of events which in the monolithic atmosphere of much of British Hellenism during the Cold War tended to discourage further academic enquiry.[5]

In Greece it was convenient for the 'winning side' of the Greek right to put forward a standardized version of events to help form the new national narrative post-1949, and detailed study of the alleged ethnic cleansing of Chameria by British resistance ally Napoleon Zervas was elided from view as part of the wider objective of strengthening what was known as 'national consciousness' and in order to produce a new historical orthodoxy resting on the assumptions of the victors, as so often happens after civil wars in all periods.[6] There are also wider issues connected to the general position of Greece in British elite perceptions. David Roessel has shown how political actors such as Woodhouse saw themselves in the central Byronic tradition of Philhellenism, where to them many of the situations and decisions of the Greek War of Independence period were exactly repeated in the Civil War, and where the foreign participants again found unanimity in their writings (anti-Ottomanism/anti-communism), while the Greeks themselves were deeply split over the issues at stake.[7]

In Albania, the Cham issue was not studied much under communism, as the new post-1944 Cham immigrants had an uncertain position in society, almost no presence in the new Enverist political or academic elite and did not have the traditions of émigré scholarship that sustained Kosovar and Macedonian Albanian intellectual life. The significant Cham diaspora in Turkey dating back to post-Versailles Treaty expulsions in the 1920s had little organic connection with Hoxhaist Albania, and

---

4 C.M. Woodhouse (1917-2001) was the son of the 3rd Lord Terrington, and from a prominent Liberal family. .

5 An interesting academic relationship can be seen in Hugh Seton Watson's standard work on the advance of communism in Eastern Europe after the Second World War, *The East European Revolution*, London, 1950. In the chapter on Greece, although he quotes approvingly Woodhouse's views on the general context, he notes the 'contrasts in wealth, an irresponsible ruling class, discontented workers and a corrupt bureaucracy' as the cause for underlying crisis throughout those years, not Russian or other outside interference.

6 It was, of course, very difficult, after 1945, for Greek or Allied nation historians to enter Albania or interview wartime participants resident there or to use Albanian archives.

7 David Roessel, *In Byron's Shadow: Modern Greece in the English and American Imagination*, Oxford, 2001, p. 272.ff. A representative work illustrating the colonial mentality at that time of the British establishment is Sir Reginald Leeper's *When Greek Meets Greek*, London, 1950. Leeper was British Ambassador in Greece from 1943-1947. Its only source value nowadays is perhaps to illustrate the ignorance in Athens about actual wartime conditions, particularly in northern Greece.

was soon to be mixed with émigrés and expelled citizens from Kosova under Tito. Albanian political organization was poor, and limited to cultural and religious societies and brotherhoods. In addition, there were very few Chams in the key United States-based Albanian diaspora. It was not always easy for members of Cham émigré families to obtain good secondary education in many places in Albania, let alone Tirana University entrance. The patterns of mutual obligation that grew up between Greece and Albania in their international relations in the late Enverist period, starting under the post-1968 Greek dictatorship and continuing under subsequent democratic governments, led Hoxha to discourage promotion of the Cham issue in all its different dimensions. In the late 1970s, and later under the PASOK government period post-1982, Greek resistance hero Manolis Glezos was a frequent visitor to Albania, and enjoyed a good relationship with Hoxha, acting as an unofficial conduit for Athens initiatives.[8]

The situation has now clearly changed, exemplified by the innovative work of Beqir Meta on the 1930s and the Second World War period, and by a degree of invigoration of study in Greece, mainly by Basil Kondis and Eleftheria Manda in Thessaloniki.[9]

In Britain, as it is now some years after the death of Woodhouse and of other key ex-SOE officers such as Nigel Clive who were active in Epirus in this period, a revaluation of the period is clearly possible. There are a number of obvious questions to be addressed. The most important is how far the expulsion of the Chams was seen in London as an unavoidable necessity in the wartime conditions at the time, and how far it was a product of ignorance and error, rather than of conscious policy decisions.

This obviously affects modern assessments of whether what is now considered genocide under international law took place. Furthermore, there is the issue of what intelligence was received in London about what was happening, how it was interpreted, and what analytical parameters were used. But perhaps the most important point is the

---

8   See Enver Hoxha, *Two Friendly Peoples*, Tirana, 1985.
9   An important milestone in Albanian studies of Cham history was the publication of *Ceshtia Came dhe Integrimi Europian*, Arberia, Tirana, 2005, and the foundation of the Institute of Cham studies in Tirana in that same year. For Kondis' views, see *Greece and Albania: 1908-1914*, Thessaloniki, 1976, and other more recent publications, also, in Greek, by Eleftheria Manta, *Oi mousoulmanoi Tsamides tis Epirou, 1923-2000*, Thessaloniki, 2003. The impetus of all recent Greek scholarship on Civil War Epirus has been to maintain a monolithic view of all Chams as all Muslims and all active Axis collaborators, although even an outdated and limited work such as O'Ballance's Cold War period book admits they were 'stirred up' by outside forces.

issue of Woodhouse's personal role, and how far he, as a prominent Hellenist intellectual who in his own view would probably have spent his life teaching ancient philosophy in Oxford had the war not intervened, angled both intelligence and policy in a pro-Greek direction.[10] Then there are also issues of most interest to students of insurgencies and counter-insurgency, with the most crucial issue that of how far Woodhouse and the British were actually in control of what Zervas and his militias were doing in murdering and expelling the Chams, and how far British SOE officers had the capacity to control their client resistance militias.[11]

It should be said clearly that there is copious material from Woodhouse's own writings which must form the starting point of new studies, and also from fellow SOE officers such as Nigel Clive and Arthur Foss who wrote books about their experiences in Epirus, as well as the similar memoirs written by SOE BLOs on the Albanian side of the border, of which the most relevant is that of Antony Quayle, who post-war became a prominent British film actor and director.[12] Woodhouse remained active in Hellenist circles in Britain until the end of his life, and for much of that time, right up to about 2001, was guardian of the approved view of events.

In my experience, much of this material from ex-SOE officers is still not very well known in either Albania or Greece. Under communism in Albania, it would obviously not have been possible to publish it, and in Greece for many years after 1945 there was little motive to do so. Scholarship did not develop in Britain as might have been expected. There are still no official histories of SOE in Greece or Albania, although some interesting work such as that of Roderick Bailey has been recently published.[13] In the literary sphere, later writers seem to have felt overawed by the heroic classical imagery of the resistance and Civil

---

10 For Woodhouse's own personal background and intellectual formation, see his autobiography *Something Ventured*, London, 1982. He belonged to perhaps the last generation of British elite leaders where classical studies were central to the educational process

11 The only Cold War period work to start to touch on these issues in a serious way is O'Ballance's book, although his evaluation is often schematic, highly ideological and depends on sketchy information. It is perhaps significant that it was written by an American counter-insurgency expert, and hence had a degree of objectivity towards the material (particularly that from royalist sources) which is often lacking in the British literature.

12 It is beyond the scope of this paper to comment on all the implications of these books, but it is perhaps worth noting that even someone so conventional and mainstream Hellenist as Foss notes in *Epirus* the continuing existence of an Albanian-speaking population in parts of Epirus in the mid-1950s, long after the 1944 massacres.

13 See *The Wildest Province: SOE in the Land of the Eagle* by Roderick Bailey, London, 2008.

War in exploits such as Leigh Fermor's capture of a German general in Crete.[14] It is perhaps illustrative of the situation in the historiography of civil war Epirus/Chameria that the first real breakthrough in the field came from a Danish scholar, Lars Baerentzen, who published the reports of British secret agent David Wallace in Copenhagen in 1982.[15] Nigel Clive joined the Secret Intelligence Service (SIS), popularly known as M16, after the war and was obviously prevented from publishing anything for many years, and when he eventually did so in *A Greek Experience 1944-1949*,[16] it was published by a very small publisher in provincial Britain with little accompanying publicity. Clive believed that the post-1945 Labour government in London had been fundamentally mistaken in continuing the essence of Churchill's wartime Greek policy, and that uncritical support for the principle of the restoration of the Greek monarchy had been a major factor in the length and severity of the Civil War.[17] The special relationship between British elite classicism, the British intelligence services, and modern Greek politics meant that in contrast to the SOE-element in the Albanian resistance, much of the Greek material and sometimes even the names of the people involved were shrouded in secrecy and self-censorship and any public discussion of events in the Cold War was difficult.[18] The Albanian situation in historiography was much better, with the full and open publication of memoirs from both the right, like those of Julian Amery and David Smiley, and from the left, like that of Reginald Hibbert, and contributed to the vigorous open debate about post-communist Albania after 1990 in London. An entirely different

---

14 See David Roessell's illuminating quotation of novelist John Fowles's views: 'All my generation had been dazzled by the exploits of a celebrated generation of odd men who had fought beside the brave Greek resistance from 1939 to 1945', *op cit.*, p. 272.

15 *British Reports on Greece 1943-1944*, ed. Lars Baerentzen, Copenhagen, 1982.

16 Published by Michael Russell in the UK in 1985, with an Introduction by Sir William Deakin. Deakin occupied a position in the SOE Yugoslav pantheon of equivalent authority to Woodhouse in Greece, and ended up as Warden of St Antony's College, Oxford. Although an Establishment figure, unlike Woodhouse he was never a mainstream Tory on the imperialist-Churchillian wing of the party, and this had a marked influence over SOE Yugoslav historiography.

17 *Op. cit.* and conversations Nigel Clive/James Pettifer between 1992 and 2000. Although they were more or less Oxford contemporaries, Clive and Woodhouse came to diverge politically, something that may have affected their subsequent view of the Greek crisis. Clive resigned from the Conservative Party over Chamberlain's Munich deal with Hitler, while Woodhouse, according to his own account in his autobiography, found he could live with appeasement since postponing the onset of war gave him more time to complete his studies. *Op. cit.*, p. 136.

18 This atmosphere continued in some quarters in London for many years, as the furore over the first Channel 4 films about the Civil War in the early 1980s indicated.

situation had also prevailed with Yugoslavia, although for different reasons. There, the eminence of SOE advisers like Deakin and Maclean, their public prominence after the war and their literary skills had contributed to open historical enquiry. The role of Woodhouse was in essence to preserve the propaganda-based orthodoxies of the wartime period in a narrative which often discouraged critical enquiry and analysis.

It was, oddly enough, with the arrival of the Greek dictatorship after 1968 that this historical logjam began to break. The small number of British communists and other leftists in the League for Democracy in Greece organization began to emerge from the isolation imposed on them by the domination of the Greek right in London Hellenism, and found a wider audience as practical opposition to the Athens junta began to develop in Britain.[19] Some of the SOE generation came out in open opposition to the junta, including Woodhouse, and were prepared to share platforms with League and non-aligned speakers, and thus split the key Cold War alliance in Greek London between the monarchists and the democratic right, something from which it is arguable the Greek monarchy never recovered and led in part to its final demise. In his personal political activity after 1974 and the end of the dictatorship, Woodhouse worked as an advocate for then Greek Prime Minister Karamanlis, and put forward generally uncontroversial political positions for Greek political democratization and modernization.[20] The role of the long-running Cyprus crisis and British centrality to the decisions taken were, in my opinion, a major background factor in the evolution of Woodhouse's views. In the early 1950s he became increasingly critical of Tory government Cyprus policy under Churchill, and somewhat estranged from the top Tory elite groups, even though his personal prestige was at a high level

---

19 The role of Marion Serafis, as a UK citizen and widow of ELAS military leader General Stefanos Serafis, was important in these debates, both within the largely constitutionalist League for Democracy in Greece, and other more radical organizations. In the period of the anti-junta campaign, the League was given a small office within King's College London, a centre of academic British Hellenic studies of many years standing. See *ELAS - Greek Resistance Army*, London, 1980, a landmark publication indicating the change in climate in London as a result of the dictatorship. There are also obviously important wider issues here affecting the historiography connected to the presence of a number of communists and non-party Marxists in the world of classical and ancient history studies during the Cold War in the United Kingdom, such as Robert Browning, Frank Walbank, George Thompson and Geoffrey St Croix, in contrast to the absence of similar scholars in the field of modern Greek historical studies. In practice, this left the field open for Woodhouse to establish and maintain a de facto orthodoxy of opinion.

20 See C.M. Woodhouse, *The Rise and Fall of the Greek Colonels*, London, 1985.

then after his key role within the SIS/CIA operation to overthrow Mossadegh in Iran and establish the Shah in government.[21]

None of this political liberalization in London led to the reawakening of the Cham issue in political discourse. That was intimately linked to the re-emergence of Albania onto the international stage in 1990 and the end of the extraordinary period of autarchic isolation of the previous thirty years. As an anecdotal illustration, I wrote a short article for the London *Independent* newspaper in 1991 about an Albanian government proposal to take the Cham issue to the World Court at The Hague, and subsequently discovered that this was the first mention of the subject in a British newspaper since the Second World War.

We need to see that Woodhouse's work was not monolithic, and that he changed at least the presentation and style of his views over time. His first excursion into historical writing was his book *Apple of Discord*, which appeared in London in 1948, when the Civil War in Greece was still going on. It sets out in considerable detail the recent history of Greece, with an account of the time of Metaxas and the Second World War in the Balkans, then a very much blow-by-blow account of the course of the Occupation and development of the resistance, and of the British role, including that of Woodhouse himself. It is very strongly anti-communist, and could be said to be a pièce d'occasion, reflecting the assumptions of the time and also very bound up with the imperative to keep British public opinion 'on side' in support of Civil War policy, when criticism of British support for the right and the monarchists was spreading well beyond the left, inside and outside Parliament. Although reporting of the Civil War was tightly controlled by the government in London, the effects of bombing on civilians in the northern mountains as well as on the communist Democratic Army was causing widespread concern.[22] As Thanasis Sfikas has shown, the Greek

---

21 There would be scope for a comparative study of the two operations. There are obvious structural similarities between the use of Zervas' EDES militia as a destabilizing force of the right against the dominance of the communist-controlled ELAS forces in Greece, and the use of street gangs and roughnecks from wrestling clubs in the counter-revolution against Mossadegh in Tehran a few years later.

22 For data on the methods used by the British government to control media coverage of the conflict, see *Memories of a Mountain War Greece 1944-1949*, London, 1972, by Kenneth Matthews. Matthews was the resident BBC correspondent in Athens and a man of a conventional centrist outlook, making his exposure of the pro-monarchist media manipulation all the more credible. Techniques pioneered in the 'spin' world in Greece were later widely used in the entire Cold War period. The Greek government also made various attacks on the media, particularly American correspondents in the 1947-49 period which after the murder of correspondent George Polk in Thessaloniki undermined much of its general credibility as a moderate responsible alternative to the left. See *The Salonika*

Civil War was a major crisis for the British left, on a much wider and deeper register than issues connected with the left in other European nations like France and Italy, where communist hopes of taking power after the war had also been dashed by events. It was also, of course, the time when the British government had effectively ceded control of the foreign military aid effort to the right in Greece to the United States, and it is perhaps not entirely a coincidence that the only currently available edition of Woodhouse's book is the 1985 American reprint. His writing is imbued with the assumptions of the Truman Doctrine, with all that means in terms of the suppression of complexity in the interests of building a united front in support of the right. Yet although it is a modern book, in that it is a reflection on contemporary history by a participant who had played a leading role in many of the events that he describes, it is impossible not to see the shadow of Woodhouse's traditional classical education in the writing, from Thucydides writing about the fifth-century conflicts in which he was an actor, right through to Roman historians such as Tacitus. The classical moral ideal of the scholar-soldier acting in defence of democracy is seen by Woodhouse as part of an unbroken Greek tradition, and the British, as holders of a special relationship with modern Greece since its 1830s birth, as political and military actors capable of re-enacting ancient dramas.[23] The little bands of heroic resistants whom Woodhouse, Clive, and Leigh Fermor describe so well are very directly descended from the Spartans who fought at Thermopylae, but with one significant and, in the end, fatal difference, in that in 1943 and afterwards they were split between left and right, and were to remain so. It is worth noting that Woodhouse had, even then, an exceptional command of the demotic Greek language, something that may in part explain the admiration

---

Bay Murder - Cold War Politics and the Polk Affair by Edmund Keeley, Princeton, 1989.

23 There are many complex issues here of political and cultural identity that future historians will need to study. In many ways, the BLOs were expected to 'become' Greeks or Albanians or Yugoslavs when attached to irregular forces in the mountains, in order to exert productive influence over the resistance militias. The well-known British proclivity for embracing particular Balkan national causes was also a factor. The unique difference with the Greek BLOs was that they were inheritors of the Byronic tradition, where involvement in the promotion of the Greek national cause was not merely legitimate, but also manly and heroic, and in British terms, wholly patriotic. To take up either the Albanian or Yugoslav national causes, as actors like Hibbert, Smiley and Deakin later found, involved a degree of cultural displacement. For an account of how these issues played out in Greek practical politics in earlier generations in the post-Byron period, see *The British and the Hellenes - Struggles for Mastery in the Eastern Mediterranean 1850-1960* by Robert Holland and Diana Makrides, Oxford, 2006. Most of these issues resurfaced in the Second World War period.

Churchill had for him, as someone who was prevented from applying to study at Oxford because of his lack of ancient Greek.[24]

The Chams are only referred to in the section of the book called 'Minor Armed Collaborators', and the entire Cham community in Epirus is thus tarred with the collaborationist brush, and described in what can only be called imperialist-racialist terms as a 'Moslem people commonly called Turko-Albanians'. In this book Woodhouse laid down the orthodoxy in which the Chams were afterwards seen in British historiography for two generations by adopting the terminology of the Greek extreme right.[25] He is not without valuable perceptions; he notes that one of the disadvantages the Chams had was that they were a wealthy community, disinclined to fight until it was too late, and that the Axis powers in the Balkans were inclined to be fairly sympathetic to local Moslem populations, as happened in Kosovo, compared to the pre-war regimes in Greece or Serbia based on Orthodox Christianity. He notes correctly that the Cham issue has some resonances with the issue of the Macedonian minority in Greece, with its ever-explosive political connotations. He considers, probably wisely, that the Chams had very poor wartime leadership in their communities. Some Cham leaders were very slow to recognize the wider political realities of international relations at the time. But there are also startling lacunae. He omits completely any mention of the small Jewish communities along the coast opposite Corfu at places like Syvota (until 1944, in Albanian, *Muros*) or nearby Plataria who lived intermingled with the Chams, and so fails to mention some of the most hapless victims of both Metaxas and then the Axis occupiers. There is also a slant on any use of the word 'Turk' in the book while Greece is always presented as an inherently superior culture. We should not, of course, forget that Greece was at one period early in the Second World War the only ally that Britain had or that Churchill - although poor at school and ignorant of most classical culture - had taken in much of the traditional sentimental Hellenism of the ruling elites at that time. The Metaxas period was seen in London as a defeat

---

24 On knowledge of Greek as a metalanguage within the British elite, and its social and ideological role, see *The Victorians and Ancient Greece* by Richard Jenkyns, Oxford, 1980. Little had changed by 1939 in many circles, and Woodhouse had received a very conservative classical education at Winchester College. For Woodhouse's own generally sensible views on this tradition, see *The Philhellenes*, London, 1969.

25 In his later academic writing he shows he understands the nature of Greek nationalism quite well, thus writing in *Modern Greece: A Short History*, London, 1982, that 'Greece included considerably fewer than half of those who regarded themselves as Greeks by virtue of their language, religion, and (less plausibly) their race. It was easy to stir up agitation in favour of enlarging Greece's borders by a progressive extension of *enosis* (union).'

for British influence in Greece, and a triumph for Germany, and the experience of the Occupation and Civil War did little to modify this perception.

In his later works, Woodhouse somewhat modifies his line on the events insofar as he avoids the use of what would now be regarded as politically unacceptable language derived from colonialist stereotypes, but the essential content changes less. *The Struggle for Greece 1941-1949*, published in 1976 with an introduction by Richard Clogg, does admit that there was an 'Albanian minority in Greece', in defiance of official Athens views that there are no ethnic minorities in Greece, but the Chams or their destiny are hardly mentioned apart from the normal perfunctory designation of all Chams as collaborators. This at one level might not be surprising if the book did not also contain an extensive and lengthy account of the general activity of Zervas in the resistance, in more sympathetic detail, on the whole, than in *Apple of Discord* where the character of Zervas' militia soldiers is not glossed over.

In his 1976 book, Woodhouse describes the Chams as 'punished' by Zervas for collaboration, but gives no details of the grim and systematic militia violence against them in places like Paramithia in 1943-44, and above all the human rights violations against civilians, particularly women and children.[26] He does not discuss whether any British attempt was made to stop Zervas' war crimes. It seems likely that there was no such attempt, in accordance with the policy of boosting Zervas in the north-west to tie down communist ELAS forces and prevent them from reinforcing other ELAS forces who were on the point of controlling Athens.[27] It may, moreover, be claimed, as some more intelligent Greek commentators do, that these events happen in wars, and are worse in civil wars, and that similar crimes were committed on all sides.

This is, of course, the case, but the laws of war existed in 1944, if in a less developed form than they exist now, as the Nuremberg trials showed. There is a case of general double standards in the recent historiography, where, for instance, a book like Nicholas Gage's *Eleni* received widespread international publicity, with some help, it appears, from at least one official US government agency, on the basis of its recording of the violence of communist-led ELAS and Democratic Army guerrillas, while the Chams' sufferings at Greek hands have

---

26 See Beqir Meta's *Tensioni Greko-Shqiptarët (1939-1949)*, Tirana, 2002, for a comprehensive Albanian viewpoint of these events.

27 For the different currents in British policy, see *British Intervention in Greece: from Varkiza to Civil War* by Heinz Richter, London, 1985. Also *Greece at the Crossroads: The Civil War and its Legacy* ed. John O. Iatrides and Linda Wrigley, Philadelphia, 1995.

been elided and obscured as irrelevant and unworthy of serious moral concern.[28]

In Woodhouse's autobiography, *Something Ventured*, published in 1982, there is a mention of Paramithia, but only in the context of a visit to David Wallace's grave, and no reference to the fate of the Chams at all, and the standard view is reiterated that without Zervas and the energy the communist-led ELAS had expended in fighting, ELAS might have been able to take control of the Greek capital.[29] The EDES Chams have become, so to speak, the Ghost in the History Machine, unseen and unspoken.

It is clear that the historical work and life of Monty Woodhouse contain many contradictions. He was not a friend of the Greek left but in his middle and later life in debates in London he did distance himself from their repression under the post-Civil War governments in Athens, above all the junta between 1968 and 1974. In his defence, it could be argued that his acceptance of a mono-ethnic Epirus/Chameria was only in keeping with policies and events that had their roots in the 1923 Treaty of Lausanne and its aftermath of mass population exchanges. At a human level, he was an approachable and serious scholar-politician who was always open to debate with those of different views, but even his strongest admirers often noted a current of austerity and abstraction in his outlook and personality that could detach him from the sufferings British policy caused in wartime Greece in the name of anti-communism. He came from an aristocratic family in Britain and had been pro-appeasement and anti-Churchill, but he was to find himself Churchill's chosen man in Greece, with enormous personal responsibilities for British policy. He knew little of the wider Balkans from personal experience but that did not stop him from making sweeping pronouncements on political developments there, and he was particularly ignorant of the Macedonian Question. Although the

---

28 The Greek lobby in the United States is often active in promoting a particular view of the history that among other things elides the war crimes of Zervas from the historical record. Gage's book was published in 1983, just when in Greece under the new PASOK government a new evidence-based historiography of the wartime period was developing.

29 Quite apart from anything to do with political events in Epirus, these claims are highly speculative from a military point of view. It is quite arguable that what stopped ELAS taking Athens was the confusion and ineptitude of the Greek Communist Party leadership, rather than a simple lack of ELAS soldiers, coupled with the effective presentation of Archbishop Damaskianos and his entourage by Churchill and the British. The KKE leadership weaknesses continued long afterwards; see Svetozar Vukmanovic (General Tempo), *How and Why the People's Liberation Struggle of Greece Met with Defeat*, London, 1985. Tempo was Tito's emissary to the Greek resistance forces and had a detailed knowledge of the personalities and political forces involved.

general SOE tradition in informal warfare was essentially derived from the Arabist T.E. Lawrence, Woodhouse had a limited and imperialist view of Islam and the Ottoman and Arab worlds that chimed well with that of the irredentist Greek right in Epirus. Private debate about Greek history was something that he encouraged, and he was not there a proponent of orthodoxy, but in the end the Chams and other ethnic minorities were not seen by him as fully Greek and so were not entitled to their full human rights and dignity.[30] The public discourse was, however, a different matter, where the maintenance of orthodoxy of view and the suppression of heretical discourse about the ethnic cleansing of the Chams - and many other issues - was always his duty.[31]

The Cham issue will need, before it is resolved, to start to write its own history, and that is bound to include some consideration of Woodhouse and his true role in British policy and reactions to events. This will include a consideration of the wider crisis of British Philhellenism in the Civil War and Cold War periods.[32]

---

30 An interesting illustration of Woodhouse's own understanding of his historic role can be found in his foreword to D. George Kousoulas' volume *Revolution and Defeat: The Story of the Greek Communist Party*, Oxford, 1965. This was the first serious attempt by a non-communist Greek historian to write the history of the KKE, and on many issues Kousoulas' views differ substantially from those of Woodhouse, but this does not stop Woodhouse from claiming in his foreword that the Greek author relied mostly on *Apple of Discord* for his orientation.

31 One of the many ironies of his activity was alienation from mainstream British academia. In his autobiography, he writes very disparagingly of prominent Oxford figures such as Isaiah Berlin and Richard Crossman who taught him at New College, and rather sourly of his time at Chatham House, the Royal Institute of International Affairs.
An important starting point will be to clarify what happened during Woodhouse's 'missing years' after he left the armed forces, and Greece, in 1945-46, and his return to activity with the SIS/CIA operation in Iran after 1950. He does not mention this period in his autobiography at all, and states that he did not revisit Greece until 1950. He was not involved in the SIS/CIA operations at that time to overthrow the communist government in Albania. But it is hard to believe his unique knowledge of Greece and the region was not drawn upon by the UK government in this critical civil war period.

32 See *The Greek Civil War: Essays in a Conflict of Exceptionalism and Silences*, eds. Philip Carabott and Thanasis D. Sfikas, Aldershot, 2004.

33 An earlier draft of this text was published by Botuese Onufri in Tirana in 2010.

CHAMERIA HISTORY
GEOGRAPHICAL SPACE AND
ALBANIAN TIME

'FOR MORE THAN TWO CENTURIES, the Ottoman Empire, once so formidable was gradually sinking into a state of decrepitude. Unsuccessful wars, and, in a still greater degree, misgovernment and internal commotions were the causes of its decline.'

Richard Alfred Davenport, The Life of Ali Pasha Tepeleni,
Vizier of Epirus[1]

On the wall in front of us is a map of north-west Greece that was made by a French military geographer, Lapie, and published in Paris in 1821, although it was probably in use in the French navy for some years before that. Lapie was at the forefront of technical innovation in cartography in his time, and had studied in Switzerland, the most advanced country for cartographic science in the late eighteenth century. It is likely that it was made for military use in the Napoleonic period wars against the British. Its very existence is a product of British-French national rivalry in the Adriatic in that period. Modern cartography had many of its roots in the Napoleonic Wars period and immediately before in the Eastern Mediterranean, when intense naval competition between the British and French for control of these waters led to major scientific advances. In turn, in the eighteenth century, similar progress had been made in both countries as a result of earlier wars in the Atlantic.

This map is titled 'Chameria/Thesprotia', and so at that time it is clear that the two traditional names for the region, Albanian and Greek, were both in common use, not only locally but by the often classically-educated officers of a European Great Power. Yet a glance at the development of mid-nineteenth-century cartography shows us that as little as twenty years later, after the time of Ali Pasha as ruler of the region, this joint terminology had disappeared and in the increasing British monopoly of regional power the Greek terms 'Epirus' and 'Thesprotia' always predominate, usually exclusively. These maps, French or British, were of course a very considerable step forward from their Venetian Empire predecessors, in that however schematically, they did begin to try to make scientific geographical descriptions of the mainland interior; most Venetian maps except of important trading centres like Ragusa (modern Dubrovnik) only alluded to places within ten or twenty miles of the coastal littoral, at most.

The great majority of this material is in the form of Admiralty charts, made for the Royal Navy. Geography can often fade into historical

---

1   Davenport, R.A., *The Life of Ali Pasha of Tepeleni, Vizier of Epirus: surnamed Aslan or the Lion*, London, 1837, p. 4.ff.

enquiry and names on maps are often very important, or even, spelling of the same name, as Kosova/Kosovo demonstrates as an issue between Albanians and Serbs, or in a different context, the current 'name' controversy between Greece and Former Yugoslav Macedonia. The colonial powers of Western Europe were not only engaged in warfare and economic rivalry, they were also helping construct the national identities of the new states that were beginning to emerge from the Ottoman Empire. Chameria then was not a name that meant anything to Great Power diplomacy as a political factor but it nevertheless did exist, as the Albanian-speaking inhabitants of the region that is now north-west Greece saw themselves as Chams. But it was a fragile identity. The term Cham has no existence in classical literature, whereas Epirus does. This was important given the centrality of neo-classical ideology in the construction of the new Greek state after 1835. After being in common parlance in the eighteenth and early nineteenth century, the name 'Chameria' gradually disappeared in the later nineteenth and early twentieth century, as the expansion of Greece's northern borders and Ottoman retreat dominated events. The absence of an Albanian national state until as late as 1913 was an important handicap to the Chams, as a friendly kinship state on the northern boundary of their historic territory.

This story of the largely subterranean survival of a Cham identity through the disasters and ethnic cleansing of the twentieth century is very little known outside the Albanian world. The historiography of Chameria/Thesprotia is a very incomplete and fragmentary narrative, even by Balkan standards. In the Albanian story, there is little sustained historical writing although a plethora of personal memoirs and essentially antiquarian excursions into the past of a particular locality or family. Compared to the rich local narrative of Kosova and Macedonian Albanian history writing, this is little indeed. In contrast, on the Greek side of the debate, there is a long-established canonical version of twentieth-century history which has been efficiently promoted in all school and education textbooks, also by the Greek Orthodox Church, and in the vast majority of the historiography of the key World War II and Greek Civil War period. Most of this narrative has become accepted as standard outside Greece, most strongly in neighbouring nations such as Serbia with their own motives to diminish Albanian influence in the Balkans.

Their view of the Cham story is very limited, and purports to be only a minor footnote in the wide and complex story of Balkan nationalities and Balkan minorities who after the end of the Ottoman Empire felt aggrieved at their status and position within a new post-Ottoman nation. The Greek narrative is in essence a simple tale, of a remnant of the Ottoman world, the Cham Albanians, who lived a tenuous life in ever diminishing numbers in 'Greek' Epirus, and most importantly, clung on (or most of them did) to the religion of the old Empire, Sunni Islam, that of the collapsed Caliphate. They were, in colloquial parlance, 'losers', with all that implies. In the historiography, Greece is seen as representing westernising modernity, and 'civilisation', against the Chams' role as fragmentary survivors of a dead empire and its backward, defeated and 'Eastern' culture and religion. As in all nationalist myths, there are some historic facts underpinning the inflated story. Faced with the modernizing realities of Greek nationalism after the Ottomans left the region in 1913, many Chams also 'drifted away' (or were forced to leave) in the interwar period, to escape rural decline, unemployment and poverty, until what is in Greek eyes the culminating Cham folly occurred that destroyed their legitimacy as Greek citizens, support of some Chams for the Italian invasion and Axis Occupation. Although Chameria had not been important in the Treaty of Lausanne deliberations in 1922-23, the Lausanne mechanisms of the exchange of populations between Greece and Turkey tended to legitimize Greek expulsions of Chams, in Greek nationalist eyes. This led to their 'final' expulsion in 1943-1944 at the hand of Napoleon Zervas' nationalist militia EDES. Virtually all Muslim Chams were dead, or had left Epirus. The remaining Orthodox Chams chose to assimilate, or were forced to do so by post-World War II Greek governments and left their Souli and other mountain redoubts to quiet anonymous lives in the growing new towns of Epirus, or emigrated abroad, or simply moved to Athens.

This Greek view of the history of the Chams in the twentieth century has dominated all international academic discourse about the subject until very recently. In both Peace Conferences held after the World Wars, Greece also tried to expand further northwards by taking 'Vorio Epirus', northern Epirus, that part of southern Albania stretching up to the Shkumbini River from Albania. The history of the modern Greek state after 1832 has been one of continuous northern expansion, so much so that some historians of modern Greece such as John Koliopoulos have questioned whether even the concept of a final and fixed northern border for the nation ever existed. Greek northward expansion was a product of the overwhelmingly strong influence of the Megali Idea, the 'Great Idea', the concept of the restoration of the 'Greek' Byzantine Empire through an ever-expanding Greek nation state after the departure of the Ottoman Empire from history.

The expansion of Greece along the Adriatic coast of the mainland opposite the Ionian Islands received a decisive setback with the establishment of the independence of Albania after 1912. It was achieved through resisting Greek and Serbian policy to prevent the emergence of an Albanian state and divide the territory between them. Yet independence was achieved. The hundredth anniversary of that event will be celebrated in Tirana and throughout the Albanian world this year. Albania has been less successful over that period in reuniting the disparate parts of its political firmament compared to Greece. This has not been only a matter of the delay in achieving Kosova's limited independence in 2008. The Albanians, reemerging, as Reginald Hibbert put it, onto the Balkan scene after the Hoxhaist years, did not have a good position in international academic and associated political discourse about the Balkans to put their case forward.[2]

Greece was able to dominate discussion about the region throughout the twentieth century. The Chams are a little known people. On the Albanian side of the border, the post-1944 refugee Chams were an unpopular group in Hoxha's Albania and few were able to obtain higher education or rise to prominent positions. In the Diaspora, principally in Turkey, many chose to abandon much or all of their Albanian identity when faced with the intensely conformist pressures of the Turkish education system under Ataturk and his successors, and Turkish national indifference then to the cultural rights of all minorities. Rulers then saw the 1923 Treaty of Lausanne as having either downgraded or abolished minority rights as an issue of concern in South East Europe. The Greek government took up the intellectual position that has been maintained across the board until recently that there were no ethnic minorities in Greece. Religious difference was also downgraded, in both Greece and Turkey. Religious people from Balkan refugee - usually but not all Muslims or of partly Muslim - origins have had a low status and regard in twentieth-century Turkey until the arrival of the Erdogan government where many prominent figures, including Erdogan himself, come from Balkan Muslim families.

The Greek academic tradition is certainly very powerful, and has been very closely integrated with state political objectives in the field of modern history not merely in the Cold War period, but for long before in many fields of enquiry, most obviously those concerning Macedonia and its identity, but the power and cogency of this tradition does not, in

---

2   See paper by Hibbert, R., 'Albania's Emergence onto the Balkan Scene', *Balkan Studies*, 38.1, Thessaloniki, 1997, republished in *Albania and the Albanians: Essays in Honour of Sir Reginald Hibbert*, ed. J. Pettifer, London, 2013.

my opinion, fully explain the absence of a Chameria history narrative, or the difficulty the Chams have had in establishing themselves on the 'cultural map' of post-communist Balkan minorities in the post-1989 period. It was difficult for the critics of the canonical Greek view of modern Macedonian history to make headway post-1989 but they certainly quickly did so, as the bitter exchanges inside and outside universities involving the work of independent-minded scholars such as Loring Danforth and Anastasia. N. Karakasidou show in the mid-1990s. Similar vigorous debate has taken place between Greek and Turkish historians over Cyprus issues. In recent years there has also been a marked improvement in the historiography in Greece itself of the Muslim minority in Thrace, culminating in recent London publication on the subject, with Anglo-Greek authorship.[3] In contrast, Cham history writing has been confined to study of the World War II period and the relationship between the Cham Albanians, Greece and Albania as states, and the Italian occupiers, and has a highly tendentious character, seeking to show that the Chams were not active Axis collaborators, and by implication, responsible for their own later misfortunes.

Why is writing the history of Chameria apparently so difficult, and publication on it seems to be so fragmentary and incomplete? It is worth remembering that in terms of classical antiquarianism, and the Grand Tour, Epirus hardly existed, apart from passing coastal interest in the site of the Battle of Actium near Preveza, and the relatively accessible ruins of ancient Nicopolis. The magnificent structures at ancient Butrint (Buthrotum) were unknown, and the area was a feverish swamp. In terms of archaeological discovery, the theatre at Dodona was a late addition to the classical pantheon, and in any case was not within the Greek state until after 1913. In Ottoman times the area was an overgrown wilderness inhabited only by shepherds. Epirus is not mentioned at all in the standard history of the Grand Tour.[4] Finding a sense of what a Cham narrative might include is as much a problem for foreign writers as for Albanian and Greek historians. At one level there are seemingly easy answers, as indicated above.

There are also deeper problems, which relate to developments with the establishment of the British Empire and British naval supremacy in the Mediterranean after the seminal event of the British defeat of Napoleon in the Battle of the Nile in 1799. The contest between French and British naval power over the replacement of Venice as the main

3   See Featherstone. K. (ed.), *The Last Ottomans: the Muslim minority of Western Thrace during the Axis Occupation and the Greek Civil War*, Basingstoke, 2011.

4   Black, J., *The Grand Tour in the Eighteenth Century*, New York, 1992.

Adriatic and East Mediterranean sea power was not new in Napoleon or Ali Pasha's time. But it intensified markedly then. Ali Pasha sought to curry favour with both powers and to trade influence in his pashlik whenever he could. Both governments placed envoys in his court, and both of them, the Frenchman Pouqueville and the Englishman William Martin Leake, acted as de facto spies for their respective governments in Paris and London. As Richard Davenport, the mid-nineteenth-century author who was Ali Pasha's first biographer, observed, 'Bonaparte counted much on the active cooperation of Ali', and when his cooperation did not materialize, French ambitions in the region never recovered.

Chameria lies on the north-west Greek landmass at a time of the construction of British naval supremacy in the Ionian Islands off the coast. The dialectic of Chameria and Thesprotia is essentially that of the mainland versus these heavily fortified and British-controlled islands. The tiny Ottoman-period ports like Sagiada on the mainland facing Corfu were of little or no importance compared to those on the Ionian Islands themselves. It is sometimes forgotten nowadays how much the development of the British Empire was a naval project, and how far political policy in London, in general, was determined by Royal Naval priorities. The fortification of the Ionians, principally Corfu, was driven by the need to construct a sea empire for British trade at a time when the nation was excluded from most of Continental Europe by Napoleon and his realms of control. The British presence became deeply engaged in the communities such as Corfu, Gibraltar and Malta and elsewhere which were under effective Royal Naval government, sometimes virtually openly, as on the Ionian-governed island of Kithira for a long period. As Robert Holland points out: 'So entrenched did the British become in significant parts of the Mediterranean that their presence became something deeper: a world of its own, though like all such phenomena, one shot through with other worlds, presences and rivalries.'[5]

British naval power was projected, particularly after about 1840, through a series of colonial island 'Alamos' of which perhaps Malta and Corfu became the most characteristic. The Epirus mainland was of little interest to Corfu government magnates like Sir Thomas Maitland, once Corfu was secured for London, and it became a place to go duck shooting and little else. Once great centres of trade like Butrint had collapsed into malarial stagnation, and they and many other places were too small and silted up to accommodate British ships. The Ionian Islands represented progress and modernity and integration into an expanding world-empire

5   Holland, R., *Blue Water Empire: The British and the Mediterranean since 1800*, London, 2013, p. 5.ff.

as opposed to the near-medieval conditions in the collapsing Ottoman world in mainland Chameria and Epirus generally. Yet it was also the case that however bad these mainland conditions were, they did not involve the persecution of Christian minorities along the lines of the conflicts that brought Great Power attention and subsequent intervention in the Crete crisis of 1867. Christian and Sunni and Bektashi Muslim Chams co-existed with Christian Greeks, Vlachs and Roma of both religions in relative harmony, compared to many Balkan Ottoman domains, and so the region attracted little attention from the liberal imperialists in the Gladstonian, post-Batak tradition. After the 1820s, the Adriatic had become a British lake in terms of power projection, and it was a matter of massive indifference what happened on most of the coastal littorals, with the exception of the ambitions of the Habsburgs centred on Trieste as the century drew towards its close.

As the nineteenth century wore on, Greece began to expand northwards towards Epirus. Towns on the southern fringe of old Chameria with substantial Albanophone elements in the population like Arta (Greek after 1881) and Preveza (Greek after 1913) and the rural areas near the enormous fortress of Vonitsa on the Gulf of Actium began to see changes in their population composition, particularly after Arta became the boundary between the Ottoman Empire and the expanding Greek state. Preveza was fiercely contested by the emerging Albanian nationalist organization the League of Prizren, and it was not finally surrendered to the Greek state until the fighting there in the Second Balkan War was concluded in 1913. This event, in my opinion, marks in practice the beginning of the end of Ottoman Chameria, at least as a potential Albanian nation state formation component, along with the retreat of the Turks from Ioannina at the same time and the mass expulsion of a significant proportion of the Albanophone and other minority populations. Historic time was changing the Albanian geographical space, to the advantage of the Greeks following their traditional 'northern' policy of border-creating war against the remaining Ottoman dominions. The British on the Ionian Islands had little detailed interest in developments, other than a general welcome for the expansion of Greece as a traditional friend of British naval power. Rival Great Powers such as the French and Germans were not involved, and Habsburg naval ambitions were not matched by practical naval construction. Ports on the southern Cham coast were unimportant except for local trade with Corfu. Very little indeed was known of Albanian nationalism in London. The prevailing view in many London institutions was heavily influenced by the outcome of the Congress of

Berlin in 1878 when Bismarck had stated that the Albania was only a geographic expression, not a nation. He was only saying openly what many diplomats and power-elite members privately believed and the Berlin Congress and its aftermath was in every sense, Bismarck's Congress.[6] The 'concert of Europe' had to follow Prussian leadership afterwards on many issues and the future of Chameria was only one very minor issue in most eyes.

On the ground these deliberations were unknown to most Chameria inhabitants, who might as well have been living in medieval China for all they knew of the external world, apart, perhaps, from a small minority of coastal dwellers who were literate and had access to some information through Ionian island links. Unlike in some other parts of the late Ottoman Empire where ethnic Albanians had taken part in revolts against imperial rule, in northern Chameria/Epirus there were few ciflik estates with large areas of fertile land and equally large heavily exploited workforces prone to radical ideas and armed revolt. The Cham/Thesprotia land is dominated by the immense Pindus and Souli mountains with scattered pastoralist populations, and towns (with the exception of Ioannina) surrounded for the most part by limited areas of cultivable land. This has remained the case since antiquity. It has always given the region a sense of being a somewhat separate world from the Greek - or Albanian - mainstreams. Geographical space is central to this. Cary comments in his Geographical Background of Greek and Roman History that 'The interior of Epirus is sundered into separate compartments by an intricate system of ridges towering over deeply sunk valleys ... its political detachment has a valid explanation in its geographical seclusion.'[7]

In the Ottoman period the region did not lend itself to the pattern of agriculture favoured by the imperial rulers and amongst other things this resulted in the relative absence of much of a Bey class of the type who formed the backbone of Albanian nationalist political consciousness from the Rilindja national revival period in the latter half of the nineteenth century through to the Ambassadors Conference and World War I. Cham Albanians who were integrated into the Ottoman world tended to be urban dwellers who owed their main loyalty to the army system and the Sunni mosques. Politically radical imams were confined to a few centres like Paramithia where nationalist ideas had

---

6   This did not, of course, mean the legacy of the Berlin Congress remained the same over the years, any more than that of the Versailles conference did post-World War I. For a near-contemporary German view, see Brandenburg, E. (trans. Adams, E.A.), *From Bismarck to the World War: A History of German Foreign Policy 1870-1914*, Oxford, 1927.

7   Cary, M., *Geographical Background to Greek and Roman History*, Oxford, 1949, p. 56.ff.

made more headway among the Albanian-speaking population. The Albanian-speaking Orthodox Christians in the Souli Mountains and nearby had no discernible political leadership at all. At a political level the detachment of the Beys from the Empire led to transference of loyalty to the ideal of an Albanian national state. Local imams were often culturally conservative. Cham-majority religion was the religion of Sunni Islam, the religion of rule of the Turks, and the tekkes and rural shrines of the dissident Bektashi sect that is very closely associated with Albanian nationalism had only a very limited presence, and in some centres, like Ioannina, they were also closely connected with the Ottoman garrison. The Chams in their small northern market towns like Filiates or a small coastal centre like Murtos, modern Greek Syvota, had few leaders of any standing compared to other parts of the Albanian world.

The isolation of Chameria/Thesprotia was eroded by the World War I period, but not dramatically so. The geographical space was not fought over on land once the remnants of the Ottoman army left from the 1913 debacle had disappeared, and Chameria remained in rural torpor in World War I, benefitting from the complete absence of harbours capable of taking large ships along the coast. The newly delineated Greek-Albanian state border that had emerged from the Protocols of Florence period held, to the surprise of many observers, and the Greek attempts to reopen the issue at the Paris Peace Conference in 1919 came to nothing.[8] Rather in the manner of the Bismarckian dominance of the Berlin Congress, Woodrow Wilson and the Americans held sway over Versailles and the subsequent installation of the League of Nations at Geneva. Washington was able to successfully protect the infant Albanian state from the ambitious attentions of the Greek irredentists, much as contemporary Kosova is protected from Serbian border revisionism by Washington nowadays. But it was not willing or able to reopen the issues of the division of the Albanian people between four countries that had emerged from the pre-1914 international conferences.

These constraints on the Cham issue remained until the end of communism in Albania and elsewhere between 1990 and 1992. Oral tradition remained strong in the Cham world, both at an 'underground' level in remote areas of the countryside where the writ of Athens

---

8   See, for a pro-Greek account of what happened, Petsalis-Diomidis, N., Greece at the Paris Peace Conference, 1919, Thessaloniki, 1978. The Greek difficulty was that the Entente powers were really only interested in questions about the future of Thrace and Asia Minor issues, whereas Venizelos saw the issues of 'Vorio Epirus' as a central issue in the future power relations in the post-war Adriatic. His major concessions to Italy have been claimed by his critics to have laid the basis for many future problems and encouraged the expansionist thinking of the Italian fascists about Albania.

has never run very far, and in the rich collections of oral material in the Cham Diaspora in the United States. In Albania a Cham party has been founded and has representation in the national parliament. Important works on Greek-Albanian relations have been published in Albania, principally the writings of Beqir Meta, which have put study of the genocide/expulsions period on a professional historical basis.[9] At the same time, important changes in the population composition of Epirus have taken place. Rural depopulation has been important, with many Greek villages more or less abandoned except in the mid-summer.[10] Albanian migration has increased, bearing out the old adage of Balkan history writing that if the borders do not move, the people often do.[11] The general Greek view has been that Zervas' actions in 1943-1944 effectively closed the Cham historical chapter, and old Cham geographical space has now become only 'historic' Greek Epirus. It must be doubtful if this will be the case.

---

9   See Meta, B., *Greek-Albanian Tensions 1939-1949*, Tirana, 2006.
10 See Vickers, M., 'C'po Behet me Ceshtjen Came?', Tirana, 2005.
11 For useful factual background, see Green. S.F., *Notes from the Balkans: Locating Marginality and Ambiguity on the Greek-Albanian Border*, Princeton, 2005.

Britain and the Emergence of the Socialist Republic of Macedonia 1942-1946: Conspiracy Theory or Chaos Theory?[1]

---

1 An earlier draft of this paper was presented at the State University of Tetovo conference in April 2008 on western Macedonia in World War II.

THE DECLINE AND COLLAPSE OF the Axis occupation of the southern Balkans in the latter stages of World War II saw the return of uncertainty over the future of Macedonia and the re-emergence of the Macedonian Question after the interwar period when it had seemed to disappear. It is a truism to state that nobody in the British Foreign Office in 1943 knew what would happen in Macedonia as a result of the uprisings against the Axis occupation of Yugoslavia and Greece. In our historiography in Britain, recent Macedonian narrative has been built almost exclusively around the story of the Greek Civil War and the development of the 'Truman Doctrine', where the struggle against communism in Greece was to prefigure the beginning of the wider Cold War. Yet the Cold War is over now for half a generation, but much of the told story remains the same. In the historical literature of the Balkan region, this process is not, of course, unique or confined to Macedonia - similar obsolete and outdated patterns prevented understanding of the post-1990 crisis in many other places in the Balkan region, as Christopher Cviic, Carol Hodges, Brendan Simms and others have shown.

Nevertheless, there were certain parameters of expectation, particularly in Britain, which as a World War I victor was one of the progenitors of the first, royalist Yugoslavia after the War. The Treaty of Versailles was supposed to have resolved the nationality issue in the Balkans by the creation of the first Yugoslavia. In the mainstream British school of thought, the creation of this Yugoslavia 'solved' the Macedonian Question, which had been a product of the collapsing Ottoman Empire. The violent clashes in Macedonia between Greek, Bulgarian and Serbian interests in the 1903-1913 periods seemed to have come to a historic conclusion, in that geographic Macedonia, as understood in antiquity, had been divided between Greece, which had found its 'final' northern borders, and Yugoslavia, which had found its southern limits.[2] It was, of course, an entirely speculative engagement with recent history, and empty as a guide to the future.

The understandings - or misunderstandings - of recent history deeply affected the British policy in World War II.[3] In 1944, there was an

---

2   See *The Macedonian Question 1893-1908: From Western Sources* by N. Lange Akhund, New York, 1998, for a good introductory account of events after the foundation of IMRO. The seminal British book forming pre-1914 London opinion was *Macedonia: Its Races and Their Future* by H.N. Brailsford, London 1906, along with the works of G.F. Abbott. For Central Power assumptions, see *Austro-Hungarian Documents Relating to the Macedonian Struggle, 1896-1912*, ed. F.R. Bridge, Thessaloniki, 1976.

3   See Elizabeth Barker's works for representative examples of post-1945 British official and semi-official thinking, as in *British Policy in South East Europe in the Second World War*, London, 1976.

intelligence crisis in London and Paris over Macedonia as much as over many recent issues in Iraq. There was little detailed knowledge of Tito's thinking about the future on many issues, and until the latter months of 1943 and the winter of 1944, it was not at all certain that Tito would in any case be victorious over the Chetnik opposition to the communist Partisan movement. [4]There were other long standing strands in British thinking for Balkan leaders to consider. One of the major areas of importance was the strength of the Greek lobby within the British Foreign Office, the secret intelligence service in particular, which had always seen Bulgaria as a basically pro-German and pro-Russian surrogate and the post-Balkan Wars Macedonian Question as an invention of the Russians to increase their pressure on Greece. A Titoist takeover of Macedonia, while unwelcome insofar as Tito was a communist and until 1948 firmly within the Russian camp, was nevertheless much better than Bulgarian dominance, provided the former did not go as far as to affect the Greeks' interests or border. A major factor in British official thinking was the image problem of the Macedonian themselves, as Andrew Rossos and others have shown, Macedonians had been involved with the assassination of King Alexander of Yugoslavia in 1934, and the heritage of IMRO, the Internal Macedonian Revolutionary Organization, was (with the contemporaneous Serbian 'Black Hand' organization) essentially that of the first modern terrorist organization.[5] IMRO was feared in its day in Europe as much as Islamic extremists are feared at the moment, and it was hardly an advertisement for British support for a Macedonian socialist republic after 1944.[6] A second major intelligence issue was the very divergent political viewpoints of the Special Operations Executive (SOE) British Liaison Officers attached to the resistance movements themselves, who almost always tended to adopt the standpoint of the forces they were attached to, so that in Albania men like Julian Amery and David Smiley working in the north were anticommunist and pro-'nationalist', while others attached to Hoxha's Partisans in the south like Reginald Hibbert and H.W. Tilman tended to see the war through left-wing eyes. This deeply conditioned the kind of information that eventually reached the Foreign and War Offices in London.

---

4   There are numerous English language biographies of Tito, most of which neglect the national question in Yugoslavia and often have anecdotal and uncritical attitudes towards the biographical subject, i.e. Phyllis Auty's work.

5   See Andrew Rossos, 'The British Foreign Office and the Macedonian National Identity, 1918-1941', in *Slavic Review*, No 53, 1994, p. 369ff.

6   This image prevailed for a long time in the United States also; see Duncan M. Perry, *The Politics of Terror - The Macedonian Revolutionary Movements 1893-1908*, Durham NC, 1988.

In Serbia, of greater direct relevance to the future of Macedonia, there was a similar split between the dominant Deakin-Maclean group around Tito, who played a key role in Tito's rise to power, and the firmly anti-communist figures like Michael Lees who worked with Draza Mihailovic's pro-royalist Chetniks, and saw the anti-Axis struggle as having been betrayed by pro-communist subversives with the Special Operations Executive in Bari regional HQ, in London and amongst the field officers.

What did London really know about what was happening? In the confused conditions of Partisan warfare and without modern communications technology, inevitably there were serious difficulties in intelligence reporting to London. But equally important were the ideological constructs that were a major obstacle to understanding. Most of the reporting from British Military Liaison Officers (BLO) attached to the Partisans came from people like Fitzroy Maclean and Bill Deakin who were physically, and in Deakin's case politically, close to Tito.[7] As with Albania, hardly any of the SOE field officers had any wider empirical or academic study of Yugoslavian society from pre-war experience. Of the northern BLO group, only one, Bill Hudson, had detailed knowledge, in his case of pre-war Serbia as a result of his work as a mining engineer for the Selection Trust organization in the 1930s. He could thus speak good SerboCroat.

None of the Yugoslav-based BLOs had pre-1939 experience in northern (Yugoslav) Macedonia at all. There was no inter-war 'Macedonian' narrative for even the most educated and best-informed British officials to draw upon, apart from that derived from IMRO terrorism and Greek nationalism which although of some influence in London, had none of the traditional Philhellenist input of the Civil War and post-1949 Civil War period with the ascendancy of the royalist right.[8] The main literary influence on that generation, Rebecca West in *Black Lamb and Grey Falcon*, saw the whole issue of Macedonia through South Serbian eyes (as she saw much else), another conditioning factor for British elite views. The Greek lobby in London was perhaps less directly concerned in this ideology formation than is sometimes alleged. In terms of the sociology of London Hellenism, the very influential Greek exile shipping community was dominated by families which originated in the eastern Aegean, who no doubt embodied the nationalist views

---

7   Deakin's politics are often rather unclear, but he was certainly well to the left of Maclean, in British political terms.

8   For a comprehensive picture of how Macedonia was subsumed within royalist Yugoslavia, see Nada Boskovska, *Das Jugoslawische Makedonian 1918-1941 Eine Randregion zwischen Repression und Integration*, Vienna, 2009.

of the Greek right on most things, but had no particular connection with Macedonia. This did not change substantially until twenty years after 1949, in the 1960s, with the arrival on the London scene of the Latsis family, with its roots in Kavala. It is also worth noting that in the internal discourse of the Civil War period, Macedonia does not play a dominant role until the so-called 'Third Period' of the war, particularly between 1947 and 1949. Before that, the pro-communist ELAS and Democratic Army forces were presented by Athens as pro-Russian and a threat to Greece as a whole, rather than specifically 'Macedonian', although a high percentage of Democratic Army soldiers were in fact from geographic Macedonia.

There was little immediate pre-war experience for diplomats to draw on. In the pre-1939 period, geographic Macedonia did not figure much in British Yugoslav policy, as it was poor and backward and apart from Tetovo region had few mineral resources. It had in any case lost its identity within the pre-1939 royalist *banovina* system where it was merely part of 'South Serbia', or of Greece. Even those with a sympathetic knowledge of Yugoslav communism - which in London official circles meant virtually nobody - could not easily foresee the emergence of a new semi-state unit called the People's Republic of Macedonia within a socialist Yugoslavia. Yet the Titoists did not disguise their intentions. The founding of ASNOM, the Anti-Fascist Assembly of the National Liberation of Yugoslavia, in 1944, with its explicit commitment to Macedonians as one of the five constituent people of Yugoslavia was of course known in London, but it was mainly seen by Prime Minister Churchill and the Foreign and War Offices as a positive move that would help galvanize the military struggle against the Axis in a part of Yugoslavia where the Partisan movement had been slow to develop.[9]

The heart of the Yugoslav Partisan resistance was in Montenegro, Bosnia and northern and central Serbia. The Communist Party of Yugoslavia (CPY) was weak in Macedonia; in fact it was difficult for Tito and Djilas to form an adequate party at all. Axis power was well entrenched, with major fortifications along the very limited number of usable asphalt roads in the tough mountainous terrain controlling all wheeled vehicle movements. In this situation, it was natural for some

---

9   There is a very large primary and secondary literature on ASNOM, embodying different national viewpoints, for the most part. For an introduction in English to official Skopje government positions in the post-communist period, see *Historical Dictionary of Macedonia*, ed. V. Georginva and S. Konechni, Skopje and London, 1998. For mainstream Greek thinking, see *Nationalism and Communism in Macedonia* by E. Kofos, Thessaloniki, 1954, and for Macedonian Albanian views under Titoism, *ASNOM-I*, ed. V. Vangeli, Skopje, 1984.

policymakers in London to see ASNOM in Macedonia in 1943 as mainly a military and resistance organization, and to not inquire too closely into what it might symbolize politically, or what influence it might have on the post-World War II Macedonian Question. Churchill, in particular, had little interest in the details of Titoist post-war policy for the entire country, made clear in his famous remark to Fitzroy Maclean that he had no plans to live in Yugoslavia after 1945, and if he had little interest in the details of Belgrade, he had none in what happened in Skopje, beyond a strong residual Hellenism that was to shape British Greek Civil War policy. In fact, as we know, in the Skopje narrative of the modern post-1991 Republic of Macedonia, the founding assembly of ASNOM is seen as the beginning of the modern Macedonian nation state - but it did not seem like that at the time, in western Europe in particular.

The history of ASNOM has yet to be written in terms of a major comprehensive study, but some issues are becoming clearer. What is very unclear, however, is how much or how little London and Paris and Washington really knew about what was happening in Vardar Macedonia. Their perceptions were formed by the fact that inter-war Serbian regimes did not recognize Macedonian nationality or the Macedonian Question, and western capitals post-Versailles did not object to Belgrade's attempts to systematically Serbianize the population.[10] The work of Rebecca West and other publicists like Nora Alexander tended to suggest that this process had been fairly comprehensive and successful, and IMRO was a hangover from the past, and their views were in turn reinforced by the heritage of Seton Watson and the British intellectuals involved in the formation of the first Yugoslavia in London University at the School of Slavonic and East European Studies. Moscow knew more but tended only to see the political struggle as important in terms of inner Comintern politics. This was true even before the Yalta Conference when Stalin knew that Yugoslavia was his for the taking after the war finished. The Comintern remained a battleground between Yugoslav and Bulgarian aspirations, as it had been prior to 1939. Many Macedonian communists saw their territory as a colony of Belgrade, and demanded radical action to correct this, but Tito did not agree. It is certain that Tito's problems with the Macedonian party had long predated the foundation of ASNOM. This is traditionally seen as that of the shortage of communist cadres, and depends on the writing of Ivo

---

10 It is, of course, arguable, that the Treaty of Lausanne was a more potent influence on Belgrade Macedonian policy post-1923, and on the Balkans generally, than the Versailles process itself, with its legitimization of mass population movements between Greece and Turkey that produced largely ethnically homogeneous new states.

Banac. But Banac can be questioned for basing his analysis too much on the 1948 crisis and the Stalin-Tito split, and it is not as applicable in the pre-World War II period.

The problem for Stalin was not new, and long predated World War II. Within the international communist movement difficulties over the Macedonian Question appeared almost as soon as the Comintern was founded, and while Lenin was still alive. In 1923, the Comintern had pronounced that the right long-term solution to the Macedonian problem was for national autonomy within the framework of Yugoslavia, but many Macedonian communists themselves were only able to envisage this as occurring within Bulgaria. The Bulgarian party continued to recruit in parts of Macedonia right through the First Yugoslav period, and some pro-Bulgarian 'heretics' were still in gaol in Yugoslavia as late as 1960.[11]

In the so-called 'Third Period' of the Comintern policy after 1928, a separate Macedonian state had been briefly foreseen, but the CPY reasserted control over the policy with the end of the ultra-leftist Third Period and the onset of the Popular Front in the early 1930s. In his book, Stephen Clissold notes on relations between Yugoslavia and the Soviet Union between 1939 and 1973 that as early as 1938 Macedonian communist groups were trying to form their own party that was independent of the CPY, and in September 1942 the controversy had reached the point where Tito had to get Comintern support for his inner-party crackdown and expulsion of various oppositional Macedonian communists. His problem was compounded by the fact that the Secretary of the Comintern for a long time had been the 'old Bolshevik' and widely respected figure of Georgi Dimitrov, who was a Bulgarian, and saw the future of Macedonia as within a Balkan Federation, rather than as a constituent unit of a new communist Yugoslavia.

Tito's main adversary pre-1939 was Metodi Satarov (known in the Comintern as 'Sarlo'), the leader of the Macedonian party who was born a Bulgarian and had once been a member of the Bulgarian Workers Party. Whatever the background, and the links between these events and the foundation of ASNOM, which is not really relevant to this paper, the salient point is that even then, long before the Greek Civil War, Tito was repressing the national aspirations of a major opinion-national group within his nascent state territory, and centralizing control of it from Belgrade. This was what interested London.

In terms of modern politics and human rights, this might be seen as retrograde but to Churchill and the British government at the time, it

---

11 Interview by James Pettifer with Georgi Petkov, Skopje, 1995.

was an entirely positive feature of Tito, and perhaps helps explain some of the strength of British support for the Partisans and - incidentally, of course – it also helps undermine the 'conspiracy theory' put forward by Michael Lees, Julian Amery and the right in London post-war. There were far deeper political forces at work than a simple pro-communist conspiracy could account for within the Special Operations Executive or elsewhere in London. It had been possible for the British Prime Minister to understand from his close relationship with Fitzroy Maclean, a fellow Tory aristocrat by background, that Tito was open to outside influences in a way many communist leaders of the period were not, and would listen to British advice on major issues.[12] Churchill was looking for a strong leadership in post-war Yugoslavia where he hoped he could cash the cheque of British support for Tito against the royalists and to turn Tito to at least a degree against Moscow. In fact the policy turned out to be much more effective than its progenitors could have ever dreamed, as events in 1948 showed. The British Prime Minister was carrying on strands of policy that long pre-dated World War II, to support a strong, centralized 'Yugoslav' government as a barrier against German influence in the Balkans, and Hapsburg influence before that.

Where did this leave the Albanian communities within what is now the modern Republic of Macedonia/FYROM? And the Albanian national question? The Albanians had benefited from the Axis occupation, and under the Italian-occupied parts of the western Macedonian and Kosovar Albanian-majority lands had a substantial degree of self-rule and various education and cultural rights that were not recovered until the Ohrid Accords in 2001. Ethnic Albanians, like the Bulgarians, were on the wrong side when the war was over, the losing side, never an enviable position in any period of history. In his memoir of his work as a visiting BLO based in Dibra in Albania, Reginald Hibbert describes the confusion in the military situation around Tetovo and Gostivar in the winter of 1943-1944, much of which was dominated by the difficult relations between the CPY and the communists in Albania itself, who were seeking to establish their authority in the western Macedonian communities.

Only a few Kosovar Albanians had fought with Tito, and fewer still from western Macedonia. British policy was very unclear. Hibbert considered that the original Davies leadership of the overall SOE

---

12 See *Eastern Approaches*, London, 1962, where Maclean sets out clearly what he felt could be achieved with Tito. It is worth bearing in mind, when studying Maclean and Deakin's works, that both felt they had been proved right by post-World War II developments, particularly after 1948.

missions had concluded that some form of 'Greater Albania' was inevitable after the war, but the Foreign Office in London had been unaware of this orientation for some time. Hibbert comments, 'It was difficult to believe the Foreign Office could have known about it, as the FO regarded Yugoslavia as an allied country towards which Britain had obligations, while it was not sure that Albania was a viable country or what would happen to it after the war.'

In these circumstances, British support of the Partisans in western Macedonia was small and irregularly distributed, whereas German aid, in troops and materiel, continued to Fiqri Dine and his pro-Axis militia until the end of the fighting. From the point of view of London, it seemed best to acknowledge what Hibbert calls Tito's force majeure in the region, and consign the Albanian fighters, both followers of Mehmet Shehu's National Liberation Army spill-over forces after the Battle of Dibra, and the few local western Macedonian groups who were actually pro-communist, to the not very tender mercies of the new order that was to be imposed from Belgrade.

In conclusion, it is possible to emphasize how much British policy rested on anti-German, anti-Central Powers assumptions, where stable central authority in Belgrade to follow the chaos of the war was largely the be all and end all, and that thread can of course be traced after the Tito-Stalin split in 1948 right through the close relationship with Tito to the support and sustenance given to the Milosevic regime in Belgrade post-1990. It was a policy that technically could be defended in terms of *realpolitik* and the British special relationship with Serbia and Greece, but it was impossible to sustain under the pressures of the post-communist violent conflicts in the region, the emergence of the national questions, and modern principles of human rights and national self-determination. The burden of this difficult history, nevertheless, remains over Macedonia, as the current situation of the state indicates.

Bibliographical References

See written works post-World War II by the ex-BLOs, such as *The Rape of Serbia: The British Role in Tito's Grab for Power 1943-1944* by Michael Lees for the first fully developed exposition of the SOE communist conspiracy theory. Also Julian Amery's *Sons of the Eagle*, David Smiley's *Albanian Assignment* and numerous other BLO memoir books, many of which rest on highly polemical views of recent history. For an authoritative view of the inner-SOE conflicts over Albania, see *The Wildest Province: SOE in the Land of the Eagle*, Roderick Bailey, London, 2007. Also, *The OSS in World War II Albania: Covert Operations and Collaboration with Communist Partisans* by Peter Lucas and Fatos Tarifa, Boston, 2006. For a general view of Bulgaria and IMRO regional interests, see *Bulgaria'*, R.J. Crampton, Oxford, 2007. On terrorism as a phenomenon, a view descended from the Sarajevo events in 1914, see *Hands of Terror*, Leonard Gribble, London, 1960, *Terror in the Balkans*, Albert Londres, London, 1935, and for Serbia, *Black Hand over Europe*, Henri Pozzi, London, 1935.

Sir William Deakin was author of *The Embattled Mountain*, a fine picture of the Titoist Partisan struggles in Montenegro and Bosnia, and other books. See Ivo Banac's work for post-1945 Comintern and Cominform background, in particular his comprehensive account of the later 1948 crisis period in *With Stalin against Tito: Cominformist Splits in Yugoslav Communism*, Ithaca NY, 1988, and his publications on the national question. For a semi-official American view, see *Yugoslav Communism and the Macedonian Question* by Stephen E. Palmer and Robert R. King, Connecticut, 1977. For collaborative material, see the memoirs of prominent British diplomat Sir Frank Roberts, *Dealing with Dictators*, London, 1972. Roberts sets out very well the London-Belgrade 'special relationship' in the early Tito period. See also paper by Sir Reginald Hibbert 'Albania, Macedonia and the British Military Missions', in *The New Macedonian Question*, ed. James Pettifer, London and New York, 1998. For the viewpoint of one of the very few Kosovar Albanians to reach leadership levels in both the Partisans and subsequently in the CPY, see Fadil Hoxha's autobiographical memoir, *Kur Pranvera Vonohet*, Prishtina, 1980. There is a recent and rapidly growing literature in Albanian dealing with the history of Balli Kombetar in Macedonia; for a useful general background, see *Distinktivi Tetovar*, Islami Arsllani, Tetovo, 2008. For the pre-World War II period with Serbian ethnic dominance in western Macedonia, see *Tetovski Sponmenar 1919-1941*, Bratislav Svetozarevic, Tetovo, 1999.[*]

---

[*]   This article first appeard in *Journal of the Philosophical Faculty*, Skopje, vol. 1, 2010, www. fzf.ukim.edu.mk

CONTEMPORARY
REFLECTIONS

THE MACEDONIAN STATE AFTER COMMUNISM

DEMOCRACY AND THE BURDEN OF HISTORY

Introduction

STATE FORMATION AND FUNCTIONALITY IN relation to minorities and collective identity have been at the heart of discussions of Macedonian history in both ancient and modern Macedonian historiography. Democracies in general and modern concepts of liberal democracy in particular have rarely been important in these debates. As the controversies among ancient historians about the nature of Hellenistic Macedonia have illustrated in relation to the 'name' dispute of the FYROM/Republic of Macedonia state entity that has emerged from the second Yugoslavia, what appear to be very recondite academic debates can affect contemporary political realities.[1] At the heart of this debate, in both the academic and political discourse, has been the question of the ethnic identity of the inhabitants and whether the society was ethnically homogenous. At first sight this should not be a difficult question to discuss or analyse. The *doyen* of British experts on the period of Alexander the Great, the late Nicholas Hammond, observed in one of his works that even in the ancient society of the Macedonian *ethnos* (nation) in Hellenistic times there had been minority tribes resident for hundreds of years, such as the Magnetes mentioned in Hesiod.[2] Non-Greek speakers also lived there, such as the Illyrian

1   In this paper I use the term Macedonia as the name for the ancient territory, as a geographical term, and the abbreviated terms FYROM/RM (FYROM - Former Yugoslav Republic of Macedonia) and RM '(Republic of Macedonia) to denote the state entity with its capital at Skopje. FYROM remains the official name of the state in some contexts e.g. NATO, while Republic of Macedonia is the name under which the state has been recognized by many countries. Both terms are used in this paper and any usage does not imply any personal view on the name issue

2   See Nicholas Hammond, *The Macedonian State Origins, Institutions and History* (Oxford, 1989), p. 7.ff. Discussion of the role of ancient historians in the protracted dispute about the name is beyond the scope of this paper, but it is perhaps worth observing that Hammond (1907-2001) was a man of the anti-communist Right who had been involved in the Greek Civil War in Macedonia as a British Liaison Officer to the guerrillas in the ultra-sensitive area of western Macedonia. See Nicholas Hammond, *Venture into Greece* (Thessaloniki, 1983). But as a great scholar his meanings often are multi-dimensional and open to different interpretations. This was certainly the case with his early study of the history of Epirus in north-west Greece, where his antiquarian topographic and also anthropological fieldwork in 1937-1938 resulted in published material that was very objective and open about ethnic Albanian settlement in Epirus but was used as part of mainstream Greek nationalist narrative-building after the Second World War. Hammond nevertheless unintentionally provided, in the conceptual structure of his discussion of the period of Alexander the Great in the 1989 OUP book on the ancient Macedonian state, some ammunition for current Skopje views of the nature of Macedonian identity. His controversy with the prominent Harvard classicist Badian is important in debate on some controversial contemporary issues linked to the 'name' dispute e.g. the nature of the Macedonian dialects in the third century BC and their relationship to the Greek

tribes from which modern Albanians claim descent, and the Dardanians (modern Kosova Albanians claim descent), and the Thracians (modern Bulgarians claim descent). In the modern period the ethnic diversity has been acknowledged by all scholars.

Yet with considerations of democratization, modern minorities with their rights based on the rule of law and based on ethnicity and language rights and the liberal concept of democracy are much more recent phenomena. In seeking the reasons for the slow progress of internal reform in FYROM/RM and the difficulty in resolving the 'name' problem and other seemingly intractable issues it is impossible to avoid discussion of the ancient identity issues as they surfaced in the scholarly controversies affecting the ex-Yugoslav wars historiography in the 1990s. There is also a continuity of intellectual enquiry. In virtually all the texts written concerning the Greek absorption of much of the ancient geographical territory of Macedonia in the late nineteenth and early twentieth century, there is little or no debate or analysis of the internal governance issues affecting the main concerns of the Macedonian people, in any historical period. This is frequently the case in the historiography of the ancient period, so that, in for instance, Hammond's seminal work on the Macedonian state, he rarely analyses its internal workings, particularly in his later writing.

The locus of modern Macedonia at the heart of the Eastern Question and as a centre of international tensions and conflict in the late-Ottoman period meant that the focus was always on the unstable and contested borders, not internal governance. This continued in the writings covering the middle and latter years of the twentieth century, so after the division of geographic Macedonia during the Balkan Wars 1912-1913 period and the First World War, sanctioned finally

---

language. This was not the case with Hammond's later work, after the re-emergence of the Macedonian Question within the Yugoslav crisis after 1990 where his expressed views always explicitly assisted mainstream Greek nationalist positions e.g. in his late book, '*Alexander the Great: King, Commander and Statesman* (London, 1995), which is symptomatic of the wider problem insofar as it almost exclusively focuses on Alexander as an expansionist military commander.

Unlike some of the other history debates that accompanied the ex-Yugoslav wars, this issue has remained divisive in academia. An example was the 'round robin' letter from over a hundred prominent American university classicists, ancient historians and archaeologists sent to newly elected President Barack Obama calling for a change of US State Department 'name' policy towards the Skopje government in 2008. Also the various difficulties Loring Danforth and others have had in obtaining platforms for their positions critical of Athens Macedonian policy, and the violent attack on Chicago University Mellon Professor of Linguistics Victor Friedman at a public event in Athens in 2011.

by the Versailles Treaty, there was little attention paid to the internal democratic life of the region. In general, the Macedonian history has not been extensively written as the history of the wider Yugoslavia, as in the writings of prominent and internationally renowned scholars such as Sabrina P. Ramet and Ivo Banac. As Nada Boskovska points out in *Das Jugoslawische Makedonien 1918-1941*, 'Die Geschichte Jugoslawische in der Zwischenkreigszeit is noch keineswegs erschopfend behandelt worden.'[3]

The main European backers of the first, royalist Yugoslavia, France and Britain, were content with the limited and controlled internal democracy of the new state, and did not alter their fundamental relationships with it after the onset of the royalist dictatorship in 1926. The Royalist Yugoslav government did not recognize the problem of the Macedonian Question and incorporated what they saw as all Macedonia within the *banovina* of 'South Serbia'. Late Ottoman Macedonia had been a byword for violent instability prior to the First World War and the scene of the long and difficult allied armies' Macedonian Campaign during it. [4]The Great Powers at Versailles seem to have been content that the region would have clear and agreed borders and be at peace, and this was the extent of their ambitions. The key criteria here were undoubtedly military. Britain and France had had close military relationships with Serbia and the Serbian army in the latter stages of the First World War, whereas the Americans at Versailles knew little of many realities on the ground, and seem to have believed democracy would evolve rapidly and without difficulty in the new Yugoslavia. French investment in military equipment and munitions production was central to the development of the nineteenth-century Serbian army, most openly symbolized by the investments by

---

3   Nada Boskovska, *Das jugoslawische Makedonien 1918-1941: Eine Randregion zwischen Repression und Integration* (Vienna, 2009), p. 23. This important book delineates various long-term issues in the nature of the Macedonian identity and state formation issues in the twentieth century which remain current today.

4   See *Official History of the War the Macedonian Campaign* (HMSO London, 1933). In general the British military were by far the best informed part of 'official London' in the inter-war period, as a result of the long occupation of Salonika in the First World War, and this affected activity and perceptions in the later Second World War and Greek Civil War periods with Special Operations Executive (SOE) quickly becoming an important force in the region after 1943. Although the 1933 volume is a very scholarly and major study, it is permeated by assumptions about the legitimacy of the northwards expansion of Greece and Greek nationalism in general that Macedonians nowadays would find difficult to accept. The entire issue of the role of the British and French military presence then in Salonika and its relationship to the establishment of the first royalist Yugoslavia and the absorption of what is now the FYROM/RM territory into the *banovina* of South Serbia under the Versailles provisions has yet to receive the scholarly attention it deserves.

the Creusot company at Kragujevac, the foundation of the modern Serbian military industries.

In her influential study of the post-Versailles Treaty period, Boskovska sees the region now in South Serbia as one hovering between repression and integration into the new Yugoslavist construct.[5] It could also be noted that this situation, which certainly was the case, also pertained in various guises throughout all southern Balkan history in the post-Ottoman period The arrival of foreign occupation in the Second World War period, the contest for the future of Vardar/ Greek Macedonia in the Greek Civil War, 1943-1949, and then the development of communist Macedonia within communist Yugoslavia did not alter these perceptions. Throughout, the nature of the various contests for physical control of the territory had the effect of stunting possible progress towards at least bourgeois constitutional democracy, and emphasized frequently the importance of military criteria not only in determining Macedonian identity but also the structure and nature of internal governance.

This continued for many years, throughout the region. The important gains for local democratic processes introduced in the Greek 'mountain government' in the EAM-controlled areas after 1943 were reversed in the monarcho-authoritarian regimes established after 1949. In Yugoslavia, under communism, the Peoples Republic of Macedonia enjoyed the status of a constituent Republic within the Yugoslav Federation, and the constitutional framework provided in the various Yugoslav constitutions culminating in the 1974 Constitution document. The existence of this Republic was a great step forward for Macedonian nationalism outside the Greek framework and accounts for the enduring popularity of Tito within the post-communist FYROM/ RM today. But obviously, as a communist governmental framework, it suffered many limitations for those supporting the liberal concept of democratic government.[6]

But there were also serious limitations on governmental and civil

---

5 Boskovska, *op. cit.*

6 An interesting illustration of this can be found in that seminal but nowadays little read book S. Palmer and R .King, *Yugoslav Communism and the Macedonian Question* (Hampden CT, 1971) Written by ex-State Department employees, it presents a cogent and well developed argument about the nature of the Macedonian 'state' entity and its emergence outside the influence of Greek-influenced thinking that has been so strong in Europe, in France and the United Kingdom in particular. It shows very clearly how Macedonian identity was promoted by Belgrade as exclusively a product of Yugoslav communism, and so 'it became heretical for any Yugoslav to deny the Macedonian nationality, it was a punishable heresy for any Macedonian in Yugoslavia to treat the new nation outside the framework of the new Yugoslavia' (p. 116).

society development within the assumptions of a communist polity. Many key communist policies were very hard to implement in the Macedonian entity, e.g. agricultural collectivization. Central efforts to force it through only resulted in many leaving the land altogether and resulting in the large areas of uncultivated fertile land that can be seen in a drive across any part of rural FYROM/RM today. The central project, as seen from Belgrade, was to tackle the serious material underdevelopment of the Macedonian Republic compared to the more northern Republics, improve social conditions and educational standards, and eradicate disease and illiteracy. The Republic was a priority region for investment in hydroelectric generation, and became an important contributor to the Yugoslav generating system. Road building was also prioritized. While no doubt these were worthy projects, they often followed authoritarian Soviet-era developmental models and were entirely under the control of the Party and Belgrade experts, and local Macedonians were not involved much in the management processes once construction was complete. The army, security service and police were popular careers for Macedonians under Yugoslav communism and important sources of employment for the better educated but in practice those involved often did not stay in the Macedonian Republic. Elite formation in Skopje and the other cities was always a problem,

In the pre-Second World War period, Tito had found it difficult to establish a well-supported communist movement in Macedonia, and frequent expulsions of dissident communists who wished to establish a Macedonian communist state outside the Yugoslav framework took place. The situation for Tito was complicated by the fact that the Comintern general secretary was Bulgarian Georgi Dimitrov who also did not support the establishment of a Macedonian republic with a communist Yugoslavia but as a component part of a future Balkan federation.[7] The same shortage of educated and politically compliant

---

7   For a good picture of Dimitrov's views and the debates in the Comintern generally, see Ivo Banac (ed.), *The Diary of Georgi Dimitrov 1933-1949* (New Haven CT and London, 2005). Stalin had little close personal knowledge of the Balkan countries and their history and seems to have relied heavily on Dimitrov for information. These are not distant and recondite academic historical debates within communist and Cold War history but have affected recent political discourse and actions e.g. the removal of IMRO founding father Gotse Delchev's body from Bulgaria and its reburial in Sveti Spas church in central Skopje. For issues of Comintern debates on Macedonian policy, see the scholarly work undertaken in Skopje by V. Popovki and L. Zhila, in publishing volumes of documents on Soviet-Macedonian relations after 1922 and on Macedonian deliberations in the Comintern, *The Macedonian Question in Comintern Documents* (Skopje, 1999) and *The Macedonian Question in Soviet Foreign Policy (1922-1940)* (Skopje, 2008), in Russian and Macedonian.

leaders showed itself after 1945 once communism had been established.[8] The 25 per cent ethnic Albanian and other predominantly Muslim and non-Slav speaking minorities were subject to major discrimination under communism, and few from those communities had the education to become local or Skopje-regional government leaders, or shared the new identity of 'Macedonianism' encouraged by the YLC leadership in Belgrade. Communism had been forcibly imposed in these areas after the victory of Tito's Partisans against ethnic Albanian Balli Kombetar nationalist paramilitary groups. Economic backwardness was endemic. Important issues of illiteracy and innumeracy remained in those communities two generations after communism had been established, particularly among women.

Within the different ethnic communities, however, many different local democratic traditions of non-institutionalized and pre-bourgeois democracy and informal decision-making existed, and some strengthened in the post-Versailles period in the absence of a respected central democracy based on the Belgrade capital city of the royalist state. To note only some examples, the Turkish-speaking people of towns in Western Macedonia like Gostivar had strong Ottoman legal traditions that survived the end of the Ottoman Empire in 1913, and property ownership rights often depended on Ottoman documents, in the absence of an efficient cadastral register in royalist Yugoslavia. The ethnic Albanians had the *Kanun* legal code and conflict-resolution guide derived from medieval times, and Orthodox Christian villages had patterns of informal rules and conventions ultimately derived from the authority their priests had acquired under the Ottoman system of *millet* religious and social differentiation. The large Roma community in Skopje and other cities had internal conventions and informal legal codes based on accumulated ancestral experience as a despised minority, almost a caste system in Skopje, in many respects. The royalist Yugoslav law courts were imposed from above, and were partly military in character and procedure and were in essence those of a *de facto* occupying power. They

---

8   There is a very large literature on this subject, in general terms, in many languages but as yet no satisfactory history of the Yugoslav League of Communists exists in any language. For the role of Tito in Macedonia, see Ivo Banac's works, in particular his seminal *With Stalin against Tito: Cominformist Splits in Yugoslav Communism* (Ithaca NY, 1988) casts light on the general problem of party leadership in the post-Cominformist split period in Skopje. As he points out (p. 190), 'With Tito's appointment as General Secretary in 1937, the KPJ at last took notice of deficient conditions in its Macedonian branch.' For a general history of the period, see Sabrina P. Ramet, *The Three Yugoslavias: State Building and Legitimation 1918-2005* (Bloomington IN, 2006). For the key institution of the army and its political origins, see M. Dimitrijevski, *Die Makedonische Armee 1944-1945* (Skopje, 1999).

were particularly dysfunctional in disputes involving property matters. Many of their cultural characteristics continued in a different guise under communism, with bribery of public officials very common.

In wider civil society terms, modern political parties hardly existed, and were illegal later under communism, and political participation was at a low level, even in local community matters. Modern printed media only existed in the towns, radio was almost unknown, and highly conservative and patriarchal relations in the family and society dominated all community life. Thus, at the end of the communist period in 1990, a highly centralized and very bureaucratic communist state mechanism existed based on Skopje, Bitola and other large towns, which itself was closely linked to the central Yugoslav government in Belgrade. The countryside and the mountains had their own traditional ways and followed them with little regard for central government.

At the same time, the Macedonian socialist Republic had undergone some very progressive economic development in the late-communist period, particularly in the tourism, tobacco, and food production industries, and this had led to a degree of capitalist development with accompanying demands for more political freedoms. The high emigration from Macedonia to nations like Australia and Canada in the Slav-side of the ethnic divide, and Germany and Switzerland and Turkey on the Albanian side, had produced a large and better educated youth with wider horizons than their parents and a consequent impatience with the restrictions and underdevelopment of the old society.,

Democratization in FYROM-Republic of Macedonia after 1990

In general society in FYROM was not generally very much disrupted by the arrival of Slobodan Milosevic in power in Serbia after 1988.[9] This relatively peaceful transition under the leadership of long-time local CPY leader Kiro Gligorov (1917-2012) continued during the early very difficult years after the independence referendum of Autumn 1991, with Gligorov as a long-time communist leader seeking to keep FYROM out of the wars involving the other republics. His general policy was strongly Yugoslavist. In practice this meant keeping much of the old highly centralized communist state governmental mechanisms in being, in terms of the formal operations of the government, although the old

---

9   For a view of this period from an informed Greek author, see Vangelis Calatychos, *The Balkan Prospect: Identity, Culture and Politics in Greece after 1989* (New York, 2013), although the author neglects the Albanian factor in internal FYROM/RM political realities.

Yugoslav League of Communists had collapsed and new parties based primarily on ethnicity were to appear quickly.[10] In particular, there was almost no change of an institutional nature affecting the judiciary, the armed forces and the security apparatus. The Gligorov government after independence had little or no intelligence or diplomatic capacity, and in practice many tasks were discharged either via Serbia, in the old communist networks, or via the very close relationship formed by Gligorov with France and Britain.

In some cases, such change as did take place was regressive, where the limited rights for ethnic minority representation under communist-period legislation were in practice dropped as Macedonian Slavs moved into all leading positions. Thus 'liberalism' as an ideal of state organization took a step backwards, and ever since there has been a consistent dialectic in Macedonian life between a centralist and basically undemocratic institutional tradition inherited from communism and modified by Macedonian nationalism, and the efforts of the international community to produce reform and modernity in the developing new nation. The European Union accession process has a number of demands in terms of legal and institutional reform and in many cases progress on these has been very limited in recent years. Modernization of the armed forces under NATO pre-accession guidelines has been more successful but only because the crisis caused in the forces by the 2001 war period enabled NATO to force through long-resisted reforms. Ethnic minority representation in the officer corps remains a serious problem.

Yet the 'stability' brought by Gligorov was welcomed by the international community, who were centrally concerned to see peace maintained in Macedonia and avoid the possibility of violent conflict involving Greece and Turkey as fellow-NATO nations. There was little real pressure put on the Skopje government to reform institutions or democratize society generally. This led to major minority community dissatisfaction.[11]

---

10 For a good summary picture of this early post-communist period, see paper by Duncan M. Perry, 'The Macedonian Question: an Update', in Studies in *Macedonian Language, Literature and Culture*, ed. Benjamin Stolz (Ann Arbor MI, 1995).

11 For a general view of the post-1990 situation and data and analysis by different expert authors on particular issues, see James Pettifer (ed.), *The New Macedonian Question* (Basingstoke and New York, 1999). In general, fifteen years later, I would not wish to modify most of the views expressed in my papers in this book, except to note that like all the authors, I tended to overestimate the degree to which 'Western' models for political parties and civil society would quickly establish themselves, and we all underestimated the degree to which events in Kosova after 1997 would determine many political developments in FYROM/RM. For a good view of the workings of the post-communist Skopje state on the key issue of civil-military relations, see B. Vankovska and H. Wiberg,

In the ethnic Albanian-dominated north-west, new political parties had soon formed after 1991, and a proportion of them were dominated by radical nationalist activists. The Gligorov government attempted to resist dealing with them, and to keep the Albanians under control through individuals from that community who had held prominent positions under Yugoslav communism. This was a strategy doomed to failure by the increasingly radical atmosphere of ethnic Albanian politics, with its background in the fact that in previous generations, particularly during the Second World War, Tetovo and region had been a strong centre of support for the Balli Kombetar ethnic Albanian nationalist movement. The most important event in these years was the overthrow in 1993 of the leadership of the main Albanian political party in Tetovo by radical leaders Arben Xhaferi and Menduh Thaci, and the refounding of the Albanian PDP party under their control. This led to much closer connections between the Albanian parties in FYROM/RM and Kosova, and the growth of nationalist feeling in the Albanian minority community in general.[12] This development was viewed with concern in the international community, who saw it as a precursor for demands that FYROM/RM be split and that Western Macedonia would form part of a future 'Greater Albania'. After violence developed in some places in 1992, the then chair of the Human Rights and Minorities Working Group of the European Community Conference

---

Between Past and Future: Civil-Military Relations in the Post-Communist Balkans (London, 2003). For discussion of the general principles of democratization as seen from the Western point of view, see Sabrina P. Ramet, *The Liberal Project and the Transformation of Democracy* (College Station TX, 2007) and the post-communist constitutional crisis, see the chapter 'Constitution Engineering and Institution-Building in the Republic of Macedonia (1991-2011) by Biljana Vankovska, in Sabrina P. Ramet, Ola Listhaug and Albert Simkus (eds.), *Civic and Uncivic Values in Macedonia* (Basingstoke and New York, 2013).

12 The best history of this period is in Zeqirja Rexhepi's short book *Partia Demokratike Shqiptare Lindja Zhvillimi dhe Veprimtaria* (Tetovo, 2004). It is particularly comprehensive on the crisis in ethnic Albanian leadership between 1992 and 1994, and is a very well researched and accurate guide to the demise of the old PDP under Halili, and post-communist Tetovo politics generally. See also James Pettifer's obituary of Arben Xhaferi, available on website www.professorjamespettifer.com Section: Obituaries, and Enver Robelli, *Arben Xhaferi rrefen Ne tetove, ne kerkim te Kuptimit* (Prishtina, 2011). Xhaferi later played a key role in the Albanian leadership in the Kosova war and was an important ally of Kosova Liberation Army political spokesman and later the first Prime Minister of Kosova, Hashim Thaci, but was sidelined by Ali Ahmeti in FYROM/RM as a result of the latter's success as a military commander of the National Liberation Army in the 2001 conflict. Xhaferi was a dominant figure in the Ohrid Accords negotiations afterwards. His last years were affected by illness and the day to day running of the party passed gradually to Menduh Thaci. Ahmeti's BDI party is dominant in the Albanian community nowadays.

on Yugoslavia, German diplomat Geert-Hinrich Ahrens, put forward a plan to bring extensive reforms involving extensions of minority rights to the Gligorov government.

Many of the provisions of this plan were eventually to be incorporated into the 2001 Ohrid Accords but at the time they were seen as potentially destabilizing by the Europeans closely involved with Macedonian affairs, principally France and Britain, and were not taken up by the Gligorov government. In many government circles in London, Germany was seen as a progenitor of instability in Yugoslavia as a result of the German role in the emergence of an independent Croatia.[13] Thus, during the 1990s little real institutional reform took place in Skopje, and little progress towards democratization along liberal lines was achieved, and the common pattern of development was for various internal changes to take place as a consequence of violence, or external stresses and strains, of which by far the most important were the long periods of tension with Greece before the Holbrooke 'small package agreement' of 1995, and the Kosova war crisis that began soon after the Holbrooke deal and accelerated rapidly after 1997 before the refugee crisis in Macedonia in 1998-1999.

These events produced seismic economic forces in Macedonia. The gasoline shortages caused by the Greek economic blockade led to smuggling on a very large scale and the breakdown of central controls on fuel supply and pricing, and then in the economy generally. Extensive financial speculation based on Milosevic-associates' efforts to steal Skopje banking assets crippled the old state banking system and in the process destroyed many people's savings in the hyperinflation of the 1992-1994 period. Later, the Kosova war led to a breakdown of central government authority in large parts of Western FYROM, a precursor to the war in 2001. The situation may be summarized by saying that there was a deconstruction of the previous edifice of Macedonian socialism, but rather than being replaced by open society liberal institutions that functioned well, 'shell' reforms of a limited character came into being in Skopje which kept the old and quite small elite holding onto the reins of power in the centre, while in the country generally the Skopje

---

13 For Ahrens' views and a very comprehensive analysis of the general issues of the time, with a good deal of coverage of Macedonian issues, see Geert-Hinrich Ahrens, *Diplomacy on the Edge* (Washington DC, 2007). He is somewhat weak on the difficult German/British/French diplomatic relationships in the Lord Carrington-chaired EU Balkans conference and does not make clear the very strong negative feelings towards German foreign policy in the Balkans in London and Paris in the post-Maastricht Treaty period, and associated recognition of Croatian independence controversies. He also appears to have a very indistinct understanding of perennially strong Greek lobby influence in London.

government was suffering a major decline in practical authority. Belgrade influences of a highly undemocratic kind grew while the Milosevic regime was in undisputed power in Serbia, with Skopje the location of much arms dealing, money laundering and shadow banking activity. These dubious practices were quite incompatible with transparent rule of law government or democratic reform.

In parallel, nationalist ideology and practice grew in the majority Slav community. The Internal Macedonian Revolutionary Organisation (IMRO) had been refounded as VMRO-DPMNE just prior to independence and soon grew to be a major political force. It was, however, a bitterly contested heritage and the movement was soon affected by splits and internal ructions caused by the intense interest of neighbouring countries in IMRO's revival and attempts by various means to influence its development and political and ideological orientation. Although VMRO-DPMNE was founded in the mode of a 'western' political party and at one level functioned for some years in the early 1990s as such, with offices in Skopje and other localities, and contested elections as a main opposition party in a peaceful and cogent way, its roots in a violent and contested past were not easy to overcome. The international community generally did everything they could to assist Gligorov's Social Democrats, for the reasons outlined above, and this gave Gligorov and his 'conservative' political allies such as Stoyan Andov with his Liberal party carte blanche to avoid facing the issues of economic and political reform. Demands for a diminution of Skopje's overriding centralism were focused within the 25 per cent Albanian community and resulted in recurrent outbreaks of minor violence, often over educational issues and language rights, and the right to fly the Albanian flag in public. An important event was the rioting in July 1997 over the struggle to obtain higher education in the Albanian language in Tetovo.

How can this period be characterized in terms of progress towards liberal institutional development? Corruption and economic malpractice became a major problem and has remained one to the present day. The importance of the 'grey' economy, the distrust of public officials, the reliance on informal family and clientistic ties and the *de facto* illiteracy and associated education issues have provided an ideal environment for corruption to flourish. This has not, however, prevented the successful privatization and sale of major industries to multinationals with high legal standards e.g. the sale of the old state tobacco manufacturing monopoly in Skopje. It has, though, burdened all local businesses with a variety of informal costs and 'taxes' and an atmosphere of coercion and local racketeering exists with some violence in the background meted out to economic dissenters. The central government ministries in Skopje have a heavily authoritarian tone in their operations, providing much irritation to the entrepreneurial in spirit and many temptations to cut corners in transactions. It has been a time of stagnation where the needs of the country for reform - which most intelligent Macedonians of all ethnic groups knew and still know was and is required - was stymied by the continuing and hostile international pressures on the country and the incapacity of the Gligorov and then VMRO leaderships to envisage a political future with different assumptions and values to the ones in which they had grown up and owed their entire political identity. The proximity of powerful neighbouring states which themselves have large 'grey' and criminal economies e.g. Bulgaria, Greece, Serbia and Albania adds to the pressures on FYROM/RM in this respect and helps impede reform. It is very hard for local regulatory authorities to control what is done in the country by foreign-passport citizens when large cash transactions are involved.

At the same time, many in the international community were blind to the general internal problems of FYROM/RM and were unduly influenced by the views of particular neighbours e.g. Greece and Serbia in particular. When in 1995 the Holbrooke negotiations in the immediate post-Dayton period took place, the 'small package' deal had a considerable and positive effect towards stabilization, but mainly through decisions on the 'symbolic issues' e.g. the flag showing the Star of Vergina, and freeing up the border with Greece for normal trade exchanges, and so on. It did not address the 'name' dispute with Greece, nor issues of internal reform within FYROM/RM, let alone those of minority rights which were to bring the country to the brink of disintegration with the small war of spring 2001.[14]

The Kosova Crisis: A Catalyst for Democratic Change

As the crisis in Kosova developed after the failure of the Dayton negotiations to deal with Kosova adequately and the emergence of armed resistance to Belgrade rule among the 90 per cent majority ethnic Albanian community, the Gligorov regime felt immediately threatened by 'spillover' concerns from the deepening crisis there. The new international border of FYROM/RM had only existed for

---

14 For detailed analysis of the wartime period see the publications of International Crisis Group, *www.crisisgroup.org* and the Conflict Studies Research Centre, at the Defence Academy of the United Kingdom, www.da.mod.uk/cdera and accounts of the conflict by John Phillips, James Pettifer, Laura Rozen, Miranda Vickers and other authors.

a few years and was effectively very porous and virtually impossible to police in the mountains. These issues intensified after the beginning of widespread disorder and armed activity in the central Drenica region of central Kosova in late 1997.[15] The Gligorov government proposed the establishment of refugee 'corridors' through FYROM/ RM that would have involved the suspension of many Albanian ethnic minority democratic rights in Western Macedonia and exacerbated the already widening gulf between this community and the Skopje central government. As the crisis continued to develop, the international community became more deeply involved with the government, and NATO established a presence there. The real authority of the Skopje government diminished considerably in this period and was never to recover as the Kosova conflict worsened, refugee flows accelerated and tented camps were established in different locations in central and western FYROM/RM under international control. Many government functions such as refuse collection and water supply that had been under the exclusive control of the Skopje government passed to the control of local mayors in the refugee localities, and on a day to day basis many crisis management decisions passed to the big international humanitarians NGOs such as Mercy Corps and CARE International that under UNHCR were in charge of the refugee relief effort.

Thus, in a very unusual way for a country in the twentieth century on the European mainland, a degree of democratic transformation began to take place, but caused by the spillover effects of a war over the recently established border (in 1991) of the neighbouring second Yugoslav state in Kosova. Naturally the majority Macedonian Slav and minority ethnic Albanian communities saw this development very differently. The Macedonian Slav community who completely dominated all aspects of the physical and ideological state apparatus, in the Althusserian sense, viewed the new free climate in the west of the country with concern and displeasure and as a threat to state stability, even possibly its future existence. The highly centralized and undemocratic system developed under Kiro Gligorov was all they had known and it suited them very well as a means of maintaining control of events. On the other side of the ethnic divide, the ethnic Albanians gladly welcomed the crisis changes, not only because it offered an opportunity for their relatives over the border in Kosova to move nearer independence from Serbia, but because it removed the burden of the Skopje apparatus from many aspects of

---

15 See Tim Judah, *Kosovo: War and Revenge* (New Haven CT and London, 2000) and James Pettifer, *The Kosova Liberation Army: From Underground War to Balkan Insurgency 1948- 2001* (London and New York, 2012).

daily life and brought much decision-making back to their communities with leaders in the main of Albanian ethnicity. Religion was becoming more important in FYROM/RM as in many other places in the world at this time, and religious influences on local politics were growing. Thus, this period in Macedonian life was dominated by the growth of informal and networking democracy based on ethnicity in particular localities, and the retreat of the mechanisms and practical power of the communist inheritance of the ultra-centralized Skopje-dominated neo-Gligorovist state. Inscribed within the ideological state apparatus connected with the rise of religion as a political factor alluded to above was the rapidly rising influence and in some dimensions practical power of the Macedonian Orthodox Church which sought to reinforce the traditional views of Macedonian identity originally developed within the Titoist state framework and maintained by Gligorov.[16]

The final stage of the Kosova war accentuated these trends, and Gligorov left the political scene. The slide towards war in 2001 is outside the scope of this paper but was caused by a combination of spillover from the Kosova conflict and the final breakdown of consent by the minority community with the old system of Skopje government inherited from communism and modified between 1991 and 2001. In the July-August 2001 Ohrid Accords negotiations, the parties were on firm ground once Xhaferi had persuaded the Albanian delegation that it was essential for them to recognize the preferred Macedonian state identity of the existing Skopje government, and to be prepared to accept most elements of the existing Constitution. The ethnic Albanian

---

16 For a discussion of how some of these issues developed after 1991, practical religious freedoms and the general situation of Macedonian Orthodoxy within the ideological state apparatus, see paper by James Pettifer The Gligorov Regime in Former Yugoslav: Macedonia and the Development of Religion', in Ines Angeli Murzaku (ed.), *Quo Vadis Eastern Europe? Religion, State and Society after Communism* (Ravenna, 2009). The most important issue since this book was published has been the rapid and continuing rise in foreign-inspired religious proselytes, both Islamic and Evangelical Christian and Pentecostalist Christian in FYROM/RM, and this has now meant there are over fifty organizations in the country claiming identity as Islamic religious institutions/ or Christian churches/or other cults by 2012. For a general account of the origins and development of the Macedonian Orthodox Church since its foundation under Yugoslav communism, see Archbishop Mikhail, *Our Holy Orthodoxy* (Skopje, 1996). Most local observers believe that this external evangelization pressure with foreign financial aid has intensified nationalist and exclusivist pressures within the Macedonian Orthodox Church, foreign-linked Islamic missions in particular affecting institutions in Tetovo. The VMRO-DPMNE party has generally assisted new Orthodox church building in the last fifteen years, and the construction of Christian symbols in prominent locations, and has encouraged the always politically important discipline of archaeology to excavate on old Christian sites, e.g. Stobi.

military leader Ahmeti seems to have been relatively unconcerned by these concessions to the Slav-Macedonian majority as he knew that he would be by far the most important Albanian leader once new elections were held. This duly turned out to be the case, and has remained the case ever since. Ahmeti entered into a *de facto* spoils system in politics, where the Ohrid provisions enabled him to set up a political machine in the west, with the agreement of the central governing majority that would share out jobs and public money on a local ethnic basis and also give a substantial influence over policing, always a controversial topic. Thus decentralization of power in western FYROM/RM came not by liberal democratic reform processes, but through war. The aftermath of the Accords saw many provisions unenforced and the decline in international attention and commitment to the Balkans as peace seemed secure and Kosova approached independence meant that this has remained the case to the present day.[17]

The international community perspectives set out in documents such as 'Ohrid and Beyond a Cross-Ethnic investigation into the Macedonian crisis' in 2002 have in many cases only remained abstract ideals nearly fifteen years later.[18] Although, for instance, the threat of a return to war from the National Liberation Army element in Ahmeti's BDI party has receded substantially - some observers would say completely - this has come at a cost, namely the development of a near-apartheid organization of society, where members of the Albanian minority do not meet or interact with Macedonian Slavs outside work and certain public-sector contexts, and where many Macedonian Slavs are still reluctant even to visit Albanian-majority towns like Tetovo or Gostivar. Education, particularly higher education, remains a difficult issue. Many ethnic Albanians are reluctant to accept even the assumptions of the reformed Skopje school curriculum and their level of proficiency in Macedonian language and writing skills is such as to rule them out of higher education in Skopje. Institutions such as the South East Europe University in Tetovo and Skopje, and the State University in Tetovo, have attempted to form an elite that would bridge the cultural and ethnic divide, but the demands of operating in three languages often limit the achievement of the students, and the shortage of jobs in FYROM/

---

17 For a cogent and well argued analysis from an Albanian point of view of the successes and failures of the Ohrid Accords, see article 'The Ohrid Peace Process' by Blerim Reka, in *Südosteuropa* journal, 62, 2014. As he points out, the nation is multiethnic but many of its constitutional and governmental frameworks remain mono-ethnic, and he considers inter-ethnic relations have deteriorated since 2006 and the signature of the European Union provisions for FYROM/RM candidate status.

18 Antony Borden (ed.), Institute of War and Peace Reporting, London, 2002.

RM means that a high proportion of the abler graduates emigrate immediately after graduation. Education in the sciences, and in history, is a particularly difficult issue, with most ethnic Albanian students finding it hard to achieve the level of Macedonian on paper needed for science, while the content of school and university history textbooks remains very contentious. The number of ethnic minority students at the key elite-forming Ss. Cyril and Methodius University in Skopje remains very low, not only from the Albanian minority but from other numerous local ethnic minorities in Skopje such as the Roma.

In the background lie the ever-present issues of international relations and dialogue with neighbours that have dominated Skopje political life since 1991. The threat of a takeover from Milosevic's Serbia disappeared with the end of the Milosevic regime, but all Macedonian citizens, whatever their ethnicity, are aware of the unsatisfactory nature of regional relationships and their negative effect on the prospects of European Union and NATO membership. The 'name' dispute with Greece is only the most prominent of these issues, and the admission of Bulgaria to the European Union - long before it was ready in the view of most expert regional observers - and the subsequent issue of Bulgarian passports of FYROM/RM citizens has heightened concerns about this relationship. Russia is becoming a more important player in Skopje, focused on issues of energy supply in the light of Moscow's success in the Ukraine conflict, and this is likely to increase. Relations with Tirana are not unconstructive, particularly on trade issues, but the still high - if declining ethnic Albanian birth-rate in both Kosova and FYROM/RM - and the low Macedonian Orthodox citizen's birth-rate is still a cause of potential long term instability. Turkey is a very important partner for the Skopje government but has been emboldened under the Erdogan governments' neo-Ottoman impulses in the Balkans to advance religious and social agendas that are anathema to the Slav Macedonian majority.

The international community policy to resist these difficult internal and external pressures has been to produce social reform under the banner of 'decentralization'. A target has been the improvement of government in Skopje with its overwhelming social and economic dominance in the country, but very divided communities. There are widely varying views of what decentralization is, and what it involves. For Albanians, it is seen, at street level, as a means to achieve in localities where they are a majority the Ohrid Accord provisions that have been difficult to achieve through central government action in Skopje. For the Macedonian majority, decentralization is all too often used to enforce cultural exclusion in areas where they are the majority, and in these places, particularly the east of the country in towns like Strumica, virtually no use of the Albanian language takes place at all. The international community can, however, claim some success in improving the political environment in Skopje itself, with strong local ethnic Albanian mayors in relevant areas, and this has diminished the radical nationalist influences coming from cities like Tetovo in the west. The relative stability and progress in Kosova since internationally controlled independence was granted in 2008 has also diminished Albanian nationalist pressures from the north on Skopje and enabled a more normal political environment to develop with less of a sense of continual minor crises than there used to be.

A sign of this progress was the skilful and prompt reaction of the Skopje government to the world economic crisis after 2008-2009 and the threat that it posed. The democratic deficit in institutions and the extreme centralization of power around Prime Minister Gruevski and the governing party did have the advantage of bringing effective and rapid action to cut public spending and stabilize the banks and associated institutions. The economic chaos in Greece not only brought a strong sense of private satisfaction to many Skopje political leaders, from all ethnic groups, but a sense of relaxation that the perceived threat from FYROM/RM's most difficult neighbour has been reduced substantially. The large 'grey' economy and the strong agricultural and mining sectors have been beneficiaries of rising commodity prices over the last five years. With more investment, there is scope for a major expansion of production in agriculture. Tourist income remains lower than in the days of the second Yugoslavia, but is improving and brings ready cash to many poor communities. Émigré remittances have held up well, as most émigré Macedonian Albanians work abroad in Switzerland and German-speaking Central Europe where economies are still satisfactory and unemployment is low, and Slav Macedonian emigration is concentrated in Canada and Australia, also strong economy/ currency countries. In general, most observers feel nationalist radicalism on both sides of the ethnic divide coming from the different Diasporas has reduced in recent years with the real - if limited - achievements of decentralization and relative economic stability during the international financial crisis.[19]

Although the Gruevski government has inherited the difficult

---

19 For a discussion in more detail of what happened during the financial crisis after 2009 in Skopje and associated matters, see paper by James Pettifer 'The effects of the Greek economic crisis on the Republic of Macedonia', in *Südosteuropa* journal, 58, 2010, p. 605ff. On the main issues not much has changed since the time of writing, except for further regional infrastructure decline e.g. the closure of all north-south rail links with Greece which have been a mainstay of Balkan trade and transportation since the nineteenth century.

patrimony of the immediate post-communist years, and the governing party and opposition parties operate in a way far from the conventional parameters of liberal democracy as envisaged in the immediate post-1990 period, the country has survived through the often appallingly difficult circumstances of the Greek economic blockade, the Kosova refugee crisis, a war in spring 2001 and the difficulties of implementing the Ohrid Accords in the following years. Corruption is high, there is a major lack of transparency in many governmental functions and there is always the possibility, in the Balkan tradition, that some minor random incident could ignite ethnic violence once again. But the government is no longer seen as the coercive and neo-communist apparatus by the large ethnic minorities that it was in the immediate post-1991 period, and although human rights violations do occur and the media is heavily influenced by the government, freedom of expression is much better than it used to be, and freedom of religion is well up to international standards. Thus the stability achieved is only relative but it does exist and in the absence of any obvious perspective of European Union membership, the current political and social 'settlement' from the Ohrid Accords may well continue.

HELLENISM IN CONTEMPORARY

ALBANIA

LOSS AND GAIN?

THE SUBJECT OF THE GREEK influence and relationship with Albania is a constant factor in Albania's perceptions of, and international definition of, itself. Ever since the foundation of the modern Albanian state just before World War I, the definition of the relationship with Greece has been complex and often unstable. This in turn rests on the difficulties of achieving a satisfactory and agreed definition of what constitutes Greekness, or Hellenism, and its place within modern Albanian culture.[1]

The question of the nature of and definition of Hellenism itself is similarly generally difficult, as it has been ever since antiquity. There is the basic difference of view, inherited from ancient philosophy, as to whether it is only possible to be a Hellene by direct blood descent, or whether it is possible to become Hellenic through taking part in Greek life and culture and learning and using the Greek language. There is the added component of Orthodox religious adherence, which is primarily inherited from the Byzantine historical experience of the Greek people. Issues of citizenship, religion, language and ethnicity all collide and interact.

For the purposes of this paper, I am taking Hellenism as an identity within Albania on a primarily linguistic basis, where knowledge and use of demotic Greek is regarded as the primary constituent of a Hellenic identity, at least in the eyes of the majority of Albanian citizens. For reasons I will set out, this way of approaching the issue is new, compared to what one might have said in a presentation of this kind twenty years ago, when discussion would probably have exclusively focused on the Greek Minority in the south-west of the country, who were assumed to be of a fully Hellenic nature on the basis of a definition based on religion and sanguinity, blood descent. Looking back to my notes for my first seminar here at Kings in 1992, that was certainly the focus in those days, when I was invited by the then Director, Professor Averil Cameron, to discuss the subject.

For a long time, all discussion of the nature of Hellenism in Albania, in Greece itself and in the Greek Diaspora, evolved around the problems of these people. In modern Greek political discourse this group is normally referred to as the Greek Minority, and under communism was primarily resident in and around the towns of Saranda and Gjirokastra (Agioi Saranta and Argyrokastro) in the deep south-west of the country. The position and numbers and nature of the Minority have changed

---

1   An earlier version of this paper was presented to the Hellenic Studies seminar at Princeton University in November 2007. This paper was given at the Albanian Studies day in the Department of Greek and Byzantine Studies at Kings College London in January 2008.

considerably over the years, and it is necessary to give some account of the history in order to understand the contemporary situation. In broad outline, although these statistics should be treated with caution, the Albanian government under communism considered that there were about 40,000 members of the Minority, while Greek experts have claimed that there were as many as 150,000 people in this category. For reasons I will set out, I do not think these statistical arguments are very important nowadays, and are part of a sterile and dated way of looking at the issue.

In Greece, and elsewhere, it is often believed that the Greek Minority as an ethnic identity recognized by the Albanian government, and as a geographic expression for this area of the south-west was a product of Albanian communism. This is not the case. The Greek Minority concept originated under the monarchy of King Zog, well before World War II. Controversy over Greek language and cultural and education rights was common then, particularly after the enforced closure of Greek language secondary schools by Zog in 1934. Cultural pressures intensified with the gradual annexation of Albania in the Zogist period by Mussolini and the Italian fascist regime. This very negative period culminated in the disasters of the invasion in 1940 and 1941. The area where most ethnic Greeks in Albania live was fought over in the Italian army's invasion. For a period the front line between the Greek army and the invaders lay across it and many villages were totally destroyed in the fighting. This caused the inhabitants, Greek Minority, Albanian and Vlach, to flee. The intensity of the crisis in north-west Greece and south-west Albania was also worsened when the ethnic Albanian Cham population of Epirus was driven out in 1943 and 1944.

Under the Axis occupation in World War II, Epirus was rent by this bitter fighting, both within Greece and also throughout southern Albania, which was the heartland of support for the Albanian communist partisans, whose first victories against the occupying forces were achieved near Korca, Koritsa. In Epirus, the Right was triumphant in the form of Zervas and his militia, whereas north of the border the communists were the dominant military force. Although some ethnic Albanian villages supported the right-wing Balli Kombetar (National Front) movement, Enver Hoxha's forces were able to destroy the Ballists militarily in the south by the late summer of 1944.

As Hoxha himself points out in his book on Greek-Albanian relations, *Two Friendly Peoples*, many ethnic Greeks supported the Albanian partisans because they were a clear opponent of the occupation, and anti-fascist.

Under communism, this resulted in a contradictory situation for the Minority. In the view of the right in Greece, and particularly the Greek Orthodox Church, the Minority constituted a clearly defined cultural bloc of universally oppressed Christian villagers, and this view has always been heavily promoted by the Epirus organizations in the United States, Canada and Australia, taking their inspiration from authors such as Chicago-based Pyrrhus J. Ruches.

But the position was more complex, and involved subtle mixtures of changing ethnic and political allegiance. Within the Minority there were substantial political differences on many issues, domestic and international. While probably a majority of ethnic Greeks supported either the partisans or had no allegiance, others sought to form an effective military movement for what they saw as the liberation of northern Epirus from any type of Tirana government control, and to open the road to unification of the minority area with Greece. They saw themselves as the successors to Zographos' 'Sacred Army' that entered Gjirokastra from Greece in the World War I period. This was the Northern Epirus Liberation Front, which fought a few unsuccessful engagements against both Ballists and partisans in the 1943-46 period, mainly in the Droppoli valley near Gjirokastra. Social tensions in some parts of the south-west were high in the 1940s as a result of the arrival in southern Albania of thousands of Cham refugees from Epirus who had bitter memories of their displacement by Zervas and the forces of the Greek right in the *andartes* resistance. In some cases the Chams were housed in new villages, like those east of Saranda below the Buret Mountains, but in other places they took over homes abandoned by ethnic Greeks who had fled the fighting in 1940-41. Within these newly arriving communities on the move, there were many internal differences.

Some Chams had collaborated with the Italian invaders but others had not and a Cham partisan battalion had been formed in 1944 and fought with Hoxha's forces against the Ballists and Zogists in the north. It is also worth remembering that the Athens monarchist government was promoting the issue of the future of Epirus as a whole in international forums at the time, principally the Paris Peace Conference in 1946, with a case based on the non-ratification of the Protocols of Florence dating from the World War I period. The Minority in the immediate post-1945 period was caught in a web of rapid social and political change in the south-west of Albania, where the material basis of life had suffered appalling damage as a result of the war and internal conflict. It took people in areas like the Droppoli valley and the villages near Skala many years to recover from World War II, and this was as true for the Minority as for their newly arrived Cham neighbours. The same was true, also, of Epirus, as the books of Nicholas Gage and others illustrate a picture of economic ruin and consequent major external emigration.

In Albania, a further ironic twist in the story of the Minority came with life under the one party state. As a result of their active support for the partisans in the anti-fascist war, and personal adherence to communism, some ethnic Greeks from Minority families were able to rise to high positions in the Albanian Party of Labour (PLA), the communist party, and within the Albanian state. A prominent example was Spiro Koleka, from Himara, who rose to membership of the Central Committee of the PLA itself for some years in the 1960s and 1970s, and became a personal contact of Greek wartime resistance hero Manolis Glezos.

This native ethnic Greek Minority presence was also augmented by inward immigration of an unusual kind. Some Greek communist families came to live in exile in Albania after the defeat of the Democratic Army in the final round of the Greek Civil War in 1949, rather than go to Yugoslavia, Bulgaria or Russia. The majority of these people, in my personal view, were often particularly committed and hard line communists as a result of their ELAS and Democratic Army experiences in the Greek Civil War, and some soon rose to high jobs in the Albanian state, with a particular influence in the Sigurimi, the secret police, in cities like Vlora and Durres. Others became prominent intellectuals. They quite often dropped Greek endings from their surnames and adopted an Albanian form, e.g. Hoxha's sometime legal expert Pascal Hakos became Pascal Haxhi. These patterns of cultural and political difference and redefinition continued throughout the communist period, with the leadership these people offered being contested by clerical figures based in Greece itself, principally the Metropolitan Sevastianos of Drinopolis. He was the author of the main popular work influencing opinion in the Greek world about the position of the Minority under communism, *Northern Epirus Crucified*.

So we see that at the end of the one party state in the 1990-91 period there was a complex situation for the Minority. The world of a homogenous Orthodox Christian rural community in the south-west that did exist in 1939 had to all intents and purposes been fragmented beyond recognition by war and social change, as much as the feudal world of the Bajraktars had been destroyed in northern Albania by the same forces. As Reginald Hibbert, Bernd Fischer and others have shown, the Axis occupation was as much an enemy of the old society as the communists, and both helped destroy it. Yet the Church leadership, particularly Sevastianos, had an image of the Minority in 1990 that suggested it had continued intact. In an odd way, some of the patterns of social and occupational stratification among Greeks in Ottoman Albania had returned, particularly that of the role of the intellectuals.

What had to be done after 1990 to try to restore the Minority community? To begin with, some of this complexity was disguised by the priority of practical tasks in restoring the Minority within the emerging civil society. A new theme emerged, of migration, with thousands of southern Albanian citizens leaving the country in the first mass exodus of December 1990 and January 1991. There is no way of knowing how many members of Minority families left at this time, but there is no doubt the pattern of migration was set for the succeeding period.

An early development was the 'coming out' as Greek of some families who under communism had felt it better to disguise their Greek origins or culture for personal or career reasons. In the main this happened in Tirana, in my opinion, and mostly involved professional people. The general collapse of education in these chaotic years also affected the Minority, since under communism some use of the Greek language and books had been permitted in the Minority areas. What would happen to education in Greek in 1992? Nobody knew. The next main event was the recovery from the state of many Orthodox churches that had been seized by the government during the pro-atheism campaigns of the previous twenty years. In the main this process went well, with cooperation in many places between Christians and Muslims in the democratization process. It had been completed by about 1994.

Thus, a major force within the culture of the Minority, that of Orthodoxy, which had been absent from the arena for two generations, suddenly re-emerged not merely as a legal cultural entity but as virtually the only local leadership of any kind, following the departure of pro-communist Minority members from the scene with the end of the dictatorship. With the appointment of Metropolitan Yannulatos, a Greek citizen, in the mid-1990s to take charge of the reviving Albanian Church, many traditional echoes from the past could be felt. This was accentuated by a steady flow of money from Greece into the Orthodox Church, and then into Orthodox pockets, with every Orthodox in Albania eligible to receive various financial benefits through Church membership. This continues today.

A key event under the post-1991 government was the process of land privatization, where in the view of most observers, the Greek minority was treated very generously by the Berisha government in the break-up of the old communist period *latifundia*-type collective farms. Yet this accretion of capital, in the form of mostly fertile land, was accompanied by gradual depopulation, as people fled the land and migrated to Greece. In my view this was a very significant factor in the 1997 armed uprising, which is explored in some detail in my book, co-authored with Miranda Vickers, *The Albanian Question*. The newly privatized land, if Greek Minority owned, was and is often uncultivated, or used only for rough grazing, while land-deficit ethnic Albanian families are living nearby. Thus the basis for the whole concept of the Minority area as a living, primarily rural community was being eroded by the free market

At the same time as this element of traditional Hellenic society was in decline, a new Hellenism was growing elsewhere, in Greece itself. Tens of thousands of migrant workers were moving to Greece, some Orthodox Albanians, some of no defined religious identity and some Muslims, nominal in the most part. As they settled down in Greek jobs, they have begun to learn the language well, and some have converted to Orthodoxy, if only often for reasons of cultural security and advancement in their occupations. Their children attend Greek schools and have adopted much Hellenic culture. There are no Albanian-language schools allowed, unlike the Greek-language private schools which are allowed to exist in Albania. Mosques do not exist in provincial Greece. Some migrants have returned to Albania to open small businesses, or have been expelled because of residence and immigration status problems. The end result has been that there are now probably more Greek speakers living on Albanian soil than at any time in history. Greek is now understood and spoken, if not written, in parts of Albania where it has never been spoken since Byzantine times, like Dibra and Tropoja in the far north-east. In this sense, Hellenism, if defined as language use. has been in simultaneous decline, and revival, since the end of communism in 1991.

The future is bound to be conjectural. The question is bound to arise - as it has done ever since antiquity: is language enough to construct the new Hellene? There is a substantial school of thought in Greece which considers it does not. Birth and blood are not very politically correct concepts in this context but still determine many popular perceptions. As a recent example of this, I would draw to your attention the difficulty Minority members of undoubtedly full Hellenic identity in language and religion – at least in Albanian eyes - have had in obtaining Greek citizenship.

Perhaps 20,000 people from the original Minority residents in Albania in 1989 have left and live in Greece, and a high proportion for many years have been trying to obtain citizenship. Quite a number left in the first big exodus in 1990-91 and have been in Greece for over fifteen years. Many have married into Greek families and have Greek-born children. They have been consistently thwarted in their ambitions, and it was only, in September 2007 that the first group actually received their Greek papers and passports. This should give us pause for thought, I think - for if this has happened with the actual Minority members, is there a real prospect of the hundreds of thousands of mainstream ethnic Albanians ever becoming Greek?

THE GREEK CRISIS

A PAUSE

The Immediate Background

'THE SECOND COMMON MEANING OF the word "Greek" which developed during the sixteenth century, was based upon the opinion of Greek wickedness, rather than of Greek dissoluteness. A "Greek" meant what we should call a "twister", that is, a sharper, a cheat, a crook, any kind of confidence trickster … this popular usage received full encouragement from learning and literature.'[1]

The onset of the financial and banking in 2009-2010 did not have a major initial effect on countries in south-east Europe. Local banks had expanded considerably in the previous ten years of the post-communist transition, usually with partnerships with EU-based banks. Much the most important nations for this activity were Austria and Greece, through Vienna- and Athens-based parent banks. The type of banking was generally of a fairly simple nature and did not involve work with the more speculative side of modern international banking. Loan levels were low, the mortgage market was only beginning to develop in a modern form and heavily leveraged products were not known. There was no close link in the movements of finance capital to affect the region. In this, South-East Europe followed the pattern of the Wall Street Crash period where the crisis then did not initially affect Eastern Europe very much.

In the current context this situation has changed dramatically, as it did in the early 1930s. This began to be the case last year when it became apparent that Greek-owned subsidiaries of Athens HQ banks in the Balkans were starting to rein in lending at a very fast rate, to the extent that some subsidiaries stopped commercial lending altogether. Deposit rates and savings rates in the southern Balkans are generally low, and there was some withdrawal of savings by consumers to enable them to repay outstanding personal and business debt, so weakening local finance capital and the capital base of the banks further.

In EU member countries like Bulgaria, which are not in the Eurozone but where the local currency was unofficially tied to the Euro, there has been a gradual depreciation of the real exchange rate, so that when the new Lev was introduced five years or so ago, it was at parity with the Euro - at least officially - whereas now the street exchange rate has more than halved in value in real terms. Other local currencies like the Albanian Lek have depreciated similarly on the grey market, in a country where there is no formal relationship with a Europegged rate.

---

1   From Terence Spencer, *Fair Greece, Sad Relic: Literary Philhellenism from Shakespeare to Byron*, Athens, 1954, p. 37

This is not the case in FYROM/Republic of Macedonia where a fixed Euro peg rate of about 60 Denars to the Euro has been maintained for several years.

Greece is the only full Euro member in the region without a local currency and has suffered disproportionately from current developments. The absence of a local currency has meant that it has not been possible for the government to allow the currency to depreciate in line with its real value in the economy, and this has had a particularly serious effect in view of the role of tourist cash in Greece. Prices in Greece for transport, hotels and food are now very high by comparison with neighbouring countries such as Turkey which are not in the Eurozone. Estimates vary but it seems likely that the Greek tourist trade dropped in real terms by 15-20 per cent in 2009. There are a number of other reasons why Greece has been disproportionately affected by the crisis. The Olympic Games in 2004 increased the already very heavy burden of debts. Some of the investments made at that time e.g. the Athens Metro have heavy revenue account running costs which do not appear to have been planned for at the time the initial capital expenditure was made.

A traditional culture of favours and public sector corruption has always existed to a degree, but the longstanding alienation of many Greeks from their government has increased tax evasion and the role of the grey and black economies are substantial. The demands of the large paper-driven state apparatus drive many small firms into the grey economy to avoid the very onerous minor legal requirements in dealings with the government. Lawyers proliferate everywhere and contact with them is expensive and time-consuming for the entrepreneur. Larger businesses have their own problems. Apart from the banks, the only industry where Greece has a major global presence, shipping, is having a hard time, and in any case many of the ship-owners' operations are not in Greece at all, from the tax and financial viewpoint, but in London, New York or Switzerland.[2]

The election of the new PASOK government brought the crisis to a head in late 2009, with the 'opening of the books' that revealed a much worse fiscal position than had been generally realized, with debt interest obligation way above the Eurozone recommended level and recently subject to continual upward revision by experts. The government clearly took the decision in the way it did to place as much responsibility for the economic crisis as possible on its New Democracy predecessor. Major

2   For general background, see Gelina Harlaftttis. 'A History of Greek Owned Shipping', London and New York, 1996. There has been some improvements in cargo trade recently. See *Financial Times*, 12 June 2010.

statistical manipulation has been admitted. This would be bad enough but unlike Iceland, where the debt crisis was based on massive speculation which, although enormous could be quickly halted and unwound, the Greek debt is not based on this - or the 'hedge fund syndrome' - but serious and long term structural factors in the economy.

Historic and Cultural Factors in the Current Crisis

It is a commonplace of studies of Modern Greek history to state that a major issue for Greece throughout the twentieth century was the need to establish a stable and generally respected system of government. The presence of what was widely seen as a foreign-imposed monarchy, the huge refugee influx after World War I from Asia Minor, the Depression and turmoil of World War II with Occupation and Civil War until 1949 have left deep scars. The dictatorship between 1968 and 1974 depended on the existence of a 'deep state' controlled from the extreme right inherited from the Civil War period with little relationship to a modern democracy. The Karamanlis government that followed the military dictatorship was the first government to openly espouse the European ideal and full EU membership followed in the early 1980s. Europeanism was synonymous with democratization. After an initial refusal in 1999, Greece entered the Euro in January 2001. At the time this decision was quite widely criticized, as the statistical basis for Greece's compliance with the Maastricht Treaty requirements seemed unclear, but the strong backing of key players in the French and German governments such as Giscard d'Estaing and Hans-Dietrich Genscher ensured that objections were overruled. On the European left, most saw Greece as deserving rewards for ridding itself of the junta and becoming democratic. Greek trade with Germany was increasing rapidly as were openings to Russia where Greece has many contacts as a result of historic cultural links through Orthodoxy and communist Civil War exiles in prominent positions.[3] On the right, this was not so. In some forms, this debate has continued ever since, a typical article in the January 2010 British press stating that 'the Greeks lied and cheated their way into the Eurozone - and letting them get away with it through a bailout threatens the Euro with collapse.'[4]

There is little in these developments that is not already well known in one sense by the international community, but an unfortunate aspect of pro-European ideology (through its positivist and determinist

---

3 By 1997, six years after the advent of Boris Yeltsin, even such an iconic newspaper of the communist period as *Pravda* was Greek-owned.

4 *The Spectator*, 16 January 2010.

ideological base) is that it tends to project the idea that once a nation has 'joined Europe', particularly the Euro, it loses its previous history and problems and its capacity to affect regional and international events. This syndrome is also widely current in some quarters in the United States, where the actual workings and realities of the EU are often very poorly understood and where it is subconsciously assumed that the EU is an entity like the US with close control over its component parts.[5] This type of ill-informed thinking played a major part in Brussels in the US lobbying for Romanian and Bulgarian EU entry as an economic counterpart to NATO membership at the geostrategic level. Greece was also generally welcomed as a Euro member in the United States as a result of the powerful US Greek lobby, the US education and background in the Papandreou family and the move within the EU towards political moderation by PASOK. The recurrent problem of terrorism in Greece against US targets did not spoil this positive perception, with plaudits for Greece's return to the democratic fold. In fact, as experience shows with these and other new EU countries, the inherited political culture continues very much as it did before EU accession so Scandinavian nations that were models of probity and transparency before EU membership remain so, and Mediterranean and Balkan nations were often not and also remain so. There are some specific aspects of Greek society that are not well understood outside the country at a practical level and are likely to be important in the future development of the present crisis.

These are, in no particular order of importance, the centrality of a few political extended families within the political elite - the parataxis of the families of both major party leaders - the strength of Marxist and quasi-Marxist ideology and political parties, the political and economic influence if not direct unmediated power of the Greek Orthodox Church, high defence expenditure caused by poor relations with Turkey, the virulent anti-Americanism among very large sections of the educated population caused by US policies in the junta period, the fiscal burden of the Olympics and Bush administration international politics, massive on-costs for the state caused by the fragmented landmass and islands and the dependence on external finance for much infrastructure construction since the end of the Civil War in 1949.

---

5 See, for instance, a distinctly odd analysis by Joseph Stiglitz in *The Guardian*, 26 January 2010. His article makes no mention of the rising costs caused by Euro entry to the Greek economy at all, and he writes of the EU as if it were a Euro federalist state with a united economy based on egalitarian principles.

Reform of the Greek state and its functions has been called for by outsiders for many years, and appears to be an uncontroversial demand.[6] It is nevertheless extremely difficult, and there is little incentive for members of the major parataxis power-families to try, as they would destroy their own political bases in so doing. The political culture is extremely conservative in many ways, the ideologies of Orthodox Christianity and Marxism are very entrenched and distrust of central government is endemic. As the serious rioting in Athens and elsewhere showed in 2008-2009, young people are often alienated from the state and unemployment is growing rapidly and, like the national debt, is probably much higher than the stated data. Immigration has been high and although the borders are better policed than they used to be, the geography of the landmass prevents really effective movement control and Greek governments do not yet seem ready for the effective and unsentimental measures against illegal migrants used by the Italian government. The external migration patterns of the educated young still exist, particularly for science and medical students, but traditional Greek Diaspora host nations like the US and Canada are now much more difficult to enter than they used to be. There are few bright signs for even the most committed friends and apologists for Greece to find in the current political and economic landscape. Recently announced measures by the new PASOK government to cut down the public sector, privatize state assets, clamp down on tax evasion, break professional monopolies and raise excise duties may be worthy in themselves but it remains to be seen what their practical effect on revenue will be. Even the most optimistic estimates suggest the economy will remain in recession for the foreseeable future.[7]

Economic Development Issues

It is agreed by most economists that the crisis in the public finances has been caused by excessive public spending, although the growth of private sector and consumer debt is also important. This is seen as beginning in the pre-Olympic Games period, accelerated as a result of the Games and then continued as a product of the continuing flow of EU structural fund money into Greece. This history is actually quite flawed; Greek debt has always been very high.[8] The results have been mixed - some

---

6   See arguments advanced in my own book, Pettifer. J., *The Greeks: Land and People since World War II*, London, 1994.

7   See *Investors Chronicle*, London, 7-13 May 2010, data in article 'Hellenic Hell Not Yet Over'.

8   See, for instance, J. Koliopoulos, *Greece and the British Connection 1935-1941*, Oxford, 1977, for a perspective on the 1930s and the post-Wall Street Crash period which has

worthy long-planned projects such as the bridge across the Gulf of Corinth have been successfully completed along with the new airport at Athens and long overdue arterial roads and Metro in the Athens area. But other building has been wasteful and seemingly pointless, such as grandiose border posts where there is hardly any traffic, and major new roads, even motorways, in northern Greece where in many cases existing roads were quite adequate. The background to this spending goes back a long time and is ultimately linked to Athens right-wing government's perceptions of national security issues. At the end of the Civil War in 1949 much of northern Greece was in an economically ruined state. The communist KKE still had strong and genuine popular support in many places, particularly Macedonia, even though their Democratic Army had been defeated in the Civil War. Insecurity remained. The northern border was a long boundary with either belligerent Hoxhaist Albania, Yugoslavia, Warsaw Pact member Bulgaria or always difficult Turkey in Thrace.

The ex-New Deal Americans who supervised reconstruction in the 1950s and 1960s saw little wrong with heavy public spending in these very large regions, and all that the much-criticized EU has done is take over the role of external financial patron that NATO used to occupy. 'Underdevelopment' in northern Greece was presented by Athens as an aid to the communists, internal and external. There was also virtually no Greek welfare state of any kind in the Cold War; much of the growth of public expenditure in the last thirty years has been linked to the PASOK policy of constructing a European-type welfare system. Even a summary examination of the data shows that in 1999, when the original Greek application to join the Euro was rejected, public expenditure was at much the same deficit level as it is today.[9] The growth of private debt has been linked to major social change over the last two generations, during which Athens has become a megalopolis, in the ancient Greek sense, with a very large proportion of the nation's population in a single region and an expectation of Western consumerist lifestyles. It was therefore inevitable that there would be very strong internal resistance in Greece to the scale of public spending cuts being demanded by external economic commentators.

Outsiders often do not always appreciate the very poor wage and salary levels of many people in Greece such as schoolteachers, let alone unskilled workers. The fact that in some parts of Athens and Thessaloniki as much as 20 per cent of the vote in the 2009 national elections went

---

many echoes of modern problems.

9   In the late 1990s, about 13 per cent.

to the Marxist parties to the left of PASOK is an indicator. In the café climate of Greek politics there is fertile ground for the argument that the whole crisis is a product of the greed of Anglo-American bankers, Jews, local monopolists and the country's own expatriate rich. Public attitudes to the Euro are hard to evaluate and often contradictory. When Greece finally became a member in 2001 there was widespread national satisfaction that the country seemed to have overcome the burden of the conflicts of the past and had become a respectable mainstream European nation. But, within a year, food and daily living costs were rising rapidly because of the Euro and tourist decline had significantly set in. The end of the Drachma was widely regretted, particularly by small business.

Providing stability in a general way could be maintained, there is in all probability now a broad constituency of opinion in Greece that would support a return of the Drachma. A devaluation of perhaps 20 per cent would be needed to bring about a currency with a realistic value against the Euro. This would have a very stimulating effect on tourism and agricultural exports but a devastating effect on finance capital and on parts of the state like the military that depend heavily on imported goods and equipment. Much of this equipment is bought from France and Germany. Those who would oppose this development are the educated with a pro-globalization outlook. The vast production of intellectuals in Greece is involved. Apart from major new centres of Modern Greek economic studies at universities like Yale and the London School of Economics, Greek students are spread all over Europe, often with a strong and exclusive focus on modern economics. A Greek role in the new Eastern Europe was posited, intended to replicate the traditional role of Greek merchants and traders in leading progress in the former Ottoman world through finance capital and globalization. The theory and ethos of globalization have been adopted by a generation of Greek intellectuals in a wholehearted way rarely seen anywhere in the world. On the other hand, there has always been (since the days of the Wars of Independence and before) a significant minority of Greeks who have looked towards Russia and a more Byzantine-influenced past rather than towards the West. Their influence may grow in current circumstances.

Return to the Drachma: A Missed Opportunity?

A central issue in the spring 2010 crisis has been the failure of the Greek and European elites concerned to consider, or even seriously discuss, the policy option of a return to the Drachma, coupled with debt repackaging and a substantial devaluation. Realistic evaluations of the real economics and politics of the recent past have only been partly made. In an article in the *Financial Times* George Provopoulos, a governor of the Bank of Greece, set out a cogent position for Greece remaining in the Eurozone.[10] He admits that the Euro has caused Greece a major loss of competitiveness since 2001, and he advances a conventional script, blaming 'rigidities in the labour market' and 'excessive spending' for the situation, like most Greek and international commentators, but without (like them) mentioning the words Olympic Games in his analysis. In terms of the conventional wisdom, criticism of the Olympic Games heritage is a taboo subject as the accompanying over-hyped campaign against terrorism and the November 17 terrorist group was intimately linked with the agenda of the right to fully integrate Greece into the globalization processes. Provopoulos' nightmare picture of the role of Drachma devaluations is likely to be unconvincing, particularly to older Greeks, who saw the social and economic progress of the late 1970s, 1980s and 1990s under the Karamanlis and Papandreou governments. The claim that a devaluation of the Drachma would be a negative factor by raising the cost of imports seems particularly unusual, as the consumer splurge on new cars and similar goods was also one of the main causes of the current problems. Social change and population movement in Greece in the last generation has emptied much of the mountain and rural hinterlands and brought a new consumerist middle class in and around Athens into being. The overconsumption patterns of this social orbit are a major cause of the current crisis, irrespective of whether those involved are in the public or private sector.

Again, the situation in Greece is disproportionately important as it brings together many threads in the international economic scene generally. The political and economic agenda established for the New Democracy government in Greece in the early 2000s was firmly set in the United States, but without flexibility in application. On the key question of currency level, successive US administrations have been able to gently devalue the dollar as part of responsible international policies, yet the principle of devaluation is closed to Greece by the European Central Bank and Eurozone membership and the absence of a local currency where the Drachma would act as a safety valve for many tensions, as has happened with currencies like the Forint in Hungary and others. The strengthening of the state required to successfully stage the Olympics also involved a big expansion of the internal security apparatus and very expensive external security contractors but the real costs involved do not seem to have been evaluated at the time.

10 22 January 2010.

The Local Political Background

PASOK had many friends among the European socialist parties and a particularly close relationship with the government in London. Some key aides in the Papandreou inner orbit have strong British links. It remains to be seen what advice will be offered, and to what extent the Prime Minister will be able to overcome entrenched resistance to draconian economic measures if the government opts to try to stay in the Eurozone. As widely anticipated, all cuts have been opposed by the powerful trades unions which, in a general sense, are closely allied with the traditionalist Greek Communist Party (KKE).[11] The KKE is very well organized and well led and presents the EU leadership with a novel phenomenon, a communist party with a significant role once again in events in a West European country. New Democracy is a stable opposition force but is inevitably tarred with the corruption brush over data manipulation in the pre-2009 period in government.

At the moment the PASOK government is in something of a honeymoon period and the need for austerity measures has won widespread acceptance, at least in theory. There are nevertheless serious internal tensions within PASOK over the cuts programme and a future party split cannot be ruled out, although probably not in the short term.

The difficulty the government has is that in the view of many economists the data are still going in the wrong direction.[12] The crisis has produced withdrawals of funds from the banks in Greece by individuals who are uncertain about the future, and their share prices have fallen steeply. Serious income deficit is appearing in a way that has not existed for a generation or more, with beggars on the streets. People are having serious difficulty in repaying consumer debt. The single most critical factor is likely to be the effect of the still relatively high Euro on the 2010 tourist season.[13] A major increase in tourist revenue would buy the government time and financial space and take some pressure off the general population. If the decline continues, social tensions are likely to rise. It will nevertheless be a containable situation in the short and,

---

11 Known colloquially as 'Kappa Kappa Epsilon' after its acronyms in the Greek alphabet, the party is the oldest political organization in Greece and has been gaining support recently. It has formally distanced itself from Russia and has published cogent and thoughtful criticism of developments in Moscow since 1990 but retains many links throughout Eastern Europe, particularly in Hungary, the old GDR area of Germany and the Czech Republic and in the Middle East in Syria, Lebanon and Egypt.

12 It is interesting to compare the reporting of the crisis in the six weeks or so between the London *Financial Times* and the New York *Wall Street Journal*. See *The Wall Street Journal Europe*, 19 January 2010, 'Greece Unlikely to Get EU Help'.

13 E.g. compared to competing tourist destinations with non-Euro currencies.

perhaps, medium term if the government operates efficiently, as despite the reduction of tourist income millions of people continue to visit Greece and some cash flow is thus always present in even the weakest businesses. The initial debt figures produced by the government in May 2010 were not bad, although what the figures really mean is bound to be open to expert debate.

The Bad Greek Paradigm

The international danger for the Papandreou government is much deeper. There are many countries throughout the world where financial data is poor and misleading and where corruption of statistics is common. There are certainly many in the EU, with Portugal, Spain and others in the limelight currently. In early June 2010 there has been speculation about Hungary's financial stability. Obvious other candidates are among Greece's near neighbours and best friends in the EU, Bulgaria and Romania, and Croatia among aspirant countries. Croatia has a developing debt spiral that appears very similar to that of Greece. If financial probity is ever going to be restored to Bulgaria, for instance, the May 2010 'bailout' of the Greek economy sets an unfortunate precedent. The current lukewarm reaction in the markets to the most recent bailout deal indicates that without facing these issues, the whole future of the Euro project is now at risk. The time has come when major EU contributors like France and Germany are unable, in a democratic electoral environment, to ask their own electors voting in a tough financial climate to make sacrifices to subsidize minor EU members where it is clear, in their view, that much of the British, French and German money is being effectively stolen. It remains to be seen what the French pressure on the Berlin government will bring - in terms of the May bailout and in respect of government stability within Germany.

Thus, the Greek crisis is being judged in a different way from that of a nation like Iceland in 2009. The honest and hard-working majority of Icelanders were traduced by an ignorant and ideologically motivated elite into a foolish blind alley, but the nation remains politically stable. It is also an irreplaceable strategic asset for NATO in the northern midAtlantic and has long-term resources in fish, tourism and renewable energy that enable it to neglect international pressure to make a fast debt settlement. However unsatisfactory this is to debtor countries like the UK there is little doubt that Iceland has the resources to pay its debts and has both the will and the time to do so. In Greece the political challenge to globalization is much more acute, as there is no guarantee the PASOK government will ever actually be able to improve the fiscal position on the ground and there are major opinion constituencies in the country that are so anti-American that the prospect of debt default and a showdown with the EU and the international banks would be positively welcome. The May 2010 bailout plan is likely to fail to stabilize the situation over the medium term for a number of reasons (see below) but perhaps the most important is that it sees the Greek crisis as one of government liquidity in the economy whereas the actual crisis is one of cash flow and potential solvency. The unknown 'X factor' in all calculations is how far ordinary Greeks will be willing to release their spare cash into the banking system in the current climate of uncertainty.

The European Central Bank is hence faced with a very hard choice. The May 2010 plan in many ways has undermined its authority (as many commentators have long claimed the French have long wanted) and given more power over issues to EU governments. In many transactions involving international sovereign debt, the numbers can be effectively fiddled, or massaged, in order to prevent debtor nation embarrassment. In effect a version of this is what the French have forced on the rest of the EU through the May proposals. French banks have the highest single-country exposure to Greek debt. A significant danger of the bailout plan is that it will only encourage these financially irresponsible tendencies in second and third tier EU countries with the practical result of an increase in inflationary pressures in the Eurozone. There has been a natural tendency to try to help the new government in Athens but it will be difficult with Greece as the whole crisis originated with the exposure of data manipulation, and the financial markets are likely to scrutinize all numbers quoted with great care. The market in March-April made its own judgement before the ECB was able to do very much, by simply driving up the price of Greek debt servicing to exorbitant levels.

The general current of sentiment, both formal and informal, should have been to be hard on Greece in order to avoid setting a precedent for other second and third tier EU nations in poor economic predicaments. The markets had got used to seeing a strong functional Euro, and did not wish to see it devalued through bailout irresponsibility, and to protect the parochial concerns of French and other bankers who had in the past taken irresponsible lending positions in Greek debt. This, of course, inscribes a view on both the future of the economic recovery in the short term and the effectiveness of globalization processes in the long term, and most of all on the politics of EU enlargement. It is a sobering thought to consider what the Euro would look like now if it was linked to failing major depressed economies like the Ukraine.

International Issues: The Security and Defence Dimension

It is unlikely that the central bankers will be considering the effect of a Greek default on neighbouring countries in isolation. The ball is firmly in the EU court. The US administration does not seem particularly interested in the Balkans, along the lines of the early years of the Clinton and Bush administrations. But the already serious effects of the Greek downturn have already been seen, coupled with strong diplomatic and trade initiatives from Ankara. As mentioned above, the crisis in Greece has already had negative effects on the many Greek-owned, or partially owned, banks in the southern Balkans. The attempts to save money by cutting defence expenditure have not so far produced concrete results, as the recent Erdogan-Papandreou meetings in Athens showed.

Although the Turkish outlook is far from ideal, and excessive debt is present in the economy along with crises in some manufacturing caused by dumping of Chinese goods, there is a basic resilience about the Turkish situation that underpins the government's current activity in both the Balkans and the Middle East. Turkey has the great strategic advantage of food exports and vast areas of fertile but unused land that are being rented to rich foreign nations in food deficit, like Saudi Arabia, and booming tourism. An independent and assertive foreign policy is developing, with much greater political distance from Israel a key beneficial factor. The border with Syria is fully open to free trade in the south-east and in the Balkans. Ankara wishes to be much more involved in the protection of human rights of local Muslim minority populations, as in Bosnia. The key Turkish role in Republic of Macedonia is likely to make progress on the name dispute unlikely, as with many other issues Balkan governments are unlikely to risk upsetting powerful local opinion constituencies to fulfil foreign policy agendas set by the international community. In international terms current Greek economic discomfiture and Turkish self-confidence make an early deal over Cyprus also look very unlikely and the possibility of a split of the island is increasing. On the Macedonian name issue, after an early lurch towards Greece in summer 2009, the Obama administration has distanced itself from the US Greek lobby and has improved relations with the Skopje government and has a coherent, balanced policy.

Macedonia and the Neighbours

Many dimensions of the Greek crisis, are detectable in Skopje. While the government has behaved responsibly in the financial crisis, almost all functional government depends in the last analysis on foreign cash flows, whether diaspora remittances in the 25 per cent ethnic Albanian community or EU and NATO money for defence, security and major aspects of governance. The Euro peg for the Macedonian Denar is set at a very high level and analysts find difficulty in seeing how the current level can reasonably continue. Public expenditure is being savagely cut but it remains to be seen what will actually happen on the ground in a climate so influenced by patronage and client networks involving corruption. Vulnerable institutions such as the universities and hospitals are suffering serious underfunding. A delicate balance with the Albanian community is being maintained but at a cost of social stagnation and the effective end of the Ohrid reform process. Gloomy prognostications about an economic crisis in Macedonia do not, though, seem well founded. Although the currency peg is rigid, a degree of flexibility is being maintained by grey market transactions that may technically be money laundering but do keep the wheel of commerce moving by providing cash flow to the banks and thus credit availability and business solvency. The Macedonian Denar is generally respected by all communities and remains a functional local currency. The Greek crisis has inevitably involved a degree of Schadenfreude about Athens' discomfort and consequence indifference to the many problems between them. A period of stagnation in mutual relationships seems likely, as with Bulgaria.

In the very short term, developments are likely to favour the Athens government. The May plan has removed the problem of unstable Greek government/bond market relationships. Debt funding will no doubt go ahead successfully for a while, although at a very high and probably increasing cost to future generations of Greeks. Many Greeks are likely to resist change now, as they will feel the May deal emphasizes the unique importance of Greece in the world and its Panhellenic heritage in a stable European Union. Greeks are grossly overrepresented on a numerical basis in many Brussels organizations and can no doubt attempt to push policy Athens' way. They are likely to be supported by officials from other second and third tier nations with dubious economies who expect a more or less eternal subsidy of elite lifestyles from first tier nation taxpayers, it would appear. Papandreou may also be gambling that some other sovereign debt crisis will appear on the international scene soon, and Greece will be forgotten if, say, there is a major Spanish banking crisis coming.

This may be misplaced optimism. Much of the crisis burden will have to be carried by important mainstream social groups, as urban workers' and farmers' demonstrations suggest, and it will be difficult to keep Greece's problems from the media and public eye. An important issue to observe will be the announcement of figures about Greek tourism. These have been vastly inflated in the past and have often been regarded by students of modern Greek society as risible. Publication of objective data would aid a realistic evaluation of the state of the real economy

Social tension is now likely to subside for a while as the tourists arrive and Greeks leave the cities for the beach and holidays, only to resume and intensify as tens of thousands of school leavers and college students come onto the job market in September and find there are very few opportunities of any kind for them.*

---

* First published on Defence Academy of the UK, www.da.mod.uk/colleges/arag, 10/07

THE EFFECTS OF THE GREEK ECONOMIC CRISIS ON THE REPUBLIC OF MACEDONIA

The Economic Context

THE ONSET OF THE WORLD financial crisis in 2007/2008 initially had little effect on the southern Balkans. Most countries - whether European Union members, candidate members or those awaiting an EU relationship – have similar banking systems in which the more speculative aspects of contemporary finance are almost wholly absent. This was not the case with Greece, where banking is closely integrated into wider globalized financial groups and where growing national indebtedness had concerned regional observers for some time.

The debt crisis that developed in Greece in 2009-2010, with the possibility of debt restructuring, a default and/or a return to the Drachma currency, along with the wider Eurozone's financial instability has inevitably given rise to concerns about the economic prospects of the Republic of Macedonia.[1] The Republic of Macedonia has a small and weak economy with many trade and business links to Greece, a relatively unstable internal political environment, and problems that undermine good governance. Major Greek investment has in fact been undertaken in economic sectors such as the Republic of Macedonia's petroleum and food and beverages industries, whereas Greece constitutes a major market for Macedonian exports such as quarrying and mineral products.[2]

In general, the gloomy predictions of many commentators in the Skopje press since 2008 about the likely effects of the Greek crisis on political and economic stability in Skopje have not been borne out by events. Such critics have underestimated the stabilizing effect of both the diversification of the Macedonian regional economy in recent years and the growing interconnections with various trade and investment partners such as Turkey, Serbia, Russia, Germany and Bulgaria. Although there was a short period of severe funding stress in late 2008/early 2009, the Skopje banks have avoided a crisis, and the early involvement of the International Monetary Fund (IMF) produced public expenditure reductions that avoided the need for a renewal of the three-year stand-by agreement with the IMF that expired in 2008.[3] The government still

---

1   The name 'Republic of Macedonia' for the state is used as a matter of verbal convention only in this article and does not imply any view on the legitimacy of the term 'Former Yugoslav Republic of Macedonia' (FYROM), which is also used as a state name by Greece, the Republic of Cyprus, and some international organizations.

2   See James Pettifer, 'The Greek Crisis – A Pause', Defence Academy of the United Kingdom, Shrivenham July 2010, available http://www.da.mod.uk/colleges/arag/documentlistings/balkan/The%20Greek%20Crisis_Web.pdf/view . All websites were accessed on 15 February 2011.

3   Economist Intelligence Unit (EIU) Reports on Macedonia. London 2008-2011; all reports are available at http://www.eiu.com/index.

prioritizes the desire to avoid recourse to the IMF in policy-making. Politics in Skopje is highly symbolic, and there is a widespread belief among all ethnic communities in the Republic of Macedonia that their democracy is subject to major manipulation by outside forces.[4] Thus avoiding an IMF intervention is a political as well as an economic priority in Skopje. Risks to macroeconomic stability remain but are not generally thought to be as serious now as a year or more ago.[5]

The current account deficit is high but so far has proved possible to finance. The current budget deficit ran about 2.8 per cent of the GDP in 2009, the largest for some years, but it has become increasingly expensive to service the debt as the international appetite for government bonds declines. Inward capital flows are very important. There was a very sharp decline in inward direct investment in 2009, as in other Balkan countries like Serbia, Montenegro and Croatia.[6] In most cases, this is because most (or all) worthwhile enterprises have been sold or privatized (e.g. the tobacco and steel industries in the Republic of Macedonia), and construction development has been a victim of the global economic crisis. There has been a significant decline throughout Europe in capital flows from richer to poorer countries as many have chosen not to finance holiday houses and second homes.[7] In Bulgaria, for instance, in the early 2000s vacation homes were the single most important foreign capital inflow in the country. The issue is less important in the Republic of Macedonia because of the nature of its tourist industry, which depends heavily on short-term stays by transit visitors and local customers who are unlikely to want to invest much in a second home. In general, the country has not suffered from a property and construction 'bubble' and

asp?layout=displayIssue&publication_id=1440000944 ; World Bank Country Reports. 2008-2010, available at http://www.wds.worldbank.org/external/default/main?menuPK==64258544&pagePK=64187838&piPK=64187928&thesitePK=523679&function=BrowseFR&menuPK=64187514&siteName=WDS&conceptattcode = 82709& pathtreeid=COUNT&sortattcode=DOCDT+desc ; International Monetary Fund, Country Reports. 2008 – 2010, available at http://www.imf.org/external/country/mkd/index.htm

4   An interesting analysis of this subject and the politics of Macedonian image manipulation is Andrew Graan, 'On the politics of Image', *Slavic Review* 69 (2010), no. 4, 835-58.

5   For more detail, see the EIU Report of September 2010 (above fn. 3). The report is comprehensive but probably underestimates the degree of 'grey' and 'black' economic activities, and does not raise the issue of government statistical accuracy.

6   EIU Reports, 2009-2010 (above fn. 3)

7   The *Financial Times* estimated that as many as 50 per cent of all British-owned second homes in Spain are currently up for sale. New inward investment has more or less stopped altogether. Holiday home Sell-off Forecast, *Financial Times*, January 2011, available at http://www.ft.com/cms/s/2/09923922-1a8a-11e0-b100- 00144feab49a.html#axzz1HRrby8Zi

associated bad bank loans, allowing the Republic of Macedonia to avoid the destabilization that struck 'bubble' nations like Spain and Portugal.

Macedonian monetary policy is controlled by the relationship of the Denar to the Euro, at a semi-pegged rate that has remained steady for some years. Until 2008/09, capital inflows meant that not only could debts be paid off, but that the Euro peg level could be maintained. This is a cause of concern for the future. The current account deficit improved from about 7.3 per cent of the GDP in 2009 to 4.8 per cent in 2010/11, and the trade deficit shrank by 11 per cent in the same period. Exports are rising, and in February 2009 were up 19 per cent compared to the previous year.[8]

Pledges of financial aid have been received from the European Bank for Reconstruction and Development (EBRD), mainly for road improvements, although the Skopje government would prefer that the funding be applied to complete the long-delayed and only partially completed rail link to Bulgaria.[9] An agreement with the World Bank is in force for a four-year partnership strategy. Financial remittances, mainly to the 25 per cent Albanian minority in western Macedonia, are down but remain at a reasonable level, as the majority of the Albanian diaspora work in the German-speaking countries in the EU and also Switzerland, where the economy is healthier than in Greece or Italy. Revenue from criminal activity continues to provide liquidity in the economic system, however undesirable the high level of corruption and lack of business transparency in the Republic of Macedonia is from the point of view of attracting foreign investment.

The relatively optimistic fiscal picture is compromised, however, by sharply rising unemployment, the intense financial pressure on vulnerable institutions such as schools, universities and hospitals, and the poor revenue position of the government, which has led to the closure of diplomatic missions, withdrawal of troops from NATO-led coalitions, and reduced public services.[10] The very low public sector salary and wage levels are an incentive to corruption. As a matter of fact, the country's generally stable economic position has been achieved only via rigid central government spending cuts. Further cuts may be required if capital inflows do not improve, and an IMF application might then be unavoidable.

---

8   EIU Reports, 2010 (above fn. 3).

9   See the coverage in *Nova Makedonia* and other Skopje media during July and August 2010.

10 See the BBC Monitoring reports on Macedonia between September and December 2010, also for documentation on the failure of 'name' discussions initiated by Matthew Nimitz in that period. For Macedonian Albanian views, see Koha and other media for the same period.

Nevertheless, industrial output rose by 8 per cent in the last year, and exports rose over 20 per cent in the first six months of 2010. Income from the important agricultural sector has been healthy as a result of rising world food prices and the benefits gained from local investment in improving product quality in areas such as the alcoholic beverages sector. In that sense, the Macedonian economy has long emphasized primary sector economic activities. Greece extended its border northwards during the nineteenth and early twentieth centuries to achieve economic goals, given that Greece then suffered from a deficit in core agricultural products like cereals.

There are tens of thousands of very small agricultural producers whose production and social value is not captured by conventional economic data; their output provides subsistence and social stability for the poorer parts of society in Macedonia, as in most Balkan countries.

The Political Background and International Relations

In the recent period there have been few major decisions or major changes affecting the political structures of the Republic of Macedonia. The framework of interethnic relations established by the international community through the Ohrid Accords, which were signed in August 2001 and ended the short interethnic war that spring/summer, remains in place. On the Macedonian side of the ethnic divide, all political structures are now dominated by the conservative-nationalist Internal Macedonian Revolutionary Organization (IMRO) government of Nikola Gruevski, which controls the presidency, the parliament and many local governments and other institutions. It governs in coalition with the largest of the ethnic Albanian parties, Ali Ahmeti's Democratic Union for Integration, in a de facto spoils system. Recent elections have been more peaceful than those in the immediate post-Ohrid period but many problems remain in achieving an international standard.[11] The relationship with the European Union remains stalled at an ostensible level because of the dispute over the state's name with Greece, but also over the lack or reform of what Brussels contends are obsolete and dysfunctional structures in Macedonian society.[12] The same applies to NATO membership, although the country has supplied troops to US-

11 Numerous documents exist concerning problems associated with elections in the Republic of Macedonia over the years. For the most comprehensive reports see those issued by the OSCE Vienna office, available at http://www.osce.org , searching for the appropriate year/ election.

12 For example, there has been very poor progress in the exploratory talks with Brussels over a projected date for the opening of full membership negotiations with the Skopje government.

led coalitions. It is an open question whether Skopje could afford the required national level of defence spending for NATO membership in the present economic and fiscal circumstances. Reform is a problem in the military sphere as much as the civilian one, so that, for instance, the officer corps of the army remains overwhelmingly Slav-Macedonian, despite numerous attempts by NATO and other advisers to engineer reforms over the last fifteen years.

In the international community, in general, all concern over these and other issues has been condensed into the arguments about the 'name' issue, which has been seen as the main obstacle to NATO and EU membership.[13] The thirteen-year-long United Nations mission of Matthew Nimitz remains active, although his new initiative involving Prime Ministers Gruevski and Papandreou in autumn 2010 did not produce any concrete results and led to some awkward diplomatic exchanges between Athens and Skopje.[14] While the name issue is obviously very important, it is often used to camouflage other, much more serious reservations about the role of the Republic of Macedonia in the world. The uncomfortable fact for the international community is that the Republic of Macedonia's ability to weather the global economic crisis, which earned the country plaudits from the IMF and other international organizations, is closely tied to informal centralized control in what is still in some senses a semi-socialist or state-capitalist economy. This is particularly the case in the agricultural and food products sectors, which are generally well run and have benefited considerably from the boom in the world food prices. Current grain prices are considerably higher on the local informal market than they are within the EU. The metals sector has also benefited from foreign investment and booming international demand. The rapid economic clampdown that saved the situation in 2008-2009 would have been much more difficult to achieve without the political centralization based on IMRO-controlled structures and informal networks in Skopje, much in the same way that Montenegrin leader Milo Djukanovic was able to use the methods of internal patronage networks.[15]

Thus there is a contradiction, in the current grim economic circumstances, between the reforms needed for EU membership progress, and the local system that so far has avoided major social economic

13 Cf. Biljana Vankovska, 'David vs. Goliath: The Macedonian Position(s) in the So-Called "Name Dispute" with Greece, *Sudosteuropa. Zeitschrift fur Politik und Gesellschaft* 58 (2010), no.3, 436-67.

14 See BBC Monitoring (above fn. 10), for this period.

15 James Pettifer, 'International Financial Crisis and the Balkans', *The World Today* 65 (February 2009), no.2, 22-24.

instability. The political ambitions of the Macedonian Albanians are usually intimately linked with the situation in neighbouring Kosovo, and it remains to be seen if the difficulties there following the recent elections will lead to the growth of Albanian nationalist sentiment in western Macedonian. This is perhaps unlikely in the short term, as the political leadership of the Macedonian Albanians is fragmenting somewhat into a greater number of parties, none of which is likely to disturb the general Ohrid Accords settlement. The IMRO government has offended Serbia by its recognition of the Kosovo border delineation, an astute move in the light of Macedonia's internal ethnic conflicts, as it has temporarily defused Albanian grievances over Skopje's non-implementation of the Ohrid provisions. The event was also a sign of declining Greek diplomatic influence in the region.[16]

At the onset of the Greek crisis, some diplomats were of the opinion that the crisis might force Greece to back down on some long-held positions and embrace a compromise deal with Skopje. This has not happened, however, for the simple and understandable reason that with much of the Greek left expressing vitriolic opposition to government austerity plans, the last thing the unpopular and psychologically insecure PASOK government wants is to incite the ire of the clerical right with a major concession over the Republic of Macedonia. The weak and uncertain leadership of the New Democracy party in Athens exacerbates this problem, as it cedes influence on many issues to the Greek Orthodox Church, which in general is strongly opposed to concessions to Skopje. Northern Greece, which is adjacent to the Republic of Macedonia, has been most seriously affected by the economic crash and is also most influenced by the Church and the clerical right. A major concession on the name controversy by Athens would prove to be very unpopular.[17]

American faith in the viability of a solution is often motivated by the increasing numbers and influence of the Albanian minority in Macedonia, most of whom would prefer a settlement and NATO membership.[18] This is undoubtedly true but it is also true that it would be potentially very destabilizing to the Skopje government to accept a semi-imposed deal by the International Community that depended on the Albanians in a way that many Slavs would interpret as a direct attack

16 Cf. Biljana Vankovska, 'Kosovo: Macedonia's Perspectives', *Sudosteuropa. Zeitschrift für Politik und Gesellschaft* 56 (2008), no.3, 412-41.
17 For more on the clerical issues cf. James Pettifer, 'The Gligorov Regime in Former Yugoslav Macedonia and the Development of Religion', in Ines Angjeli Murzaku (ed.), *Quo Vadis Eastern Europe? Religion, State and Society after Communism*, Ravenna, 2009, pp. 197-206.
18 Such opinions were articulated in discussions with the author by US diplomats and officials in 2009 and 2010.

on their national identity. The UN Mission of Matthew Nimitz remains dedicated to finding a top-down solution, but how sensible this policy is, given the recurrent political stresses in Skopje, remains an open question. Nimitz's mission is, in essence, a holdover from the Vance-Owen period of international activity in the Balkans, when deals could be brokered between strong international negotiators and undemocratic leaders like Milosevic or Tudman and then handed down to local populations. The development of better formal democracy in the Balkans over the last fifteen years has made this perspective rather obsolete. In a reasonably formally democratic state like the contemporary Republic of Macedonia this is a very dubious strategy, as the discussions about the need for a validation referendum indicate. In Greece, with its long, if sometimes flawed, tradition of parliamentary government, this is even more the case. In Greece only the Marxist left favours a major reorientation of policy towards Skopje, but although support for the Communist Party (KKE) and smaller Marxist parties is increasing steadily (as the recent Greek local election results in autumn 2010 indicate), they do not exert much ideological influence on Greek policy on this issue. It has been a dangerous issue for the Greek left dating back to the Greek Civil War (1943-1949) and is a low priority at the moment.

In the years since its creation as a new independent state in 1991/1992, the Republic of Macedonia has shown a sure survival instinct in often highly difficult circumstances, including the early Greek economic boycott, difficulties in attaining international recognition, the loss of its original flag and other issues in the 1995 'small package' agreement with Greece, the appalling strains of the Kosovo war refugee crisis, and a full-scale armed conflict with the Albanians in 2011. It has shown generally good sense in addressing the current world economic crisis, and for the international community to exert pressure on either government to force through a solution to the name conflict could prove very destabilizing. A better strategy may be to attempt to increase informal economic and regional cooperation to steer both countries through their acute economic difficulties.[*]

---

[*]   First draft published in *Südosteuropa*, Regensburg, 58, 4, 2010, pp. 604-12.

THE MAKING OF THE

GREEK CRISIS

ONE[*]

The Alchemist's Years: 2000-2008

'The enterprise was then entrusted to two distinguished British
officers, Lord Cochrane, who had seen service in South America, and
Sir Richard Church, who had fought in Egypt, Italy and the Ionian
Islands, where he had been wounded at Santa Maura and had made
the acquaintance and gained the respect of Kolokotronis and other
Greek chiefs. In the spring of 1827 these two foreigners were appointed
respectively to command the naval and military forces of Greece.'

William Miller, *The Ottoman Empire and its Successors, 1821-1927*

The European Union and International Monetary Fund negotiators
who have sat in financial authority in Athens since 2012 have many
antecedents. Men and women completely ignorant of the Greek language
have played their parts in the making of modern Greece, with varying
degrees of success. Their activities have taken place in historical time,
with chronological dates. Some of these dates have been more important
than others. Through the manner of his death at Missolonghi in 1824 in
the War of Independence, Lord Byron 'made' modern Greece for many
of his readers. He was following in the footsteps of many antiquarian
explorers before him. They played an important part in building the
philhellenic movement in support of the independent Greek state that
emerged from the Ottoman Empire between 1821 and 1832.

Yet for many visitors, and some scholars, the beauty and drama of
the Greek landscape seem outside Time, changeless. They follow the
ancient philosopher Plato in thinking that the Beauty is the Good. Greek
material life glides by in seascapes, olive groves, rocks, honey cakes and
white Orthodox churches. 'Greece' seems to have existed eternally (as
the advertisements for vacations also say). But now Greece in early
twenty-first-century historical time in global capitalism is in a financial,
social and economic crisis that will affect the future of all of Europe.
Why has this happened?

Greece is for many visitors the most Mediterranean nation of all,
without the ambiguities of Italy, or the dominating concrete of much of
the south of France. The pastoral way of life of the shepherds continues
with goats and sheep plodding home in the evenings along tracks that
have been used for thousands of years. But since the Second World
War Greece has experienced an urban revolution, accelerated by the

---

[*] The first draft of this text was published digitally by Penguin, London, in 2012.

effects of the European Common Agricultural Policy which after 1981 bankrupted tens of thousands of small farmers. The period of forced urbanization and tolerance of mass illegal building in the post-Civil War years after 1949 allowed Athens to become a refuge for political radicals who could survive and find work there when they would otherwise be persecuted by the police in the countryside. The city that grew had little or no public space, massive slums and overcrowding (central Athens had a population density to rival some African cities), and has continued to be dysfunctional. But from the point of view of political radicals, it is ideal, it preserves many of the conditions of a city like nineteenth-century Paris. Many other displaced rural people moved into Greek towns and cities after European Union entry in 1981.

Athens region has become a megalopolis with a very high proportion of the population of the entire country packed into it. But the later years of urbanization also seemed to be good years. Ever voluble Greeks crowded the cafés in the warm summer evening streets. It seemed a touch of an earthly Paradise had returned. The time after Euro entry in 2001 seemed to confirm the view of optimists that the problems of Greek twentieth-century history had been 'solved'. In philosophy, perhaps a marginal pursuit in some EU nations but never in Greece, positivism had triumphed. The world of Germany, where labour reforms enacted after 2003 produced a significant drop in the workers' share of national income, was very distant then from Greece.

For anyone middle aged or older, the difficult years of the Colonels' dictatorship of the late 1960s and early 1970s were far away. A growing rhythm of stability and progress had come to daily life. Some streets in Athens once full of bad tempered traffic were pedestrianized. Greece seemed to be catching up with the rest of Western Europe, a dream of many Greek secular intellectuals since the eighteenth-century Enlightenment. It was an attractive picture. Roads had improved out of all recognition, a basic welfare state was constructed, expensive bottled water was everywhere, and the Olympic Games were held without mishap in 2004. Immigrants thronged into Greece both from Balkan neighbours and as far afield as Iraq and Afghanistan to work in the growing economy. As the financial writer Jason Manolopoulos noted in his book *Greece's 'Odious' Debt*, in those years Greece 'got lucky', and

> an unreformed Greek economy was accepted into the fledgling European Single Currency. The reasons for this were overwhelmingly political, with economic data fudged, as the EU's leaders emphasised establishing as wide an area as possible

for monetary union as part of the European movements drive for full integration. Greece's *annus mirabilis* was 2004: three years into Euro membership, the founding country of the Olympics hosted that year's games. Economic growth had continued since entry into the Eurozone.

Although Manolopoulos is writing from the perspective of a hedge fund manager and within the assumptions of high capitalism, his unsparing and unsentimental account of the crisis in the financial superstructure is a commentary that casts much light on the mechanisms that drove events between 2001 and 2005. It also illustrates why even after the 2012 'bailout' the crisis is not over. Greece suffered from the 'Grand Illusion' of European federalism as much as it had suffered from the Grand Illusions of nationalist expansionist policy in the period around the end of the First World War when the Greek army invaded and occupied a large part of Ottoman Asia Minor. Athens governments had sought to 'redeem' Greeks living outside Greece and bring them within an enlarged Greek state but the military campaign after the First World War ended in disaster. Modern Greek history has been punctuated by periods of overwhelming cosmic optimism followed by defeat and disillusion.

The Euro currency 'project' that is central to the current crisis did not originate in Greece. As Victor Hugo observed in 1855, the notion of a single European currency, like all bad ideas, has been around for a very long time. Most of its genesis has always been French with Napoleon Bonaparte an early advocate. As Bloomberg writer Matthew Lynn has pointed out, there are plenty of examples of currency unions to avoid, like the Latin Monetary Union that was created in 1865 and included France, Italy, Belgium, Switzerland and even then, Greece. It finally collapsed in 1927 after a shadowy existence for many years. But history is not taken very seriously in many financial circles. In Greece, Europe and the single currency have meant something very different. The European project, for Athens, depended on a view of the unique Greek cultural mission in the world to spread Hellenism throughout the European Union. In more recent world history, perhaps only Mao's 'Great Leap Forward' in communist China between 1958 and 1961 has a comparable mixture of political voluntarism and indifference to basic cultural differences and economics. After all, ever since antiquity, Greeks have never agreed exactly what 'Hellenism' is. The use of the Greek language? Orthodoxy in religion? Democracy in government? Yet beyond these apparently interesting if not immediately fruitful speculations, the dark shadow of catastrophe was emerging, like a storm cloud over the Aegean Sea.

Imagining catastrophe is difficult. Modern social-democratic European politics has little room for the imaginary, in any shape or form; it is a terrain of social control, flipcharts, number crunching, endless economic forecasting and mass production of technocrats. The collapse of Lehmann Brothers would have been hard to imagine even a couple of years before it took place in 2008. Financial regulatory authorities did not anticipate it at all. It was outside the bounds of possibility. In the Greek political tradition, almost anything political is possible; in the European Union little is possible if outside the limits of centrist technocracy. Yet the scale of the current disaster would have been hard to imagine even in Greece itself. If anyone sitting in Syntagma Square in central Athens in May 2005 had been able to see ahead to their national crisis beginning five years later, and told their friends in the *kafenio* that over their ouzo glass they saw national bankruptcy and mass impoverishment of a sizeable proportion of the population, they would have been regarded as drunk, or mad, or both. Yet five years later the café chairs and tables may have been destroyed by out of control fires and the customers choking on tear gas. Or perhaps their place no longer exists, gone bankrupt like thousands of other Greek businesses. Yet this crisis did not drop from the sky as an eagle in Epirus might drop a sick lamb. It was made within European capitalism as the illusions of political elites in both Brussels and Athens fed on each other. A hopeless over optimism about what the European Union was or could ever be dominated their judgements and a sweeping belief in their own propaganda overtook them.

The causes of the European crisis are complex, and are not confined to Europe itself. It is sometimes forgotten nowadays that the United States has been a strong supporter of the processes of European integration, from the days of the post-war Marshall Plan when the nascent European Economic Community in its early days was seen as the economic pillar of NATO. More recently, countries like Bulgaria and Romania have become EU members long before they were ready in part because of American pressure on Brussels. Washington policies which continued the Cold War concept of the EU as the economic arm of NATO into the post-Cold War world have not always resulted in failures; at the time of Polish EU membership negotiations the US pressure to do a fast deal was widely resented in Europe but Polish membership has subsequently turned out to be unproblematic. European enlargement has taken on many of the characters and values of a civic religion in the liberal establishment in the United States, where criticism of the project in Brussels, or rational discussion of what it actually means has become very difficult, particularly since the advent of the Obama presidency. The wish to reject the American Exceptionalism of the Bush period has meant an often uncritical adherence to often superficially understood mulitilateralist ideas in international relations and abandonment of some aspects of US legitimate claims to world leadership.

The European Union is a transnational ideal. The reality of Europe is often very poorly understood even within the most educated and well informed parts of the American political elite. European enlargement and integration are often seen, consciously or subconsciously, as a process akin to the formation of the United States, where individual states agree to group together and give up local sovereignty to become component parts of a larger federal state. It often does not seem to be understood in Washington that this is, in terms of the inner debates about the future within the EU, a profoundly Euro federalist perspective that is only shared by a small, and diminishing, proportion of the voters in European parliaments and electorates. It also took a long time, over two hundred years, for the United States model to develop into its present form, and included a very bloody civil war along the way. The Euro federalists around Jacques Delors in 1992 attempted the same objective within a generation. Americans also frequently do not understand that the EU cannot tax its citizens centrally, unlike the US, and the European Central Bank (ECB) is something quite different from the US Federal Reserve Bank. It remains so after the modifications to its role and powers brought on by the Greek crisis. Obama administration policy has thus tied itself to a political position only held by a tiny minority in Europe, even within the political elites. Recent crises have also tended to diminish the size and influence of this always small federalist lobby, as the votes for anti-EU parties in the 2014 European elections indicate.

Some of these concerns may seem very remote from the realities of daily Greek life as either the inhabitant or the visitor experiences them. At a small village in the north like Agios Germanos near the border with FYROM/Republic of Macedonia, the years since 1981 and European community entry have seen a steady improvement in life. The fish of Lake Prespa are still plentiful, unlike Greek sea fish, EU money has improved production of the local staple crop, beans, and a growing trickle of visitors come on ecotourist holidays to watch the bird life or walk in the vast deciduous forests. Local Greek tour buses bring church parties to see the Byzantine frescoes around the rocky cliffs above the lake. Old men devour lake trout for lunch while tubby black-dressed wives discuss a coming wedding. The priest makes sure everyone gets back on the bus and nobody is left behind. The star attraction for foreign ornithologists is the Dalmatian pelican. In August the village thrives. Village exiles come back for summer holidays from the Czech Republic, Hungary, Australia and Canada and the church has been rebuilt and a proper graveyard constructed. Visitors stay the night in well built stone traditional houses that were also a tribute to European Union investment in the politically-sensitive border region. At the end of the Civil War, a generation earlier, the village was in ruins and virtually uninhabited as the mostly communist-supporting people left for life in exile in Skopje and Prague, either voluntarily, or through coercion.

Rural Agios Germanos would nowadays be unrecognizable to them. External help from northern Europe has been central to these achievements. Yet there is a worm in that bud. Whatever income comes to the village from tourism or other visitors tends to stay there. All payments are in cash and Athens is a distant government where corruption is widespread. Paying tax to the authorities there is not in the local tradition, and tradition, *adet*, rules the Balkan mountains. Paying tax to repay debt to external powers seems a fatuous and strange concept.

External determinants from major powers are not new in Greek twentieth-century history, or national policies based on over-optimism about Greece's place in the world. The sweeping optimism about Greece's destiny in Asia Minor led to the catastrophe at Smyrna in 1922, and the arrival of hundreds of thousands of Greek refugees who would never see their old homes in Turkey again. In the Second World War highly charged optimism about the possibility of a restored monarchy, on the right, and the possibility of a successful transition to communism, on the left, led to years of civil war, much of it depending on foreign powers with competing agendas for Greek politics. Stalin betrayed the Greek working class and peasantry at Yalta. And overshadowing it all, as in much of the nineteenth century, has been the burden of debt. As a result Greece had to turn away from democracy in the 1930s, as John Koliopoulos has shown in his masterly study *Greece and the British Connection 1935-1941*. Recurring debt crises had punctuated political life in nineteenth- and early twentieth-century Greece.

In the post-Civil War period, debt was contained within the New Deal and Marshall Plan framework, but was an ever-present problem in the background. Many infrastructure costs, such as those that involved strategic roads of military interest in northern Greece, or port and airport modernization, were effectively paid for by the United States or NATO. With the end of the Cold War and the Warsaw Pact, this funding role was taken over by the European Economic Community and then the European Union. Ever since the Greek state was established in the nineteenth century, infusions of foreign capital have been required at regular intervals to support state economic viability.

In the years since the admission of Greece to the Euro currency zone in 2001, it seemed many aspects of the Balkan-European dichotomony of the early PASOK government period under Andreas Papandreou had been overcome. The period of the ex-Yugoslav conflicts had ended in 2001 without unduly affecting or destabilizing Greece. The 'name' issue with neighbouring FYROM/Republic of Macedonia remained but was increasingly politically quiescent in the light of growing economic links. It was twenty years since Greece had joined the European Economic Community in 1981 as its tenth member, and in the intervening period Greeks had taken many leading roles in Community and then Union institutions. Greek lawyers, economists and similar professionals proliferated in Brussels institutional jobs, and became experts at channelling EU funds Athens' way. Greece had acquired the rhetoric of Europe, and for a period opinion polls showed that the Greek public was among the most pro-European in the Union.

Yet at the heart of the current crisis is the issue of the failure of a European language. Europe provided a new terminology and rhetoric in Greek politics, but not a new consciousness, at least not outside some professional and intellectual circles. The European Economic Community certainly provided a new material reality to its members in the early years but its capacity to do this with new members has diminished exponentially as Europe has enlarged. The countries in economic ruin at the end of the Second World War had discredited and often absent institutions, after the fascist past and its aftermath. It was not difficult to build new institutions on a common European model in nations such as Belgium and Germany. This has proved to be much more difficult with later members. In the case of Greece, when full membership came along in 1981, a traditional parliamentary democracy had been restored, but not a West European party system. The Karamanlis government after 1974 was certainly formally democratic in parliamentary terms but the parties inherited many Levantine traditions of patronage, corruption and clientism. Few people cared about this at the time, after the nightmare of the dictatorship. A rough and ready transition seemed much better than what had preceded it.

The Question of Rhetoric

Greece is a very complex society but with a secure rhetorical basis. It is based on a shared speech, the unique magnificence of the language, echoing in every shop, every café, and every field. Greek society has had prevailing patterns of language which have held it together, dating back to classical antiquity. Verbal dialogue and argument have been at the heart of society. The eminent nineteenth-century Swiss historian Jacob Burckhardt observed in his *Weltgeschichte Betrachtungen* (*Observations on World History*) 'the continuation of rationalism and exploitation of the language and rhetorical-dialectical capability... This capability survives the polis, public life in the gymnasia and theatres and all art: the tongue is the last to survive.' Burkhardt was an admirer of the apparently insignificant and minor factors of Greek daily life in his quest for historical understanding, writing in the same work that even trifles could illuminate Greek culture, and that 'the stamp of the rich Greek spirit penetrates even the most worn out reproduction'. Every modern visitor to Greece knows this, the magic of opening the first *Karelia* cigarette packet after arriving at the airport, the scent and taste of ouzo after the first swim. It is a sentiment that the often half-empty souvenir shops of Athens would reflect. Rows of statues of naked gods and goddesses collect dust in the absence of clothed tourists to buy them. They have surrendered to the gaze of the western Other, but the Other has not arrived to look at what they reveal of themselves.

In the modern urban world popular rhetoric and the tongue means the café and the street, and attempts to control this rhetoric by government had been a modern tool of rule. Governments use rhetoric, spin, to persuade their citizens of a right course of action, as Aristotle observed over two thousand years ago. Greece in the twentieth century was a laboratory for these rhetorical techniques, and not only recently. The first modern government media management campaigns in support of unpopular late imperial wars were devised by the British Foreign Office and the US State Department for the Greek Civil War, as post-1945 BBC Athens correspondent Kenneth Matthews has shown in his memoirs of the period. For many years after 1949, the rhetoric of the right had been a means of social control, and throughout the Cold War and dictatorship period. It was replaced by a new language in the PASOK years. The PASOK government had a prevailing rhetoric of populist socialism, sympathy with Third World struggles and anti-Americanism, at least in the initial government period. Although the reality was considerably less radical, it was the Papandreou anti-imperialist language that formed the international image of Greece and so offended sensibilities in Washington and elsewhere. After the death of Andreas Papandreou in June 1996, and his replacement by the quiet and uncharismatic Kostas Simitis, a subtle change in the language of Athens politics began to appear. The genuine, if sometimes eccentric, internationalism of Papandreou was replaced by the ever increasing commitment of the government to a federal European future. Greek nationalism was to be subsumed within the new Euro nationalism of the European Union. At the heart of this major policy change was the forging of a new Greek-German relationship. There would be little market for this in the rhetoric of the Greek street. The Athens media has always reflected this, and as a leaked Wikileaks cable emanating from the American Embassy in Athens in 2011 observed, 'analysis of European Union decisions is scarce' in the Greek media, and it made disparaging reference to Greek 'ethnocentricity'. This may appear a rash comment coming from a diplomat of a nation where so many citizens have so little interest in foreign affairs, but it is accurate.

What was the origin of the Euro federalist illusion in Greece? Prime Minister Kostas Simitis, the architect of the Greek entry to the Euro had been a university teacher in Germany when in exile from the junta before 1974, and had very deeply absorbed the cosmic idealism about Europe that prevailed in the German Social Democratic Party at that time. In his personal culture, he had become in some senses a 'German', just as George Papandreou was later seen as an 'American' in their power structure by many Greeks. The way to modernization and progress seemed to lie in enmeshing Greek finances with those of its strong northern partners, and the financial rewards were obvious, where growing Greek debt could effectively be 'lost' within the wider European financial system. For progressive Germans in the governing parties who still retained a degree of traditional nineteenth-century philhellenic idealism, it was a moral imperative to help Greece in those days, after the darkness of the junta years. Greeks were coming to work and study in Germany in increasing numbers. Far fewer went to Greece's traditional philhellenic allies in Europe, France and Britain, although France and French-based Greek exiles had been very important in the genesis of PASOK and the resistance to the junta. Many Germans had also been involved in opposing the junta, although perhaps without the commitment of some British members of the League for Democracy in Greece who moved explosives from Oxford into Greece for the resistance.

With a much smaller EU, before the costs and problems of German reunification, and in the days before the Euro and loss of budget control, Greek membership did not appear to be financially difficult. Some Greeks knew this. Then, many ordinary Greeks saw the Germans as a better protection alternative to the United States, whatever the problems of the Second World War period. In the 1950s Washington had manipulated Greek politics at will, and installed governments on a purely Cold War basis involving tolerating an underlying police state to protect the right. The Colonels' dictatorship would not have come into being without Washington support, at least initially.

In August 1989, no fewer than sixteen million personal police files amassed by Athens governments since 1945 were burnt in a steel plant outside Athens to try to expunge that memory. European Union participation was seen by many Greek liberals and democrats of all political colours as a sure antidote to any return of US-sponsored authoritarianism. It is also worth reflecting on the fact that in terms of practical political options for the internationals in the current crisis, the authoritarian option had been excluded by the abuses of the Cold War period except for the neo-fascists in the *Chrysi Avyi* (Golden Dawn) organization and assorted nostalgics for the Colonels' junta.

Yet, even then there were many deeper, darker issues below the surface. At that level, every Greek knows that Germany has never paid full reparations to Greece for the costs of the Axis occupation, unlike many countries. Greeks will never forget the forced austerity of the Axis occupation that caused mass starvation in 1941-42 as the German authorities shipped food out of Greece to use in the Nazi war machine. The occupation and the resistance to it were very intense. At Distomo, a little mountain village near Delphi, 214 civilians were massacred by Waffen SS troops on 10 June 1944 in a reprisal attack against 'partisan' activity. Despite a judgement of the Greek High Court in 2000 that Germany should pay 28 million Euros in compensation, nothing has ever been paid. The German constitutional court ruled in March 2006 that the country did not have to pay compensation to individuals seeking settlement of war crimes issues on grounds of 'state immunity'. The wounds of the Second World War period are still raw in many places, particularly in northern Greece.

Very few war crimes trials concerning the Axis occupation of Greece ever took place, exemplified by the controversy in the mid-1980s about United Nations Secretary-General Kurt Waldheim's wartime activity, and Simitis' policy seemed to be a way to obtain morally due money for Greece from the Germans without much difficulty. Nobody in this period except a few financial zealots in Brussels was interested in statistical detail. At the time of the Euro initiative in 2001, the fact that Greek budget data were significantly 'massaged' to meet the Maastricht criteria did not seem to be a major issue for those involved. The German Foreign Minister Hans-Dietrich Genscher had recently acquired a holiday home in Greece and relations seemed to be excellent. Germany and France themselves had difficulties with the Maastricht budget control criteria. The way seemed clear for a rapid and thorough modernization of Greece within a socialist project that was functional and Europe-wide.

What did Europe mean to ordinary Greeks in this period? To those of Simitis' anti-dictatorship generation, who in their early lives had been excluded from many jobs as a result of the 'bad biography' problems of their fathers and mothers (Simitis' father had been a minister in the EAM/communist 'mountain government' in the Axis occupation period), Europe meant legitimate and deserved modernity, as opposed to the 'backwardness' of Greece. It was a highly technocratic vision, on the surface a universe away from the nineteenth-century cultural concerns of those German intellectuals, for whom, as the philosopher Nietzsche pointed out, ancient Greek culture became a religion. Germany then drew widely on ancient Greece, as in aspects of the tragic drama models for Wagner's operas. The gold of the Ring of the Nieblungs was replaced in the late twentieth century with the Euro banknotes, but unlike the gold in the opera, there was an apparently infinite supply. Modern Greece needed funding and loans from Germany and northern Europe, a utilitarian project, and classical languages and mythology seemed redundant and 'superseded'. For the associates of Simitis, a new vocabulary and rhetoric of politics was available, which appeared to embody cost-free modernization of Greece. The alchemist's formula had triumphed. The bare limestone rocks on the Greek hillsides had been transformed and had become stores of value.

But the electorate did not quite see things this way. Corruption and clientism were beginning to run riot and the working class was not seeing much of the new money. The Greek upper middle class was often obsessed with consumerist greed. Families who needed maybe two cars owned six or seven. Rural depopulation speeded up as the Common Agricultural Policy marketing rules drove small farmers off the land and into urban poverty. PASOK's achievements in Brussels and Germany were being increasingly taken for granted. And the Greek public which had not enjoyed higher education was largely unaware of the wider world. As the cultural critic and philosopher Constantine Cavarnous has observed, Greeks have in general little appetite for determinist ideas and the ceaseless secret planning of the unelected Eurocracy around the new currency attracted little interest in Athens. The growing atmosphere of national optimism in the middle class and wealthy strata coincided with the end of years of PASOK government and the arrival of a New Democracy government which had natural links with the Republican administration of George Bush in the United States. Another rhetoric of politics was suddenly available after 9/11, that of the war against terrorism. The ever-present fear of Islam, a thread in Greek political psychology traditionally focused on Turkey, was reactivated. It would drive Greek politics to the right, assisted by genuine popular anger at the violent assaults of the 17 November terrorist organization. The PASOK rhetoric already seemed outmoded; as long ago as 21 June 1996, soon after Andreas Papandreou's death, the *Athens News* newspaper had commented that PASOK was 'a ruling party in search of fresh slogans'. It had not found them. Yet Greece was joining the wider world community in the globalizing mainstream, it seemed, using an international currency and sharing the wider objectives of the international community in the period of the 'war on terrorism'.

A symbol would be the staging of the long awaited Olympic Games in 2004 in Athens. It is impossible to understand the underlying causes of the decline of Greece in the present period without reference to this Olympic Games and its background. The staging of the Olympics and the real costs involved have become a hypersensitive subject in Greece, and discussion of the subject has been difficult. Why is this so? The most persuasive case has been put forward by Greek-American author Alexander Kitreoff in his book *Wrestling with the Ancients: Modern Greek Identity and the Olympics*. He sees the Olympic Games as part of a Modern Greek historical narrative of invented tradition, 'whose complexities surpass the issues of sport or athletics alone'. The Olympic Games were an important step on the road to the abandonment of economic reason. In any society, capitalist or communist, there are accountants and bills have to paid accurately, but it is a law of life that was abolished for a while in Greece prior to the 2004 Olympics. The staging of the first modern Olympic Games in Athens in 1896 was a symbol of the success of the process of national independence and reunification that had gone on for the previous three generations. Greece had more than doubled in size between 1835 and 1895. The staging of the Olympics for Greeks in 2004 was not only in this tradition of national redefinition but a part of the continual dialogue within Hellenism between its ancient and modern components. Greece acts within the international Olympic movement as a guardian of ancient tradition, in terms of a very specific endorsement of an ideal vision of the vitality of secular classicism, untainted by the passage of late antiquity and the detraction of the physical in late antiquity and Byzantium.

In material and workaday Greece, by 2001 progress with the Olympic project was not good, despite Euro entry. The Simitis-led PASOK government was in crisis. Terrorism remained a threat and was changing the international rhetoric of politics. Thirty-three Greek-Americans had lost their lives in the World Trade Centre attacks in September that year. St Nicholas Greek Orthodox Church in New York, one of the oldest in the US, had been obliterated by the collapse of the South Tower. Yet at first it all seemed a very long way away from Athens, where terrorism and social protest seemed to be on the back foot. In 2002 the security outlook had apparently brightened. The process of arrests of the 17 November (17N) Group had begun, accompanied by a good deal of grandstanding and self-congratulation by British Scotland Yard officers who were involved. US officials' views among those in the security world were more circumspect. The 'spin' factor in the press coverage and exaggeration of what was really achieved has been collaborated by Wikileaks material indicating the views of US anti-terrorism experts in 2008 that N17 had only been weakened by the 2002 arrests, and that it remained a threat. In prison, 17N members retained their security mechanisms and were 'intent on revitalizing' their organization. The American security agencies had information that key 17N weapons had not been recovered and information from prisoners that important 17N people and assets were still active and at large. Yet at the time this did not seem to matter, as cosmic optimism affected the world of anti-terrorism in 2002 in Greece as it also affected the economy.

It was nevertheless at the time of the Olympics site construction that problems of economics, finance and debt began to reappear again in the mainstream Greek media, after a long absence. Clouds were forming over the economic landscape. Economic difficulties began to intrude into public discourse, and government life. Above all, the budgets for venue construction were running out of control and in 2002-3 it was far from clear that construction work would be completed in time for the event. The enormous financial burdens of hosting the Games were beginning to take their toll on the body politic of a small country, not only in terms of current expenditure, but also at a deeper psychological level. It seemed as though in Greece money did not matter if the project was desirable. Economists disagree about how far the direct costs of the Olympics contributed to the later debt crisis but what is unanswerable is that normal government financial controls began to collapse in the 2003-4 period as international pressure on Greece rose for Olympic work to be completed on time. Controls were never restored after the Games, as first PASOK and then New Democracy in government effectively abandoned budget scrutiny. The revenue running costs of new capital projects such as the Athens Metro seem hardly to have been considered. The immensely powerful lobby of the civil engineering industry within the two big parties feasted on the Olympic development money and became ever more powerful. They had grown fat on a flood of European Union Structural Fund money over the last five years. The Athens joke of the time was that although Greeks had named most possible systems of government such as oligarchy and monarchy, there was now a new term to be coined, of government by civil engineering contractors. The seeds of an expenditure bubble were being planted. In the background was a gradual loss of international competitiveness to low-wage nations like India and China that was destroying what remained of traditional manufacturing in areas like Greek textiles. The Olympics were also a bonanza for many German engineering companies in Greece.

The commitment to the Olympics project was a symbol of the rightward movement of the government, and in particular, it appealed to the American corporations whose major players connected with big sport like Nike and Coca-Cola had become sponsors and advertisers. The Olympics embodied the culture of health, anti-smoking campaigning, intense and unbridled Darwinian competition and many other neo-conservative social objectives. The Olympics could give Greece a new and respectable international image after the anti-Americanism of the PASOK years. Yet a degree of national pride was involved in the exercise that crossed political boundaries. Distinguished US diplomats with a very deep knowledge of Greece like ex-Ambassador Tom Miller knew perfectly well the risks in staging the Games in Athens but also felt that the Greeks deserved their Games and should not be obstructed from having them. Most leftists in PASOK felt exactly the same.

Although Andreas Papandreou had no interest in sport, he presided over the original Athens application to stage the 2004 Games in 1996. His son George Papandreou when he was Foreign Minister did much of the spadework to bring the Games to Athens in the period running up to the International Olympic Committee's decision in favour of Greece in September 1997. There was a substantial 'London' factor in the Greek decision victory. George Papandreou's closest adviser was Alex Rondos, a South African origin Greek with extensive British connections, and he was later to play a central role in many later PASOK foreign policy developments. He helped the Athens government to a more positive evaluation of the Kosova Albanians' case in the war that was then developing in 1997, and was a well informed and capable individual.

But he was nonetheless seen in Greece as 'London's man', and with the difficult history after the Second World War still alive in many older minds that meant a link with the exiled and still unpopular Greek monarchy. Rondos was later to help organize meetings of the Serbian opposition to Slobodan Milosevic in Athens that were widely believed to be funded by London Greek money. Later the London link took on a more tangible form, as the role of the royalists with London backgrounds in securing the Olympics nomination showed.

For PASOK there was little alternative but to swim with the Olympic stream. It seemed to present several different opportunities for the nation. The Olympics project was a way to appropriate the traditional rightist themes of identity and history and classicism, where previously the more traditional Greek left had always treated classical Greece with the suspicion that it embodied the core values of the right. Left-wing Greeks are often much more at home with the Byzantine element in their historical tradition than the classicism of fifth-century Athens. At a deeper level, the political elite in Athens have never been slow to sacrifice the interests of living modern Greeks in favour of the dead ancients, as Oxford scholar Peter Mackridge has observed when he noted how the Vrysaki quarter in Athens was demolished and the inhabitants ejected in the 1930s to make way for the excavation of the ancient Agora (market) area by the American School of Classical Studies. In the same way, in the previous century, numerous distinguished Byzantine churches were demolished in the development of Athens after 1833 because they impeded the view of classical ruins.

The marked discouragement of rational discussion about the 1997-2001 'Olympic period' does not therefore take place because there is a direct and exponential financial link between Olympic debt and the current Euro crisis. The Olympics were very expensive and not enough visitors came to see them, but in a healthy economy this can be managed. The wealthy Canadian city of Montreal is still paying the bills for its 1976 Olympics many years later. The Athens Olympics period is important because it indicates the failure of a species of capitalist modernization in Greece based on debt finance where the host economy was too small for the burdens involved. In Greece the political elite privately believed the bill would ultimately be picked up elsewhere.

In this, the government was reproducing at international level much of the traditional *modus operandi* of the Greek peasant or citizen at any time in history who when faced with a problem, seeks a powerful patron, or person of influence, who will help him find a solution. The leaders of the European Union outside Germany never seem to have never understood until the current catastrophe how they were being groomed for that role by the Greek elite in the two main parties, as powerful international patrons who would 'fix things' in the financial sense for the Greek citizen, and remove the burden of the difficult past history. It is a pity that members of the European Central Bank, or the Commission, have probably never watched a traditional Greek shadow puppet play, where the cunning Greek *Karagiozis* outwits the Turkish overlord and runs off with the kudos, the moral victory, the joke, and most of all, the vizier's money. Many features of the plays can be immediately recognised in Greek-EU current turmoil.

Turkish viziers lose gold in these folk narratives. In the current crisis, foreign observers are often puzzled about what has happened to the billions of marks and then Euros that poured into Greece after 1981, and most of all in recent years. There are some tangible monuments, such as the great bridge over the Gulf of Corinth at Rio and Antirrio, which has displaced the old ferry with its colourful Roma bands and grubby smoke-filled lounges. There are the Athens pedestrian and Metro schemes, which have produced underground stations as beautiful and useful as any in the world. The number of universities has doubled in thirty years, although not the number of jobs for graduates. Litter bins recycle goods from households like a German city, although much of what is collected is never recycled because there is no recycling industry in much of the country. The VAT tax is collected with the rate marked on receipts as in Britain but not much of it ever reaches the government because businesses keep two sets of books, one for the tax officials and one for the business itself. This was a tradition in Greece and elsewhere in the Balkans that goes back to the predations of the Ottoman tax collectors. Greeks have been understandably blamed for tax evasion in the contemporary crisis but it can hardly be a main cause, or the Greek economy would not have looked as good as it did at various times in the recent past. Not much tax was paid between 2001 and 2004 but no one in Brussels seemed to be concerned about it then when the growth numbers looked good. In remote and small communities there is little incentive to pay taxes if the government does little or nothing for you and your family. The traditions of a remote, arbitrary and authoritarian local state were very bad throughout Greece until 1981 and the first PASOK reform programme. This abolished the archaic early nineteenth-century system adopted from post-Napoleonic France of the Prefect, a figure with vast and often undefined powers. The PASOK concept of the local state much more resembled the traditional designation of the Greek father, 'the man who has his hand in his pocket', and who would spend to enable the poorer strata have better lives.

In reality, much of the EU money goes to continue what there is of a welfare state in Greece and so is spent on revenue costs. This was built in the 1980s after the intense class struggles of the 1970s. Public debt was about 22 per cent of GDP in 1980 which rose to 58 per cent in 1985 and 79 per cent in 1990. It is not a coincidence that the national pension fund is now one of the most vulnerable aspects of government finances in the current crisis, and hospitals have been the hardest hit public institutions. Before PASOK and its European achievements in the early years, female country dwellers had no old age pension, for instance. Again, this hardly seems to have been understood in northern Europe in the early years of Greek membership, in that the financial relationship with Greece was based upon what would have to be eternal internal transfers within the Union to the poorest members, a socialist project in every way. There are many reasons why this crisis was made in the way it has been, and has been so protracted but one of the most important is that the underlying relationship between Greece and Germany in the Genscher-Simitis period was conditioned by conscious and unconscious socialist political assumptions that have never been articulated in the rhetoric of the media and politics outside a very limited circle, and that mostly in Germany. The socialist assumptions inscribed in the Greek-German relationship then have now been overtaken within the Brussels political elite by the current neo-liberal orthodoxy and social conservatism. Germany is central to the future of Greece as the original deals were made there, long before reunification, when Bonn was still a small-town capital and before Berlin was a megacity on the world stage.

Some scholars studying Greek culture have speculated, in the footsteps of the early twentieth-century Hellenist turned critic of Greece Arnold Toynbee, that the absence of much real understanding of the past was an asset to the classical Greeks, but this is not an advantage open to contemporary Greeks who are saturated with knowledge by their education system and oral tradition of their history. This may or may not be the case, but it is surely a pity that many northern European political and elite leaders have lost touch with any sense of Greek history and tradition. Classical studies are in a defensive and often beleaguered state in otherwise cultured and progressive nations. If European politicians had more contact with the Greek past, it would not be so easy for them to have believed in the current rhetoric where Greeks are being made a scapegoat for the failures that were always inherent in the Euro project from its foundation. The Euro project is ultimately doomed because it is impossible to chain together

27 different economies to one currency and one central financial institution without any tax or revenue raising capacity. The fact that it is doomed to fail was not the fault of the Greeks. Their fault was to believe in it more than most European nations did.

Yet for such an educated and political people as the Greeks, critical perceptions were available. Unease at the direction of events led to the downfall of PASOK in the general elections of 2005 and the replacement of the government by a New Democracy successor. The Prime Minister, Kostas Karamanlis, was the son of a famous and distinguished father but in a similar manner to George Papandreou this also created difficulties for the son. As head of a powerful *parataxis*, a political dynasty based on his long-prominent family, he inherited a series of high expectations from the public but a host of unaffordable spending commitments. His reaction was generally to pretend the issues did not exist, and carry on borrowing. Nevertheless it was still a time of easy money and funds were still flowing to Greece, although the national debt as a proportion of GDP was beginning to rise rapidly. High local prices caused by the inexorable rise of the Euro against the dollar and other currencies were taking their toll on tourist revenue. The effect of Euro membership on the economically central tourist industry never seems to have been considered anywhere in Brussels before Greek Euro zone membership.

International competition for tourist visitors was also intensifying. The fascination with the new Euro money in Greece did not last long after the early days when people turned coins over wonderingly to see which EU nation had made them. Cheaper long haul flights were taking the backpacking young away from Greece, and motoring holidays from central Europe have only partly recovered from the strategic setbacks of the ex-Yugoslav wars period. The modernization of the Turkish tourist industry was providing strong competition in the East Mediterranean region, where Turkey's lira, as a non-Euro currency, could generally undercut any Greek price. Although Athens' relations with Ankara were improving, the defence budget remained high and New Democracy initiated expensive new military equipment programmes, mainly from French and German suppliers. The security bills inherent in the post 9/11 world continued to grow as elsewhere in the world, coupled with increasingly strident European Union demands for better border controls against illegal migrants. At every juncture, costs and expenses in the Greek economy were rising and in most areas revenue was stagnant or falling. At the same time, even for many Philhellene visitors, there was a sense of overall mismanagement affecting daily life, so that buses that used to run reliably did not appear, and islands which used to have plentiful fish supplies allowed them to be fished out for short term gains. The peaceful idyllic Greece that intellectual visitors had always enjoyed and had been the traditional backbone of tourism was sometimes destroyed by drunken youths on noisy jet skis. The response of the government was to effectively abandon the mass market to the Turks, Egyptians and Thais, while seeking to develop more upmarket specialized tourism. This was not a mistaken perspective but Greece seemed to be swimming always against the stream, with rising costs and stagnant standards and facilities. European Union legislation and funding has brought many good things in this period, such as the arrival of ecotourism and the restoration of historic town centres, but European Union visitors have not always followed in any great numbers.

In the near-abroad world up to and after 2001, considerable progress was also being made from the point of view of Athens and traditional Greek foreign policy objectives, and this contributed to the atmosphere of complacency and neglect of deepening economic questions. In the Balkans, Greek regional economic leadership was reasserting itself after the removal of the Milosevic regime in Serbia and the quest for EU membership by ex-Yugoslav new nations. Greece seemed to provide a successful developmental model. As 2003 wore on, it became clear that the divided island of Cyprus had fulfilled all the necessary formal conditions for EU membership, and with several key EU governments strongly in favour of Cyprus membership, the absence of a solution to the island's political problems would not be an obstacle. The interminable negotiations over the separation of the communities which the United Nations had brokered for many years resulted in a referendum in April 2004 on the Annan Plan, which Turkish Cypriots supported (as many saw it legitimizing the division of the island) but it was rejected by the Greek Cypriots. Their vote was not taken as an obstacle by the European Union, and Cyprus duly became an EU member that May. This was a great victory for the traditional right in Greek politics that in the past had supported *enosis*, union with Greece, and where there were strong traditional and emotional attachments. It also meant, from all points of view in Athens, that there were now two Greek-speaking states in the European Union, and the energy, money and commercial and military importance of the Cypriots could only assist Greek foreign policy objectives in Brussels. With the strong communist party in Cyprus and developing Russian business links, the Marxist left in Greece also found much to praise in Cyprus developments that year. It was becoming a great triumph;

the alchemist had made gold out of Euro paper notes. It seemed as if Greece had been able to turn its traditional burden of a weak paper currency and debt into prosperity and economic growth.

Yet the power of the alchemist and rhetorician was transient, as recent developments have shown. Rhetoric and spin are bound by history. The nation appeared to have united around the Olympics as much as it ever might, and yet the ingredients for a crisis that could lead to a new national schism based on a revival of class conflict were becoming present. The cheap commodity-promoting physicality of the commercialized Olympics was a shadow of the Greek spirit.

TWO

From Greek Crisis to European Crisis: 2009-2012

'In the revolution, not even a shop window will be broken.'
Aleka Papariga, KKE General Secretary, December 2008

Nineteenth-century German intellectual culture was obsessed with Greece as part of a search for order. Greece was mostly ancient but also modern. Sometimes the two met. A German king had reigned on the newly-independent Greek throne; German archaeologists like Heinrich Schliemann at Troy made astonishing discoveries from antiquity. In the Peloponnese the Olympia archaeological site and its wonderful museum echoed with German links. German universities provided the model for classical philological studies. German cities were remodelled during nineteenth-century national unification on severe neo-classical architectural models. It seemed as though Germany knew everything about Greece that could be known, and was a most admiring friend and acolyte.

Now, at the beginning of the twenty-first century, most Greeks believe nothing whatsoever is understood about Hellenism in Germany. A long suppressed popular resentment against Germany has surfaced all over Greece in the current crisis, from octogenarian anti-Axis resistance hero Manolis Glezos joining militant street demonstrations in Athens under banners with anti-German slogans to restaurants refusing to serve German customers. In Evia in the summer of 2011, a Hamburg couple waited hours for a meal, only to be given an empty plate with a sheet of paper with '1940' written on it. They left immediately. Elsewhere on the island, a bishop offered to exorcise an ex-German-owned holiday flat so it would be spiritually clean, a *catharsis*, and thus suitable for a Greek family to inhabit after it was sold. Many Greeks, including the educated, also believe the large Turkish *Gastarbeiter* turned resident community in Germany has had some influence on Berlin policy. The Turks wield some power now in mainstream German political parties and most of them have little liking for Greece or sympathy with its problems. From the Berlin perspective and that of the German tabloid press, all this blame seems bitterly undeserved; in their view at least the depths of the Greek crisis was clearly understood at an early stage, instead of the shallow wishful thinking that pervaded many EU capitals in the 2009-2010 period.

Yet however bad the current crisis becomes, a period of de facto German or EU control of Greece is not a practical possibility. The European Union does not have a government or administrative cohort of its own that can be imposed on problem member nations. The issue serves as a psychological metaphor for the general loss of sovereignty involved in the current debt and financial bailout discussions, and for the failure of the European Union over the years, in Greece and elsewhere, to articulate a popular and credible alternative identity to that of component national states. What beckons? Greeks see money still draining out of their society daily. A return to a period resembling that of the 1950s may occur, a time described by the Australian historian of modern Greece David Close as one of 'dependent development'. In his view, between 1950 and 1973, formal political independence was maintained under a cloak of economic subservience to the US and the West and electoral and other political freedoms were in serious deficit. The culmination of this process was the Colonels' military junta between 1968 and 1974. The EU now has to stay on a liberal constitutional path and this removes the authoritarian options.

When did the fissile development stage of the current stage of the Greek crisis begin? Most orthodox financial commentary dates it from early 2009. The general banking crisis that culminated in the end of Lehman Brothers in New York had dominated the media in 2008-9 and its universal scale meant that little attention was paid to the problems of weaker and smaller countries within the international financial system. Sovereign debt was not then a public issue, compared to the stability of the mainstream investment and commercial banks. British newspaper headlines had been dominated by news about the aftermath of the crash of Northern Rock. The Greek economy contracted by a mere 0.2 per cent in 2008, but the economy nevertheless went into recession, like many others. It was not news. This was at the end of fourteen years of continuous growth, and did not seem critical in Athens; nevertheless by the end of 2009 debt stood at 127 per cent of GDP, with rapidly rising borrowing costs. Tourist numbers were very poor, continuing a process of decline that had been in motion since as long ago as 1995 and which had accelerated after Euro entry. The scenario that would dominated those years was now in place. Travelling in northern Greece in September of that year, just before PASOK returned to power, I discovered there was suddenly a shortage of ready money in society. A bank in Kastoria seemed to have run out completely. Insecurity was spreading to the moneychangers on the street corner by the lake, who would not take large denomination Euro notes. ATMs were often empty. Yet the walls of the town were plastered with PASOK campaign posters claiming, 'There is Money!' It was a strange election.

In Athens in October 2009 the newly returned government of George Papandreou promised, and started, an 'opening of the books', which revealed substantial statistical manipulation and a burden of rapidly rising debt. The national responsibility was linked to the boom in consumer borrowing in the Euro membership years, and the New Democracy loss of financial control and the issue of the funding of the Olympic Games was clear. The original cost estimate for the Olympic Games was about US$6 billion, the actual cost turned out to be US$15 billion or more. Vast sums of international funds had been ploughed into Euro-denominated Greek government bonds in previous years, ever since Greek entry to the Euro zone in 2001. Yet the money seemed to have vanished. The government response was to raise taxes and begin an 'austerity' programme, which was strongly criticized in parliament by New Democracy as well as the left. The seeds of the current crisis of Greek capitalism were being sown. There was no preparation of public opinion for this bad news, another significant factor in how the crisis was made. Although Greek workers and peasants were to be the victims of the imposed austerity, they were not responsible for it, and they knew that clearly.

A very strange and frightening situation was developing. Those who could remove their money from Greek banks were beginning to do so; it was being replaced by effectively virtual money which hardly ever found its way into the hands of the ordinary person, with Greek banks buying more and more government bonds with money that in origin had come from the same government. Bond interest rates escalated. The poison pill was in the system. But Greece was a small country and attention was still focused elsewhere, although Athens was moving into the crosshairs of the rating agencies. In that month of October 2009, Greek government debt received its first major downgrades from Moody's. The sovereign debt crisis that was beginning to reach Greece intensified suddenly the following month with the bust of the Dubai property boom and associated shocks. A Fitch downgrade of Greek debt to BBB+ soon followed and the economic crisis affecting the ordinary worker was beginning to bring protestors onto the streets. On 11 December a Standard Bank report speculated that Greece and Ireland might soon have to leave the Eurozone. To the ears of economic historians, it was a familiar music. It is arguable, as the Swiss investor Felix Zulauf has observed, that Greece has been in some kind of default on its debts for about 105 of the last 200 years. The days of alchemy were over (again). But what was to come after them?

If the first years of the twenty-first century had been the time of the alchemist, the bankers wanted Greece to be rescued by the careful scientific practice of the financial chemist, rebalancing the system like the kidneys balance chemistry in the human body. The only political certainty would be that as the cuts intensified and more and more public sector workers lost their jobs, PASOK would find itself in serious difficulty. Government supervised by accountants is not the PASOK ethos. Although New Democracy and the small parties have their patronage networks, none of them remotely compare to the labyrinthine and complex PASOK 'coat tails' of patronage, handouts, bribes and favours that Greeks call 'Rustaferi', a word dating back to Ottoman times, along with straightforward corruption. Yet extreme moralism in finance would work against stability, as international capitalism needs a social democratic party as an alternative government in Athens. The figures that were beginning to emerge were nonetheless extraordinarily high, with Transparency International estimating that bribery cost Greece no less than US$632 million in 2010, while 75 per cent of the people interviewed in the survey thought corruption was increasing. About one in ten people admitted to bribing a public servant to obtain something, often to jump a queue, in the last twelve months.

This international agenda with its strong northern European moralistic content (after all the Roman and Byzantine Empires had bought and sold public offices and jobs for over fifteen hundred years and had great civilizations) was beginning to seep into mainstream world public opinion, and to be Greek has resumed its old sixteenth-century British meaning of being generally dishonest and 'tricky'. There was no organized media campaign prior to default in the international press against Athens but it worked that way without a public relations agency spinning in the background. The vocabulary of entrenched Greek corruption had entered the international rhetoric of the crisis.

It is ironic that much of this rhetoric emanates from Brussels, a city with a notorious 'favours' culture, with a country, Belgium, that is itself fractured on linguistic and cultural lines.

In the eyes of the radical students, criminals and Bohemian anarchists of the Exarchia district of Athens who were at the forefront of the violent street demonstrations in Athens in July 2010, these moral concerns making leading article fodder in northern European newspapers were far away. Exarchia resembles the old Five Points of nineteenth-century New York as a quarter where anything goes. There is a reason for this. Local people have been resisting gentrification through central urban planning directives for many years. A strongly oppositional and confrontational political culture had developed. The anarchists' priority was, and is, to fight the cops, as visible and local representatives of the capitalist state. They see Exarchia as liberated 'radical space'.

In the previous winter of 2008-9 there had been widespread violence in central Athens after the murder of Alexandros Grigoropoulos, a student resident in Ermou Street in the Plaka district, at the hands of the police. The radical and oppositional street culture that then was the preserve of a minority of unemployed ex-students and social outsiders caused considerable damage and upended temporarily the statue of Churchill's clerical magnate Archbishop Damaskianos in Cathedral Square but had seemed a self-contained phenomenon. Now the Athens street and, more importantly, streets all over Greece were changing as gradually more and more mainstream people became involved in ever-growing demonstrations. Banks were blown up in the summer of 2010. A sense of looming national malaise was intensified by the raging forest fires that, as in 2007, destroyed thousands of acres of forests throughout Attica and other parts of Greece in August 2009. The international image was of a country that was allowing speculators to start fires to provide building plots and then was unable to put them out. In the natural landscape, it was a symbol of the bonfire of the financial vanities in the Greek government bond market.

It seemed time for a new politics and new politicians. To the young, it also seemed a new modernization was needed, that elusive quest that had dominated Greek twentieth-century history. But the roots of the radical parties of the left in memory lay in the Civil War period, a time of great pain and suffering, the *emfylios*, the war of Brother against Brother. To many the Marxists also represented the failure of a tradition. The parties of the left had nevertheless been gaining considerable strength in Greek large cities in recent years with the decline of PASOK in government and as a radical party, and in some parts of Athens and

Thessaloniki the communist KKE and other left-wingers like the newly emerging SYRIZA led by Alexis Tsipras were polling together as much as a quarter of the vote. The KNE communist youth organization had grow to numbers not seen since the post-junta years. The KKE had successfully modernized itself, then with a charismatic and very clever female leader in Aleka Papariaga, modern websites, a KKE television channel and many new members from among the disaffected young. Its old-fashioned internal structure which for so long had seemed outmoded became a strength as alienated oppositionists sought a firm political base. SYRIZA offered a political home for a variety of other non-aligned leftists. Once unorganized immigrant workers from the millions who had flooded into Greece were joining parties and trades unions, to the extent that the KKE now has Albanian and Kurdish-membership sections. The Euro-communist SYRIZA attracted those from more culturally diverse backgrounds, although their capacity for practical political organization was then limited. There was, and remains, little difference between the political outlooks of rank and file KKE and SYRIZA activists, and loyalties are often formed by whether in previous generations family members went into exile after the Civil War ended in 1949, or carried on the struggle within Greece.

In the campaigns of those years it was initially thought that the private sector trades unions would not support the public sector unions, with their almost exclusively Marxist leadership, but the speed and momentum of events on the ground drew them together in common solidarity. Class politics had revived in Western Europe, with a dramatic unveiling of a banner across the Acropolis, with hammer and sickle and the slogan 'PEOPLES OF EUROPE RISE UP'. The media-savvy KKE had written it in English, as well as Greek. Modernist Greek communism had arrived at one level, but in another dimension the KKE completed the rehabilitation of Nicos Zarchariadis, its controversial hardliner leader, from post-Civil War days.

The previous months of 2010 had been dominated by the revelation in the international press of the degree of Greek debt concealment, which in turn began to affect European bank credit ratings. Orthodox finance demanded cuts in government expenditure and mass sackings of public sector workers. Important foreign policy success for PASOK and for the region was symbolized by the very effective visit to Turkish Prime Minister Recep Erdogan in May to sign a swathe of unprecedented bilateral cooperation agreements, but these were eclipsed by the fiscal and economic crisis. In the blue skies over the Aegean, less changed. The daily tussle for airspace violations between the Turkish and Greek air force rolls on, with near-misses at regular intervals. Despite the diplomatic gains at the meeting, little happened to encourage the Greek government to cut the rising defence and security budgets

In Brussels a Greek bailout plan was developing. A meeting of the French and German leadership before the European Union heads of government summit put together a deal, an aid package of loans and a degree of International Monetary Fund economic supervision. Only after it was signed did German Chancellor Angela Merkel first raise the issue of Greece leaving the Eurozone, and with that event, the need for the banks involved in Greek debt to take a massive write-down (haircut) on the value of their debt. The current script that has dominated the last five years was being written. A new public rhetoric of the crisis was developing, a language of cuts, balanced budgets and deficit reduction and a return to 'normality' and growth. History was once again being abolished, as only those with no knowledge of the history of Greek indebtedness could use these words. Not all budgets were subject to these reductions. In May 2010 the new defence budget still showed rising expenditure, much of it going on new weapons from Germany and France. At just over 3 per cent of GDP, the Greek budget was then one of the highest per capita in the West, higher than countries involved in international conflicts such as France.

By summer and autumn 2010, the 'soft default' process had begun in practice, but that was not allowed to be mentioned within the public language of the European Union. The rating agencies and the markets did not share this vision. Standard & Poor's were writing by April 2011 that a 50-70 per cent 'haircut' would be needed on Greek bonds and there was a one in three chance of a final default. The bailout was clearly designed to reinforce the stability and clout of the Papandreou government but in practice set in motion the forces that would destroy it. The realistic view of S&P was a prominent indicator but what is significant is that nearly all the information on which it was based had been in the public domain for at least the previous year and much of it since 2009 or before. Greece has been *de facto* insolvent since at least that period. The exposure of French, German and other banks to that insolvency has been continually rising. The advocates of an early return of Greece to the old drachma currency and exit from the Eurozone were criticized in 2009-10 for pessimism and failure to understand or believe in the Euro and the European Union but in reality the relevance of raising this issue has been borne out by events. A Greek Euro exit in 2009 followed by a generous European aid and reconstruction programme could have done much for the real economy and confined the crisis but it would have meant major losses for the banks and bankers. The punishment of the Greek people to protect these interests had begun.

In practice, as American financial commentator Edward Harrison has observed, Greece has been in a debtors' prison, with creditors seeking to get as much out of Greece as they can before default, or in metaphorical Dickensian terms before that catastrophe for creditors, the death of the debtor. The elite belief seems to have been that the Greek people would be a largely passive onlooker to this process, while the assumption in Brussels seems to have been since 2009 that while there might be demonstrations in some streets, as there was when Argentina defaulted in 1998-2001, they would not affect the stability of the main body politic. This has been a very serious miscalculation on the part of the EU, as the election of SYRIZA to power demonstrated in 2015. The size and efficiency of the Greek trades unions and the left-wing parties has been underestimated and the popular resistance to growing impoverishment has been sustained.

Many foreign observers do not seem to have understood that the extreme centralization of Greek society and politics upon Athens and one or two other large cities, itself a product of the rapid urbanization of the last generations, has dramatically reduced the power of the lower middle class in the provinces who have been a bedrock of conservatism and conformity in Greece since Ottoman times. Economic change since 1980 has meant that swathes of little shops and local businesses have been closed by the advent of the foreign-owned supermarket and the out of town shopping mall. The last three crisis years have rapidly accentuated and speeded up this process. New Democracy has been weakened in this process, but not to the degree of PASOK whose opinion poll ratings at the dropped into single figures, and did not recover in the 2015 election.

The people have moved into activity because as unemployment has risen, during the crisis prices have continued to rise, particularly food and energy prices, in some cases because of world prices moving up but also because of a string of EU-IMF imposed taxes on the essentials of daily life and associated transport and infrastructure costs. Foreign tourist visits were reduced then by bad publicity with the street violence in Athens and price rises. In a despairing analysis of the situation in a speech in Munich in April 2010, ex-Prime Minister Simitis had described the threat to the 27-member Union and called for greater central coordination of economic policy but was short on policy suggestions on how this might be achieved. In the same city, less than twenty years before, his shared Euro federalist rhetoric with his German partners had seemed easy – now there was little shared language at all.

The Crisis Intensifies: International Intervention in 2011

The governmental crisis came to a head during 2011 when it became clear to all concerned that neither the first bailout (March 2010) nor the second (June/July 2011) had worked. Debt contagion within the Eurozone had reached Italy during the summer with soaring yields on Italian bonds as well as those of minor nations like Ireland and Portugal, and the collapse of the Eurozone beckoned. In the eyes of the international community – if that term has any meaning in this context – the removal of disliked national leaderships and the implementation of reforms by a technocratic government seemed to provide an answer. History was beginning to provide some disturbing symbols from the past where Greek democracy has been threatened. As in the height of the 1930s Depression, an unexpected series of events suddenly destroyed a once honoured Greek political leader. As Mark Mazower has written, then it led to the crisis election of 1936 and the subsequent intervention of the military. But from the point of view of the international bankers, none of this history mattered, including the democratic legitimacy of the Greek and Italian governments. However unsatisfactory they might be from many points of view, they were at least democratically elected. The prime ministers who followed were not elected by anybody.

Silvio Berlusconi was removed in Italy by 11 November, and PASOK leader George Papandreou was forced to resign in Greece in dramatic events at the same time. Papandreou was replaced by the unelected financial technocrat, Lucas Papademos. He was the chosen instrument of the international banking oligarchs to impose near-colonial status, as Larry Elliott of the London *Guardian* wrote on 20 February 2012, several months later. As it was Greece, the politics of the street had determined the details of the agenda although it appears Washington had been thinking of deposing George Papandreou for several months before his final days. Relations between the Obama administration and the PASOK government had been tetchy since the refusal of the Americans to make a big purchase of Greek government bonds in the summer of 2010. Papandreou hoped he could draw on the capital of important Greek-American lobbies in Chicago who had helped Obama's presidential race, and get them to mobilize Greek-Americans to put pressure on Obama, but the Greek leader was to be disappointed. His visit there was a failure. The crisis ground on. The dramatic climax in autumn 2011 was, fittingly, on the northern Greek streets, on the Via Egnetia, where so many armies have marched throughout millennia. A military parade scheduled for 'Oxi Day' on 27 October is held every year in Thessaloniki and celebrates Greek resistance to the Axis invasion. It is in normal times a cheerful patriotic event where Greece's ill-paid and often forgotten soldiers parade in their best kit and drive armoured vehicles through the city. It had to be cancelled when faced with a massive counter-demonstration by workers and students. In a febrile atmosphere, the Greek president was insulted as protests by Greeks against the austerity measures demanded by foreign lenders blocked the parade. Demonstrators shouted 'traitor' at President Karolos Papoulias and other officials. Similar protests took place at smaller parades across Greece. It was the first time the full parade in Thessaloniki had ever been cancelled and it was a humiliating day for the military, with Greek army commandos shouting, 'Macedonia is Greek' and other slogans as they dispersed, and, 'Greek blood flows through Macedonian veins. We won't give the name to the Skopeans.' Leftists called for the downfall of the 'plutokratia', the plutocracy, the rich and, above all, the bankers. The Thessaloniki police were professional and well prepared, and had already seen in September 2010 a major confrontation when Prime Minister Papandreou came to the city to open a trade exhibition. The city centre was then locked down successfully by heavily armed paramilitaries. In the eyes of the radical students and young, it looked as though a police coup had replaced the threat of an army coup. In 2011 the police lost control of the streets and the lockdown failed.

The Thessaloniki street voiced several rhetorical patterns, but all of them were leading to an assumption of looming social conflict. Many slogans called for bank nationalization without compensation. International alarm bells were ringing at the direction of these events. The 1967 military coup had originated in northern Greece, and although the army had been downsized and brought under civilian political control since those days, a nasty echo of the past arose. It appears the United States was well informed about the risks of an army coup attempt that were emerging, the Europeans less so. Most diplomats and intelligence officers spent little time in northern Greece, old Cold War cultural institutions like the British Council and American library in Thessaloniki had been closed down in the years of optimism, and little was known of the violent confrontational atmosphere there.

The foreigners' 'troika' in Athens needed a scapegoat and the figure of George Papandreou as PASOK leader was the obvious target. He was forced to resign and make way for an open 'bankers' government' under unelected technocratic leadership. It was a national humiliation, but perhaps an event that had long been coming. As long ago as 1993, Adam Nicholson had observed that the end of the Cold War had made the Greek national project much less important and interesting to the

Western Allies. Yet it had taken many years for this perception to be understood well in Greece. He wrote in the London *Spectator* that year that 'Greece, from being One of Us since the War, has become one of Them (Balkans).' The international community narrative since 2009 has been made on this basis. An earlier and very knowledgeable author, William Miller, in his *The Ottoman Empire and its Successors 1801-1927* had written a definition of the Eastern Question as the filling of the vacuum created by the gradual disappearance of the Turkish Empire from Europe. The European Union as a transnational entity is still trying to fill that gap on modern Turkey's border, and in that sense Greece has become a Balkan borderland country and therefore a 'legitimate' target for international 'supervision' as much as war-torn Bosnia or Kosova have ever has been.

The arrival of technocratic government was necessary, in the eyes of the foreign lenders, but it had little to do with democratic processes. It was the end of a democratic strand of rhetoric. Aristotle writes in his work on the subject that 'rhetoric exists to affect the giving of decisions – the hearers decide between one political speaker and another ... you must make the audience well-disposed towards you and ill-disposed towards your opponents.'[1] The European Union and the troika of representatives of the European Central Bank and the International Monetary Fund have frequently claimed that their policies are in the best interests of the Greek people but they have yet to convince a majority that this is so, and in many ways currently appear to have given up the attempt to persuade and instead are using brute financial force to implement their policies. Again, it is hard to avoid the memory of the International Control Commission that sought to control Greek finances in the last great Depression in the 1930s. Depressions bring as well as unemployment and poverty the breakdown of the language of progress and democracy. The words of paranoia and fear take their place.

As in the 1930s a characteristic response has been the resumption of emigration. The numerous young people leaving colleges and universities are unable to find jobs in the professions they have trained for and seek employment abroad. There is nothing new in this in Greece, and it goes back to antiquity, exemplified in the old phrase 'The Mountains lose their Men'. There are many ancient models of exile, including the Latin poet Ovid and Aristotle himself. Greeks' first emigration choice from the village is the town or city, usually Athens or Thessaloniki, and then the familiar nations abroad where there are established Greek contacts and

---

1   Aristotle,'Rhetorica'11.1 (ed. W.D. Ross), Oxford, 1924.

communities, like South Africa, Australia, Canada and the United States. But even this route out is not as easy as it used to be. Countries like Canada have an assessment system for potential immigrants that in practice only encourages the well educated, and even Australia is more discriminating than it used to be. The parts of Australia with large Greek populations like South Australia and Victoria have economic and job issues of their own and immigrant Greeks have to compete with Asians and others for the available openings. The days when Greeks could shelter under the 'White Australia' policy are over. Emigration also has a new stigma in many families. It was widely thought in Greece that the old days of buying a cheap flight or boat ticket abroad were over, and in the 1990s Greece became an immigrant receiver country and newly-mobile Bulgarians, Albanians, Romanians and others flooded in. Now they are leaving, even to the extent that the Albanian government in Tirana has set up an agency to help returning emigrant *Gastarbeiter* settle down. The post-communist world in south-east Europe has been a world of popular migration but elusive and often temporary prosperity. Some returning Albanians from Greece have money and may become an economic asset to Albania, while others, such as construction workers, may well join ever-lengthening dole queues in the streets of Greece's poorest northern neighbour.

A heavy and disproportionate burden in the crisis has been borne by Greek women. The savage cuts to public sector jobs have hit women particularly hard, but on the other hand if they have a job, and no one else in the family does, they have to combine work and family duties in an exhausting rigmarole. Although the Greek family is still the domestic fortress, and there are support networks of extraordinary flexibility and strength, it has suffered from mass urbanization, and often there is no longer a Granny in the village to support the young with her produce and clothes making. Even favoured villages have suffered depopulaton, like those around Patrick Leigh Fermor's old home base of Kardamyli in the Mani. When I first went to little hilltop Exohorio in about 1983, very old ladies sang songs and wove rugs on looms that had changed little since Homeric times. Now on nearby beaches you are as likely to hear the programmed chit chat of Whitehall civil servants from London or Zehlendorf doctors from Berlin, and where the loom once stood is an ugly chrome exercise bike in a second home. Few of these north Europeans bother to learn any Greek at all, and some like the parsimonious Dutch are notorious locally for bringing their own food from Holland in their neat motor caravans.

Life is also changing for Greek children in the crisis. Where once they were showered with different clothes and toys by an adoring family, now austerity means hand me down clothes and worn out anoraks. In summer in poorer streets it is possible to see children without shoes, for the first time since I first went to Greece in 1968. School classes are more and more overcrowded as retiring teachers are not replaced, and standards are not rising. If you are a child in a poor family, and the family falls on hard times, only charity stands between you and destitution. The Greek Orthodox Church is currently feeding over a quarter of a million people in soup kitchens and lunch clubs, and the numbers are rising every month. A Greek childhood, even in a poor urban family, used to be one of the best childhoods in Europe and it laid the emotional foundations for a good later life. It is now threatened by the endless decline as much as any other part of the fabric of society.

Children are the future. What kind of Greece will they grow up into, in perhaps twenty or thirty years' time? An important determinant is likely to be the manner and character of the national debt default, if, or more likely, when, it comes. Few serious economic commentators shared the quixotic optimism of French President Sarkozy who hailed the March 2012 bailout as a 'final page that has been turned on the crisis'. Defaults on government debt are a messy business and there are few rules on how they are conducted, only historic precedents. If the Argentina default of 2001 is taken as a model, creditors will still be chasing their money for many years and may never see it. The default, even if prepared for in a sophisticated media campaign and well organized, will involve runs on banks and bank closures are inevitable. Savers with any sense of what is coming will withdraw their funds and store the money under the mattress or abroad. Effective border exchange controls will need to be established, although whether given the nature of the Greek terrain that is possible must be open to doubt. A new Drachma would need to be quickly introduced, at a fixed parity rate, presumably, to the old Euro, although that would be difficult given uncertainties on how the Euro would itself behave in a Greek default period. Nevertheless people would muddle through. Most Greek families have been anticipating a possible default for at least the last eighteen months, and have moved money to relatives' bank accounts abroad, or into gold. Some families with abandoned land in a home village have unemployed family members resuming cultivation. Those who did not bother to pick their olives, like many in the mountain and Mani region of the Peloponnese, now do so and make some cash by selling them. The surplus cars that some Greeks built up in the alchemy years have been sold, and the bicycle has reappeared in Greek towns and cities. There are positive 'green' elements in the situation, as well as endless financial despair. If the crisis helps reverse the almost insane urbanization of the Athens region that has taken place over the last generation, some good will come of it.

One of the few certainties in the current situation is that the elections that have been held in 2015 have produced further political complexity. The decline of PASOK has produced a result with the sweeping victory of SYRIZA that is going to make a resolution of the crisis with the EU difficult. Some commentators have argued that this may lead to a 'failed state' possibility in security terms. This seems alarmist and unlikely. Whatever their political differences, Greeks nearly all have a serious loyalty to the national ideal, and it is drummed into them systematically in their primary and secondary school education, and then most of all in the military service period. The Greek nation does in the end hold together although students of Greek history, in all periods, often wonder how. This enquiry started with Thucydides hundreds of years before Christ was born.

Could modern Greece fragment like Yugoslavia? When the crisis broke in 2009, a separatist movement arose on the island of Corfu, a reflection of the high contribution Corfu tourism makes to Greek government finances. Like most Greek taxpayers, Corfiots feel they do not see much for their money. Some minorities, like the Albanophone Chams who lived in Epirus in the north-west, have very serious grievances arising from the Second World War period, and could try to unite their fate with their mother country, Albania. The issue of Macedonian identity and the Macedonian minority north of Thessaloniki simmers in the background, as always. Many aspects of the EU's so far clumsy and heavy footed behaviour towards an elected government in Athens, however unsatisfactory, recall the Union's dealings with the last stage of the Markovic rotating presidency of Yugoslavia around 1989. There is the same mixture of moral certainty about the superior wisdom of 'Europe' and practical ineptitude. Immigration was a key issue. The question of minority issues became more difficult and relations with the massive immigrant population still augmented daily by thousands of people every month crossing into Greece from Turkey. The Evros delta on the Greek-Turkish border in Thrace is a mass of displaced people clinging to primitive lives around the regional town of Alexandropolis. Many will leave for other parts of the EU, but others will stay. It is not racism to observe that the urban crisis in oppositional districts would not have become as intractable as it has without the existence of minorities with high unemployment and no common language with the police and state authority. Once again, another aspect of the crisis can be seen as a crisis of collapse of shared rhetoric.

Life for the next generation will be harder and may reproduce many of the qualities of life that grandparents thought had disappeared with

European Union membership. The wealth of the national environmental heritage was threatened by proposals of the troika for a state land auction. It is likely that this proposal turned many middle-class voters towards SYRIZA. The way of life in a little town like Loutra Edipsos on the north coast of the island of Evia may offer clues to survival. Edipsos has only ever had one industry, its old sulphur spa dating from antiquity and visited by the Roman dictator Sulla and the author Plutarch. It clings to the coast under high wooded hills and is determinedly unfashionable, with cheap rooms where working-class Athenians try to improve their rheumatism and skin complaints in the warm waters. Yet it is stable. Throughout the crisis, little has changed there. As few foreign visitors ever came, it does not matter to Edipsos that numbers have diminished during the early stages of the crisis and have only slowly recovered. Most products are sourced locally, like fish and fruit and vegetables and so are much cheaper than in urban areas. Pleasant flats are cheap to rent. Many people grow their own tobacco to cut smoking costs and drink unbranded local wine, and avoid paying much tax.

In the world of the many communities similar to Edipsos throughout the country, self-sufficiency and return to traditional agricultural practices are the key. The crowing cock early in the morning is back in even big cities, after silence for many years. Backyard chicken keeping is booming, and pig keeping on smallholdings. Meat is often eaten only once a week. While the pre-CAP days of a trade surplus in agriculture are unlikely to return, there is room for an improvement in production along 'green' lines. Local informal credit unions are providing loans, even mortgages, and the banks are becoming moribund institutions. Saving for needed large ticket purchases like cars may replace most loans altogether, and house mortgages will be difficult. Travel will became more problematic as energy costs rise, and will spiral if there is a default. After 2014, some areas have introduced local currencies to sideline the Euro. Who will benefit? Certain producer groups whose hands have been tied by EU rules will certainly do so. At the moment, much quality Greek olive oil is sold into Italian surplus and then bottled anonymously for northern European supermarkets. Agriculture could become one of the motors of the new post-Euro economy, along with tourism, once the Euro is no longer driving up prices every year.

The family is likely to consolidate and become even more important than it has been in the past – if that is possible – as a defence against individual economic misfortune. A nationalized central retail bank will probably eventually emerge from the wreckage of the current motley organizations. Bank nationalization is one of the most popular proposals in the Marxist parties' platforms. Other traditional Greek institutions will do better. No doubt the Greek Orthodox Church will keep its central position in national life, for many reasons. It has been an indispensible help to the physical survival of many impoverished people in recent times, particularly in the big towns and cities. The hierarchy has avoided getting involved in the wrong kinds of national politics, unlike on many occasions in the past. It will take on its normal historic role as a protector of the national identity and tradition during foreign political 'occupation'. And there are also deeper resonances, a sense of growing inwardness, and a search for a practical spirituality to sustain life in hard times. Monasticism will thrive, as it has developed over the last generations with the renewal of Athos. It is sometimes forgotten that Greeks are, like the British, a democratic island people in their psychology, and interest in their relationships with the ever-difficult Balkan mainland will diminish, as it already has in the last few years. The post-1995 Dayton Accord days when Greece was pushed by Washington and Brussels as a model for the Balkans to follow seem millennia away. Relations with Turkey will hopefully continue to improve although the growing economic power of Turkey is beginning to dominate some regional equations. It is quite possible that without their Turkish investments some Greek banks might not be open in 2012. The extraordinary resilience of the Greek people at ground level will carry them through as it always has done.

Many Greeks are looking towards Russia, co-religionists and always a protector of their national aspirations in theory although the practice has often been very contradictory. Greek nineteenth- and twentieth-century history is full of examples of events where Athens placed hope or confidence in Moscow, only to have those hopes disappointed, principally over the development of the Macedonian Question, Russian-Bulgarian links and the legacy of the Greek Civil War. The Greek crisis certainly presents President Putin's government with wonderful opportunity to substantially increase its political influence. Economic influence mostly through energy supply has been increasing for a long time, and thousands of Russians have holiday and urban second homes and other investments in Greece. Relations between the Churches are always close, augmented by the fact that the Orthodox Church still refuses to recognize the legitimacy of the Macedonian Orthodox Church, and sees it as schismatic from the Serbian Orthodox mother church. Greek hopes for an oil pipeline with its southern terminal in the Greek Thrace city of Alexandropolis have so far not materialized, but they could be revived. But Russia is interested in major world power and Greece, while a useful asset is a very small – if strategically important – potato in the international sack. Political relationships are not straightforward. The Greek communists and leftists in SYRIZA have many criticisms of the return to capitalism in Putin's Russia and the KKE has published a cogent and well researched document on the subject. After all, Greece now has its own oligarchs, in many eyes, with a dominant individual seeming to overshadow all others in particular industries. Even though Greek money owns some important businesses in Russia, the wonderful Orthodox Utopia of sun and sea and exquisite physical beauty that the novelist Dostoevsky imagined is far from the perspective of Putin's entourage. Russia has much influence in Former Yugoslav Macedonia/Republic of Macedonia and increasing power in Serbia, to the north, and a very strong position in Cyprus. It does not need to risk confrontation with NATO over Greece, but attractive opportunities for Moscow to increase influence may arise.

Greeks are very used to occupations in their history, in many different periods and by many different overlords. Greeks are past masters at dividing their occupiers, and the faction fighting that wrecked the Genoese occupation of Chios in the medieval period has its parallels in the internal difficulties the troika already has in agreeing Greek policy. Like the rambling Genoese fortresses on Chios, the European Union and IMF offices in Athens are islands dominated by heavily armed security staff, and much of the official's life is life under siege, driven in fast armoured limousines from one meeting to another with no opportunity to ask an ordinary Greek what they think of the situation. It is no wonder they live among a hostile population when there is so little mutual dialogue or shared rhetoric. The European Union presence is vague and undefined and ultimately depends on a power vacuum in Greek political institutions. This was the case between 2012 and 2015 but it is likely the new SYRIZA government will fill it. Writing of a period as long ago as the First World War, Veremis and Koliopoulos note that 'This clash – the so-called National Schism (*Dichasmos*) – revealed how fragile representative institutions had been in Greece; a disagreement over foreign policy and a division at the top, without any deeper social roots destabilised the whole structure and turned elected governments into quasi-dictatorships.' Different foreign governments of course have different priorities. London has thrown in its lot with the most extreme monetarists by the imposition of a British legal framework on the post-March 2012 Greek bond issues. French priorities are to protect the French banks, while Germany is seeking more realism about the next stage of the crisis.

The future of the political party system is also hard to foresee. The international capitalists would no doubt like to see the emergence of a stable two-party system, the disappearance of PASOK and the Marxist left and many other things but all – or any – of these seems most unlikely. The period from 2012 and the arrival of the New Democracy government on the scene was a period of marked political instability and jockeying for position as old leaders retired and others tried to take their place. Writing of the First World War period and its aftermath, Mark Mazower has observed that then 'the main parties had no roots at the base except for those secured through personal ties: and if such roots could extend far they were also weak. Once he lost his influence at the top, a politician risked seeing his clients and followers look elsewhere for help.' Even for those with the most benign view of the German and associated EU leaders' intentions in Athens, it is an inescapable fact that whatever happens next in the crisis, the old patronage networks have been badly damaged and in Greek history in the past this has always meant the risk of authoritarianism. The British-dominated International Control Commission in the 1930s paved the way for the Metaxas dictatorship. Once again, all the European Union manoeuvres in Greece have been undertaken with little regard for the history of the not-so-distant past. It echoes in the minds of those who know it, but they are a small minority, both inside and outside Greece. For the EU officials with no contact with Greek culture and tradition or modern or ancient history, often from newly joined-EU members that many Greek citizens have scarcely heard of and others from Brussels nooks and crannies who have suddenly found themselves trying to reshape Greek political as well as economic culture, it must seem a doomed project. The jobless figure is almost 21 per cent and rising, and is much higher among the young. New Democracy leader Antonis Samaras comes from a family with political roots in Messenia dating back to the nineteenth century. The plethora of new parties that are currently being formed indicates their rejection. Venizelos was elected the 'worst finance minister in the EU' by London's *Financial Times* readers in 2011. These are the facts the electorate faced in January 2015, and the attempt of the European Union to create a totalizing transnational rhetoric to obscure the truth about the struggle of the Greek people failed. The Greek way in politics is through struggle between opposites and the rationalist consensus the European Union would like to impose on the country proved elusive. The Greek spirit has been in the world much longer than the European Union.

THREE

Years of Stagnation: 2012-2015

'Today, turning to the European crisis, the crisis in the United
States and the long term stagnation of Japanese capitalism, most
commentators fail to appreciate the dialectical process under their
nose. They recognise the mountain of debts and banking losses
but neglect the opposite side of the same coin: the mountain of
idle savings that are 'frozen' by fear and thus fail to convert into
productive investments. A Marxist alertness to binary oppositions
might have opened their eyes.'

Yanis Varoufakis, SYRIZA Finance Minister, London,
18 February 2015

The narrative of the last three years is a depressing story, where some
progress on the international agenda has been achieved but at an ever-
rising cost for the Greek people. In May 2012 Greece held a parliamentary
election to try to form a stable government after the 'technocratic
government' ended. In the homeland of democracy, democracy began
to reassert itself over international supervision. The election result was
inconclusive, with a collapse in the PASOK vote and rejection of the
Papandreou heritage not being matched by much of a swing to the
centre right. The violent protests in central Athens in February 2012 with
arson attacks on buildings, particularly banks, had left their mark on the
electorate, and although the new troika-designed austerity package was
just passed in Parliament, New Democracy had not found a new path
forward sufficient to form a stable majority in the spring election. The
party polled over 29 per cent of the vote but had no majority of seats. As
the political process seemed near to collapse, another election was held the
following month, which enabled a coalition including New Democracy,
PASOK and DIMAK to coexist in a new coalition government. PASOK
had accepted what was to turn out to be a fatal poisoned chalice from New
Democracy leader Samaras, participation in a government that accepted
the harshest yet austerity package produced by the troika.

Within weeks of the decision entire branches of PASOK, particularly
in northern and central Greece – out of sight of most Athens-based
foreign journalists – began to leave the party and join SYRIZA. It was
not apparent at the time, but in the summer of 2012 some of the most
important building blocks of the SYRIZA election victory in 2015 were
to be put in place.

It was not long before the centre of gravity of politics returned to the Athens street, with violent protests resuming on 5 November 2012 against a new austerity package. It was almost exactly a year after the resignation of George Papandreou as PASOK prime minister but no onlooker could yet anticipate the dramatic crash of PASOK as a major Greek party. Yet the process has its roots deep in modern Greek history; time and time again a party has risen on the basis of charismatic individual leadership, only to fall from power and disintegrate as that leader lost favour with the electorate.

Unemployment rose steadily throughout this period, from about 16 per cent at the end of 2011 – according to official figures, which probably underestimate the numbers – to about 26 per cent at the end of 2014. If the tens of thousands of emigrants and those active in the 'grey' and underground economies are included, perhaps only 60 per cent of the economically available workforce had a job by the time of the election in 2015. Under Samaras, New Democracy in these years ploughed an essentially lonely path with only the upswing in tourist numbers after the dire 2010 figures a cause for popular optimism. Prices in hotels and restaurants had been cut, according to a national initiative to attract foreign mass market tourists back to Greece, but with the concomitant effect of reducing the income for many small businesses and cutting their ability to repay their debts. The quality of the data on tourist numbers, as always and as in many countries, is open to question. Regular business visitors are reported as if they are tourists and the tens of thousands of cruise ship visitors are included, even though many of them only have a quick port visit on a coach to visit an archaeological site and do not stay a night in Greece. The influx of tourists from new EU nations in Eastern Europe us useful, but they often do not spend very much.

Nonetheless, in some areas of national life under New Democracy government there were tangible and visible improvements. The scandal of the near collapse of border security with Turkey along the Evros river in Thrace leading to mass illegal migration and the swamping of towns like Alexandropolis was brought under control. A high border fence was built and police and army patrols reorganized to counter human trafficking gangs and illegal economic migrants. Although the treatment of migrants was, and is, rough and ready by international standards, the police work has had a dramatic effect in reducing refugee and asylum seeker numbers unlike the Italian navy force south of Sicily which has acted as a magnet for illegal shipping transfers of migrants. The Greek navy has little presence in most coastal areas except near Turkey. The peaceful nesting storks on the telegraph poles along the Evros riverside had looked down for some years on a wild and disorderly border but New Democracy, with support from European Union border monitors, helped bring order. This issue was not simply a matter of illegal migration control. The sense of a loss of control over national borders had been important in the growth of support for the neo-fascist Golden Dawn party, with its Nazi image and amended swastika flag. The border improvements brought about under the ND government helped cap the Golden Dawn vote at under 7 per cent, where it has remained for the last four years. This was a real achievement for the Samaras administration, as was the fiscal improvement which led to Greece returning to the international bond markets in April 2014. Anecdotal evidence suggests that Golden Dawn had achieved – and to some extent retains – significant support particularly among the police and security section workers, an ominous sign for the future of democracy in Greece if and when the crisis deepens. The last thing Greece needs at the moment is a revival of the so-called 'secret state' of the Cold War period, based around extreme-right sympathizers. Work was restarted on some stalled infrastructure projects, some of which had been abandoned as long ago as 2005, as soon as the Olympic Games construction boom ground to a halt.

The New Democracy government attempted to rebuild the state apparatus. The price in terms of civil liberties has been high. Striking subway workers had been ordered back to work almost as soon as the New Democracy government had taken power, and one of the few parts of the government machine to enjoy an increased budget was the secret service and police apparatus. Surveillance of dissidents and activists among the population has increased, and discriminatory laws introduced so that it is illegal for the KKE, the main communist party, to receive donations from Greeks abroad. One of the effects of this move was presumably exactly the opposite of what the ND government intended, in that funding from leftist sources, domestic and foreign, was diverted to SYRIZA, facilitating the opening of new SYRIZA party offices in many areas that were once PASOK strongholds, and assisting the radicalization of the left in those localities. Adherence to SYRIZA for the unemployed young has much of the same frisson and commitment to rebellion that attracted their parents to vote for the KKE in the aftermath of the junta, but without the stigma KKE adherence has for some Greeks with memories of the Civil War period. The 16 per cent of the vote that SYRIZA held in 2011 had over doubled to 36 per cent by the time of the 2015 election and these structural changes in the political parties were at work all the time.

Who is Alexis Tsipras, leader of SYRIZA and architect of one of the most dramatic rises to power in Greek politics since the Second World War? He was born in 1974, only a little while after democracy was restored that year with the end of the Colonels' junta. He is frequently presented as an archetypal young Athenian communist activist turned social democrat, who some think only left the KKE because he was very gifted and ambitious and its old-fashioned structure and organizational conservatism would have prevented him from reaching the leadership until late middle age. He is officially presented as an Athenian, growing up in the pleasant northern inner suburb of Ampelokipoi with its *rembetika* clubs, university teachers and restaurants serving snails and other dishes beloved of Asia Minor-origin people. In cultural terms, migrants to Athens bring many separate heritages with them and the Tsipras family is no exception. Political inheritance through the family and accompanying ideology are very important in Greece, as in many places, and can often embody much of the turbulent history of twentieth-century Greece in a single family. Greeks do not often change their political ideas as a response to changing personal circumstances. Both Tsipras parents both came from the north-west provincial town of Arta and his civil engineer father was part of the great migration and urbanization of Attica in the post-war period. Tsipras' partner Peristera (Betty) Batziana is also highly political, some think a more ideological Marxist than he is, and her family has a similar provincial radical background, in her case from near Kavala. But their family roots a further generation back lie far from Arta, in another layer of the Tsipras history. Arta is a historic town and has a long and distinguished story, with its late Byzantine churches and monuments and its towering elegant Ottoman bridge, a single grey arch balanced over the rushing shallow river. Ruined mosques lie obscured by leafy forest undergrowth on the outskirts. On the boundary of the Ottoman Empire for a long time with substantial Vlach and Albanian-speaking minorities Arta joined Greece after national victories in the short war over Ottoman Thessaly fought in 1881 under the Treaty of Berlin as Greece expanded northwards. With surrounding fertile land, and rich fishing in the Ambracian Gulf, there were not enough Greek-speaking inhabitants in the eyes of Athens governments and the area was a major centre for Greek refugee reception after the 1923 Catastrophe in Asia Minor and exchange of populations between Greece and Turkey following the Treaty of Lausanne.

It was government policy to 'Hellenize' the ex-Ottoman areas, and the exchange of populations provided a perfect opportunity to do so. The Tsipras antecedents would probably have arrived as penniless and disoriented refugees, in this case from near Edirne in Thrace, and people from Asia Minor retained something of their origins in their families for many years, living mostly with other similar families in purpose built refugee suburbs, recognizable even nowadays on the edge of many northern Greek towns with their rectangular semi-military layout and very modest white concrete box houses with endlessly productive vines and vegetable gardens. Refugee-origin families were often solid supporters of the left, making up a substantial part of the Communist Party leadership after it was founded, and the basis of Tsipras' radicalism lies in this inheritance as much as in intellectual Athens, or in his partner's serious Marxist commitment. Oral tradition is central to the transmission of historical knowledge in Greece, where for two generations school history textbooks were manipulated to provide a narrative that obscured much of what had happened. The events of the Second World War and the consequent civil war remain determinant, as in so many places in the Balkans. In this context, Epirus had a particularly brutal and oppressive Nazi occupation during the war, and was the scene of the onset of the Greek Civil War after 1943, with the British-sponsored rightist EDES militia of Napoleon Zervas fighting the communist-controlled ELAS resistance in the Threspotia mountains.

Most older Epiriots generally have, at the very least, strong private reservations about Germans wartime conduct, and the question of unpaid war reparations is still open in many remote village tavernas, along with the failure of post-war Greek governments to call for the prosecution of individual Germans and Greek collaborators involved in the occupation for war crimes offences. Surprise was expressed in some quarters about the nature of the first ceremonial act by Tsipras on taking power, the visit to the Kaisariani monument where two hundred Greek communists were murdered by the Germans in cold blood on May Day 1944. The stance of the Greek government has touched a raw nerve in Germany for understandable reasons, and may make any secure long-term resolution of the crisis more difficult. The government position is a general claim for wartime reparations that, according to a recent report in the *Financial Times*, would amount to as much as 160 billion Euros. The claim for the Distomo massacre would come to 28 million Euros. The Greeks are also pressing for repayment of a 476 million Reichsmark loan the Nazis forced from the Greek Central Bank in 1943, now estimated at US$11 billion in value. On the latter the Tsipras government has, it believes, a very strong position, as the Nazi government itself began to make repayments before the war ended.

So far Berlin government spokesmen and ministers have stated that they regard the matter as closed and consigned to history, and from a legal point of view the German position is reinforced by the little known treaty that was signed with the old Allied occupying powers at the time of German reunification, where the wartime Allies abandoned all claims on Germany. From the point of view of the Athens government, pressing this issue has various positive elements. It certainly has a case, and it is an interrelated set of complex issues that will inevitably take time to resolve. The Tsipras government believes that time is on its side in the debt negotiations. The plethora of prominent liberal US economists such as Jeffrey Sachs, Joseph Stiglitz and Paul Krugman directly advising or offering public support to Finance Minister Varoufakis gives the government credibility with the Obama administration, although whether the full political implications of blanket support for SYRIZA are well understood in Washington in geo-political terms seems doubtful. The same point is valid over tacit French support for at least some of the SYRIZA programme, and the distinctly Parisian intellectual culture of many of the SYRIZA leadership. It is not every European government that has ex-pupils of Marxist-Leninist structuralist philosopher Louis Althusser and fellow radical thinker Jacques Lacan in the government. It suits Paris at the moment to use the claims of the new government in Greece to help reduce the overwhelming Berlin dominance within the EU over 'austerity' policy, when France itself has its own serious debt problems. But it is an open question whether the fundamental and profound radicalism of SYRIZA as a political movement and the general strength of the left in Greece nowadays have been fully understood, with the Olympian world of journalists in *Le Monde Diplomatique* at some distance from the realities of the Greek street.

Reparations form an issue on which virtually all Greek public opinion will support the government, and help solidify popular support behind it. The maximalist nature of the claims fits into the Marxist-Leninist political problematic of making demands that transcend the possibilities of reformist politics within capitalism to then develop the consciousness of the working class and move the political struggle to a higher stage. This pleases the powerful left within SYRIZA who have in some cases expressed reservations about the original tactical concessions made by the government immediately after the election. It is an issue that will appeal to some Jewish opinion, particularly in the United States, with their influence in the international English-language media and the Obama administration. It helps construct the narrative of Greek 'victimhood' which may be effective in some opinion constituencies, as surprisingly sympathetic press coverage in some uncommitted EU members, and those with strong Eurosceptic constituencies like Britain has already shown. It is impossible to avoid the comparison between the psychology of support for Greece and Israel in some parts of the US Democratic Party, particularly in Greek Diaspora strongholds like Massachusetts and parts of New York and California, where a small country with difficult neighbours that appears to embody exceptionalist inherited historical identity and has had a raw deal from Germany is seen as a priority candidate for US political support.

So far the strategy seems promising, and all public opinion measures show that the government is gaining popular support, although also with critical resonances about the government failing to achieve the full policy objectives of the 'Thessaloniki Programme'. For a government aiming not only for a debt settlement but a fundamental transformation of Greek society along new lines this is centrally important. The same impetus to set a new and unpredictable agenda that the EU will find hard to handle comes also with new foreign policy initiatives. The media role of Finance Minister Yanis Varoufakis is important; as a member of the key 'Aegina' inner circle around leader Tsipras, he has worked towards the deconstruction of the European economic rhetoric, an exercise symbolized by his radical personal style agenda, his post-modernism reaching EU financial discussions. The opening to dialogue with Russia has naturally attracted the most international attention, with newspapers like *The Wall Street Journal* publishing analyses of the real or alleged pro-Russian orientation of some SYRIZA ministers, but of perhaps as much long-term importance was the very early involvement of the Cyprus government in dialogue over policy. The Cypriot banking and social crisis has disappeared from the media after the short blanket coverage in 2013, and the economy still remains very fragile. Russian investors – not all *Mafiosi* or money launderers but ordinary Russians with second homes and normal bank accounts – suffered what they have seen as *de facto* sequestration of their assets then for the benefit of western financial institutions. The rate for the Euro that was decreed against the Cyprus pound in the banking settlement was very high and has left Cyprus a crippled economy, with deep popular resentment at the closure terms forced on the Cyprus government from Brussels. In this climate, it was not surprising that Athens' new government turned straight to talks with Nicosia as soon as it was elected. There is a long history of Greek disagreements with NATO at policy level, going back to the Cold War and issues such as the Soviet intervention in Afghanistan. But the issues now are different, with the crisis and cuts in the defence budget making it harder for the armed forces to defend the country in the way they have been accustomed. Procurement is particularly difficult, and a Russian avenue for influence may be in the provision of spare parts for military equipment.

The geopolitics of the Eastern Mediterranean are changing with consequences that are at the moment impossible to foresee but which may well increase the centrality of Russia to future political deliberations. The Putin government in Moscow has been given a new lever to exert pressure within the European Union if in time the risks appear to the Moscow leadership to be worth taking. The US bases in Crete and elsewhere in Greece are keystones of NATO power projection in the turmoil of the Middle East, as is the NSA and British electronic intelligence collection capacity based in the Cyprus sovereign base area at Akrotiri.

In the intense debate over the short-term financial crisis, the views of economists have naturally dominated public discourse and the media. SYRIZA happens to have an exceptionally large number of economists among the leadership, even by the standards of Greek left-of-centre parties, and some groups were important in securing such a large poll victory. The ex-PASOK group of leading figures in and around Thessaloniki with an economics background is an important one, and brought many last minute votes from the disintegrating PASOK to SYRIZA in the conclusion of the election campaign.

It is against this background that the 2015 debt crisis is best understood, where the economic crisis is made much harder to resolve because the complex issues of nationalism, identity, ethnicity, the growing influence of Russian orthodoxy within the Orthodox world including Greece and Cyprus and unresolved issues from the Second World War which have all come to play a major but unspoken part in the official discourse. Greek capitalism is the weak link in the European Union construct, but the crisis is not only simply about debts and fiscal matters. If Greece goes for 'Grexit', or defaults on its debts, or both, many of the current issues will remain on the table the following day. As the author Hugh Poulton pointed out many years ago, the fault lines of religion are often the determinants of events in south-east Europe. Some EU nations like Spain, where Roman Catholic federalist lobbies and clerical nationalist centre-right parties dating from the Cold War years are influential, may welcome 'Grexit' as opening the door for further federalist and centralist integration.

The well-meaning Samaras government was paralysed by failing to distance itself from the official rhetoric of the European Union, and has left the ex-prime minister still as leader of the main opposition party but nursing many grievances against Berlin for what he sees as the lack of EU support in his attempted national revival period in government. It remains to be seen if key advisers during the government period, such as ex-Synaspismos (in his youth) strategist Chryanthos Lazaridis will remain in active roles while the party is in a difficult period of opposition. The current heated discussions on the financial crisis may or may not come to a temporary resolution and Greece may or may not leave the Euro but relations with the rest of Europe will remain central to Greek foreign and economic policy. Almost whatever is decided it is unlikely to satisfy many of the basic needs of the Greek people and with the exhaustion of the social-democratic model it is likely, perhaps inevitable, that the political agenda will move much further to the left. The view of financier George Soros, that Greece and the EU are in a 'lose-lose' situation, is likely to be influential.

In more conservative opinion constituencies, this will be seen as opening the Greek door to Russia but it is unclear if this will necessarily be so. The Putin government refused to come to the aid of Cyprus in the 2013 banking crisis where the rewards for Russia may have been much higher than is likely in Greece. But there are many strategic options opening for Russia other than direct financial aid, and early contacts between the two governments suggest energy issues will pay a large role, with the revival of thinking about the so-called 'Orthodox oil' pipeline to bring Russian oil into Greece, and the end of EU sanctions on Greek fruit growers that closed the Russian market to them in 2014. The SYRIZA government concept of Greece as a bridge between the West and Russia is likely to intensify pressure upon it from Brussels, where there are important power centres who do not want SYRIZA to succeed as a democratically elected body, and do not want a new policy towards Russia, and will do all they can to cause SYRIZA difficulties.

Religious links will be important, and it may not be a coincidence that the red carpet visit for Prime Minister Tsipras to Moscow in April 2015 came at Easter, the most important festival in the Orthodox year. The Greek Church is an important background player and the Patriarchate in Istanbul has its own precarious and pressured relationship with the Erdogan government in Ankara. With the approaching Great Council of the Orthodox Church in 2016 the Patriarch in Istanbul is unlikely to welcome undue growth in Russian Orthodox influence in Greece itself. Russia is not as attractive for the European left as it used to be, as an economically conservative country deeply embedded in international capitalist structures, and is actually termed 'imperialist' in some Greek communist literature. But energy supply brings enormous political and ideological influence nowadays in Eastern Europe, as the growth of Russian influence in Serbia shows. The Greek radical bookshops that sell Marx and Althusser do not sell biographies of Vladimir Putin or books praising 'New Russia', but they do sell anarcho-syndicalism thinkers like Proudhon, Durruti and Bakunin.

Louis Althusser observed – commenting on Karl Marx's own intellectual development – that it took many years and a long struggle before the philosopher achieved the rupture with the ideas inherited from his upbringing and forged a new consciousness. The election of SYRIZA has caused international concern and excitement in radical circles because the media and analysts – if not many in Brussels, and in the mainstream economists' institutes – have understood that it represents a step towards a break with the ideological past, not merely in terms of technical policy issues but the *modus operandi* of Greek state and government itself. The last five years have not only destroyed much of the credibility of the old political elite but the actual state structures themselves – never very strong – have become discredited. A main component of the ideological state apparatus, the Greek Orthodox Church may find SYRIZA unwelcome but is very unlikely to enter politics as it did in the Civil War period on the side of the right providing that SYRIZA respects its essential interests.

Localism has been a strong response. The liberating practice of new local currencies, Bitcoin and digital currencies, and the possible return of the Drachma as a stabilizing secondary currency to the discredited Euro do not seem to presage the advent of a return to Stalinist models of collectivisation but a more deconstructed if still capitalist economy where much of the state is bypassed. Many Greeks now see no alternative to SYRIZA, something embodied in the surpringly understanding statement issued by ex-King Constantine soon after the election, to 'give SYRIZA a chance'. Whatever develops in the current crisis negotiations, to use an analogy from Greek mythology that is universal in every EU language, Pandora's Box is open and will remain so in Greece. Although Alexis Tsipras is the leader of SYRIZA and its charismatic central figure, SYRIZA is not PASOK where the leadership can be easily manipulated by international forces based on the essentially elitist concept of the *parataxis*, the political extended family. Tsipras has no such apparatus, but instead a voluble, well-educated cohort with many inner loyalties he does not control, even if he wished to do so. In these conditions, as the early development of the government and its relations with foreign powers have shown, events will have a momentum of their own that are hard to control.

The international 'troika' years have destroyed the credibility and legitimacy of the old state ideological apparatus in the eyes of much of the population, as in conditions of political struggle the Greek people have become more aware of the true nature of their situation. The early negotiations with Germany depend for their reality on a projected major economic revival in southern Europe, and a capacity of the Greek state to reproduce many of the features of the PASOK era where state investment on the Keynesian model led to growth. With an estimated 140 billion Euros of capital now abroad and very unlikely to return, and purchasing power down by the 25 per cent cut in wages over the last five years, it is hard to see any real basis for the revival of the economy within the problematic of conventional bourgeois economists policies. If this is the case, and when the patience of the Greek people with these policies of accommodation with the EU is fully exhausted, the political destiny of Greece may well move onto another plane, towards a rupture, an epistemological break with the failed policies of the past and towards a collective anti-statist, post-capitalist economy based on strategic dialogue with Russia and its allies as much as the United States and the European Union.

CHRONOLOGY

1967   Coup d'état in Greece brings junta dictatorship

1971   Closure of Halki Theological Academy, Istanbul

1973   Athens Polytechnic student uprising against the dictatorship

1974   Turkey invades Cyprus; fall of Greek junta

1981   Greece joins European Community

1980s   Politics dominated by Andreas Papandreou's PanHellenic Socialists (PASOK)

1990   New Democracy Prime Minister Constantine Mitsotakis in power

1991   Collapse of communism in Albania and refugee crisis

1991   Referendum votes for an independent Republic of Macedonia

1993   PASOK returns to power

1995   'Small Package' agreement changes flag and Constitution in Skopje

1996   Kostas Simitis becomes prime minister in Greece; pyramid banking crisis begins in Albania

1997   Armed uprising in southern Albania

1998   Kosova Liberation Army starts war for Kosovan independence

1999   NATO intervention in Kosova

2001   War in western Macedonia ended by August Ohrid Accords

2002   Greece abandons drachma and joins the Eurozone

2004   Cyprus joins the EU; New Democracy returns to power in Greece

2007   New Democracy re-elected; recession and austerity begin

2008   Violent anti-government demonstrations in Athens

2009   PASOK wins a snap election; fears grow of a debt default and run on banks

2010   Sovereign debt crisis in Greece; government introduces new austerity measures

2011   General Strike against austerity; new EU debt bailout; collapse of PASOK government

2012   Crisis election results in no overall majority

2013   Sixth year of recession

2014   Leftist party SYRIZA wins European elections

2015   SYRIZA wins national parliamentary elections; in July voters overwhelmingly reject EU bailout proposals; SYRIZA does not respect the referendum result; August bailout to avoid ejection from the Eurozone and debt default

2016   Republic of Macedonia closes border to migrants

2018   SYRIZA government signs Prespa Agreement on Macedonian name

2019   SYRIZA loses power to New Democracy

INDEX